Hate-Work

Other books by David W. Augsburger
from Westminster John Knox Press

Pastoral Counseling across Cultures

Conflict Mediation across Cultures

Helping People Forgive

Hate-Work

Working through the
Pain and Pleasures of Hate

David W. Augsburger

Westminster John Knox Press
LOUISVILLE • LONDON

Unless otherwise indicated, Scripture quotations are taken from *The New English Bible*, © The Delegates of the Oxford University Press and The Syndics of the Cambridge University Press, 1961, 1970. Used by permission.

Scripture quotations marked RSV are from the Revised Standard Version of the Bible, copyright © 1946, 1952, 1971, and 1973 by the Division of Christian Education of the National Council of the Churches of Christ in the U.S.A., and are used by permission.

Excerpt from *And the Sea Is Never Full* by Elie Wiesel, translated by Marion Wiesel, copyright © 1999 by Elie Wiesel. Used by permission of Alfred A. Knopf, a division of Random House, Inc., and HarperCollins Publishers Ltd.

Book design by Sharon Adams
Cover design by Lisa Buckley

First edition
Published by Westminster John Knox Press
Louisville, Kentucky

This book is printed on acid-free paper that meets the American National Standards Institute Z39.48 standard. ♾

PRINTED IN THE UNITED STATES OF AMERICA

04 05 06 07 08 09 10 11 12 13 — 10 9 8 7 6 5 4 3 2 1

Library of Congress Cataloging-in-Publication Data

Augsburger, David W.
    Hate-work : working through the pain and pleasures of hate / David W. Augsburger.—
        1st ed. p. cm.
    Includes bibliographical references.
    ISBN 0-664-22682-5 (alk. paper)
        1. Pastoral counseling. 2. Pastoral psychology. 3. Hate. I. Title.

BV4012.2.A873 2004
179'.8—dc22

2003055562

Contents

Tables

Introduction

9/11. These two numbers suddenly serve as shorthand for violent attack and vitriolic hatred, not only in America, but in virtually every country. As a result, we face the disturbing challenge: *Either we will come to new understandings of hate, hate's causes, hate resolution, or we will accelerate and perpetuate it. Either we will learn from the tragedies of unbridled hate—we did not learn enough from its most heinous event, the holocaust, to stop genocides— or we will continue to transmit it generation to generation.*

I began this study of the puzzling issue of hate with a dissertation on anger thirty years ago; then wrote three books on forgiveness, in the '70s, '80s, and '90s, that touched on its healing. I grappled with the tangled skeins of hate while doing family therapy and mediating conflicts; explored its different faces while researching intercultural counseling and conflict resolution; observed its mysteries while consulting around the world; explored its power in my own soul through therapy, puzzled over it with a lifelong concern about mental disorders and their three key passions of control, resentment, and vindictive triumph; then finally turned my full attention to reading all available literature on hate. The nearby research library at Claremont University lists almost *four thousand* titles on the subject of love, I discovered, but on the subject of hate? *Forty-one.* And only half of them actually addressed the topic. The contrast of a hundred to one, the surprise at the lack of interest, the hunch that denial plays a role in this silence about hate, the shock that so little writing—particularly recent work—addressed this set of issues so crucial to civility and community plunged me into reading everything I could find to explore its intriguing dynamics.

Then, in the midst of this writing project, came September 11, 2001, and the *Los Angeles Times* offered as many reports of, references to, and projections of readers' hate as any clinical book. Since history began, the world has been a living laboratory for the exploration, justification, or glorification of hostility, but the constant availability of images, emotions, and actions reported on television in every household makes denial more difficult and projection on the other hand more automatic. Hate shows no signs of waning.

Although hate is frequently mentioned, and almost universally condemned, reflection on *why* hate springs eternal, *how* hate takes control, *what* is hated, and *which* hate is expressed seems rare. Our confusion on the various types of hate, from raw repulsion at one end of an imaginary scale to conscientious contempt of moral evil at another, makes the process of sorting out which hate is being named by an author or critiqued by a commentator a bit difficult. The family of a victim at a murder trial may express simple outrage, vicious malice, desired revenge, demanded retribution, righteous judgment, moral lament, or passion for justice. Listening to the stories of hate arising from injury, attack, or atrocity reveals a clear series of differing colors of hate that spread across a spectrum of negative attitudes and prejudices and describe a graduated scale, from hate-filled sentiments and hateful behaviors to something unpredictably different. After 9/11, snatches of words leaping out of conversations vary from "I hate all Muslims" to "I hate Muslim extremists" to "I despise any kind of terrorism" to "I hate evil and injustice of any kind" to "I abhor violence, the violence of the powerless and the powerful alike" to "I'm looking for something beyond hating, something that works for a just world of Muslims and Christians and all others seeing each other as humans."

Such a spectrum of differing kinds of hate, which I will list here but define in chapter 1, includes: (1) *"Simple hatred" (Disgust)*, an intense dislike of something profoundly unpleasant; (2) *"Spiteful hatred" (Resentment)*, what one feels when nursing a grudge; (3) *"Malicious hatred" (Revenge)*, the passionate wish for unlimited revenge; (4) *"Retributive hatred" (Retaliation)*, the stubborn insistence on repayment, or the satisfaction of seeing the other punished; (5) *"Principled hatred" (Deliberative hatred)*, rage that makes a case, creates a rationale of hate justification; (6) *"Moral hatred" (Moral contempt)*, a hate of injustice or evil that begins to separate the actor from the despised action; (7) *"Just hatred" (Just contempt)*, hatred for deliberate injustice or violation of persons. The injustice hated is clearly differentiated from the unjust perpetrator.

Seeing the many colors of the spectrum, recognizing the radical differences between one repulsion and another, allows us to carry on a deeper conversation about hate and its problems and pleasures. Those working with anyone caught up in overwhelming hatred need a way of speaking about and identifying the particular hate felt if they are to intervene astutely in this volatile issue. A counselee's experience over her long journey of healing and recovery demonstrates this spectrum.

> "I loathed my father. A million nights I relived my terror at the sound of my door opening. I dreamed of the day when I would hurt him as much as he had hurt me. When I finally told the school nurse, and he went to prison, I felt safe. I started to live again. But for years I was afraid of . . . I hated all men. Never again would I be a victim. I thought of a thousand ways to get even. I felt totally right in all my rage. One day, after he got out of prison, my husband and I went to see him. I expected the monster of my nightmares. I found a pitiful wreck. I said everything I had waited so long to say, he just shook his head, "Yes," and I left. But the world began to look different. I could see a space between the awful things people do and the miserable bastards they can become. In time the gap grew wider. I still hate what happened with a passion, but murder is completely gone out of me. It changed how I work, how I care about others, how I think about perps, how I care for people who have suffered like me, and how I demand justice for them." (Name withheld)

In this story, the movement from spiteful hatred (2) to malicious hatred (3) and then retributive hatred (4) is slow, the formation of a rationale for hating inevitable (5), then the encounter with the actual human being creates a space between act and actor (6), and the breakthrough offers the freedom to begin to feel just contempt with human compassion (7). What a journey!

This book is addressed to those who care—caregivers such as pastoral counselors, pastors, mediators, attorneys, social workers, and the many nonprofessional caregivers who work daily with raw emotions in others and consequently in themselves. It will be of special interest to those preparing for any of these fields, since we tend to be drawn to serve in areas where the estrangement witnessed is no stranger to our own inner struggles. It is written from the perspective of Christian chagrin, since the propagation of hatred is no stranger to us, even to Anabaptist pacifists such as myself. It will offer a fresh paradigm for naming, defining, and confronting the power of malignant negativism that lurks in the human soul.

The argument of the book builds throughout the chapters as follows: A new understanding of the spectrum of hates from simple disgust to a complex passion for justice is set forward in chapter 1. In chapter 2 I argue that this more informed perspective on hate can help us move from a reflexive, automatic, reactive hate, often called subjective hate, to the more responsive, empathic, mature hate we call objective hate, which is closely akin to impartial love. Chapter 3 looks backward to explore how hate is learned to help us begin the active hate-work of unlearning and relearning behaviors of hostility and hate. Chapter 4 looks inward to the union of hate and memory to offer guidance in exploring and resolving hate that lives eternally in the inner judgment halls of memory. Chapter 5 continues the inner journey into the dark side to empower us to open and assimilate the reserves of our mysterious unconscious sometimes called "the shadow," where hate lives on, awaiting its moment to emerge. Chapter 6 identifies the need to soften our persistent tendency to make godlike demands for absolute answers, unquestionable opinions, and unassailable positions in the rationales, reasons, and justifications for continuing hostility and hate. Chapter 7 recognizes that no discussion of hate, since the holocaust, dares omit a long look at the ultimate consequences of hatred, since that greatest of tragedies reveals what horrendous hate and monstrous evils we humans are capable of perpetrating. The revelatory work of holocaust survivor and prophet Elie Wiesel is especially helpful here. Chapter 8 explores the dynamics of enemy formation, revealing that we cannot reduce our captivity to hate without reconsidering our fears and gathering the courage to face our attitudes toward the enemy. Chapter 9 outlines a path from a personal philosophy and practiced theology of contempt toward a renewed vision of mercy, compassionate concern, and empathy. Exemplary of applied theology, the Psalter is examined as a model for moving toward a just hate. Finally, the appendixes contain exercises that invite the reader to risk doing the hard work of hate-work that leads toward transformation of the shadow darkness within. This is an arduous journey, to be sure, but a journey that you will, I hope, find inviting and compelling.

At the beginning of each chapter, the proposition for the next step of the developing argument is concisely stated, grounded in the preceding chapter, and followed by story, event, history, theories of psychology, sociology, and theology to demonstrate the formation of a wider and deeper perspective on hatred. This is an introduction to the study of hatred, an introduction needed since we have cut off many of the impulses and passions of our souls in seeking an easy truce, a too simple peace with the forces within our souls, our relationships, our families, communities, society, and nations.

Those who work to reduce hate through service in mediation, in law, in child protection, in the various parts of the criminal justice system, tell me that they are puzzled by the deep contempt they often feel, contempt for senseless abuse and violence, contempt for all that dehumanizes, but they lack a language to discuss it cogently. Those who pursue a personal struggle for justice after injury—having been abused as children, or violated in incest, for example—speak of their outrage in hushed tones because the hate they want to describe requires the use of words that fall into the same language file as the emotions and actions of the perpetrator. These who look back on the horror of the holocaust, or the other genocide atrocities around the world, search for appropriate language to speak of the abhorrent loathing they feel, but that loathing remains inadequately named. We must talk about our horror to create metaphors that possess the power to name the horror; we must speak the unspeakable if we are to stop repeating the unrepeatable.

Any discussion of hate by its very nature, since 9/11 for Americans, since Hiroshima for Japan, since the holocaust for all religious thinkers, since the Cultural Revolution for China, since Stalin in Eastern Europe—the list can go on and on—unites local and global. The outrage one feels at personal injustice, the hate one recognizes when those one loves are injured or violated, is inseparable from the pain one sees in the evening newscast, the suffering one witnesses in any honest look at the real world—the first, second, third, and two-thirds worlds included. All caregiving takes place in this larger context which is now an increasingly small, inseparably enmeshed, inescapably interdependent little world. We will have to move back and forth between the personal and the political, the individual and the social, as we discuss hate if we are to recognize this interconnectedness. How I deny or decry the violation of women in Asia and Africa cannot be separated from how I am oblivious to the obvious in my church or town. Similarly, how I contribute to environmental or energy crises by driving an SUV cannot be split from my hopes for the world I leave to my grandchildren. All caregiving in a postmodern world recognizes that the large picture and the small picture are not two, but one.

Hate, even when we experience it in the more mature forms, offers us both *pleasures* (have you felt the rush of "rightness" when dislike is clearly justified?) and *problems* (or perhaps you've felt the chagrin of "Oh no, the other's actions may make sense after all"?). Frederick Buechner writes of hate's pleasures: "Hate is as all-absorbing as love, as irrational, and in its own way as satisfying. As lovers thrive on the presence of the beloved, haters revel in encounters with the one they hate. They confirm him in all his darkest suspicions. They add fuel to all his most burning animosities. The memory of them can be as sweet as young love" (Buechner 1993, 63). The pleasure of standing on the moral high ground in superior disgust seduces us, the problems of managing the lingering feelings and attitudes of repulsion dismay us, we face a sentiment which even at its best expression has two faces. These two faces—righteous outrage and resistant repulsion—each has its problems, each offers a certain pleasure, each requires maturation. These two sides to our deep negativity are both essential to our human hard-wiring, but not always useful. The impulse to hate is inevitable, but hate is not necessary. The assessment of hate in most literature from classic times to the present, from one hemisphere to another, is consistently negative. "Hatred punishes itself" is a proverb common to a number of cultures. "Hatred is like rain in the desert—it is of no use to anybody," an African proverb, warns of the futility of hate. But most proverbs have a mate affirming the direct opposite as equally true, and the second is: "Who cannot hate, cannot love." Similarly, the "Preacher" in Ecclesiastes: There is "a time to love and a time to hate" (Eccl. 3:8). What if these are not separate times, but both feelings and actions are needed to temper and correct each other? Working through the complexity of these sentiments is the hard work I have called "hate-work." Be warned that hate-work will require a disciplined effort to identify, own, and then rework some of the negative recesses of the soul. In the final appendixes I offer a series of resources for exploring and experiencing personal transformation, which provide several paths for working through both the pain and the pleasures that hate seductively offers.

Around 700 B.C., the book of Leviticus commanded, "You shall not hate your brother in your heart" (RSV). The summary of the Torah given by Jesus calls us to refuse hate and choose love—"'You shall love the Lord your God with all your heart, . . . with all your mind, and with all your strength.' The second is this, 'You shall love your neighbor as yourself.' There is no other commandment greater than these" (Mark 12:30–31 RSV). The uniqueness of Jesus' understanding of love is that genuine agape is not simply a benevolent, sacrificial, generous concern for the welfare of the neighbor that expresses itself in equal regard, but nothing less than enemy love. This compassion for the foe illuminates the gospel of reconciliation in the teaching of Paul, empowers the arguments of the Johannine tradition, and shines incandescently throughout the Synoptic

Gospels. It calls us to constantly renew all attempts to bring together passion for good and moral contempt for evil with courage and consistency.

Compassion without contempt for all that is vicious and virulent is weak and thin. Empathy with both the offended and the offender does not preclude clean and clear hate. Is hatred an essential component of compassion? Does moral contempt have its own—too rarely trod—pathway toward transformation, to a unique metamorphosis into empathy? Is it possible for any or all of us, acculturated to hate as we are, to change?

In Ramallah, West Bank, Palestine, Daniel Barenboim, Israeli conductor and pianist, slipped past a military checkpoint in a German diplomatic vehicle to play a concert for two hundred seventh- through twelfth-grade schoolchildren in September of 2002. The sight of an Israeli without a gun was a new experience for many of these kids. "We hate them," a twelve-year-old volunteered. Barenboim took the stage wordlessly and launched into Beethoven's "Moonlight Sonata." When he finished and the standing, shouting, whistling ovation subsided, he said, "I think each of us has a responsibility to do what we think is right. . . . What I can do is play music. . . . By these few moments maybe we can build down the hatred." "Music breaks all barriers," fifteen-year-old Nadia Avouri said in response. "I don't look at him as a Jewish person or an Israeli person. I look at him as a musician" (*Los Angeles Times*, September 11, 2002, sec. A, p. 3). Emotional breakthrough from hate to empathy for the enemy happens as she sees a human being, not a part of a war machine. Hearing the art, seeing the artist, feeling the deep connection of shared beauty, she realizes their common humanity. This offers a clue we shall pursue in the chapters that follow.

Chapter One

The Many Ways of Hating:
A Spectrum of Hates

I have one great fear in my heart—that one day when they turn to loving they will find that we are turned to hating.
—Alan Paton, *Cry, the Beloved Country*

There is a time to love and a time to hate; whoever does not hate when he should does not deserve to love when he should.
—Elie Wiesel

I tell you there is such a thing as creative hate! A contempt that drives you through fire, makes you risk everything and lose everything, makes you a long sight better than you ever knew you could be.
—Willa Cather, *The Song of the Lark*

Proposition for Chapter 1

There are many kinds of hate. Hate is not a single sentiment, a discrete tendency. We learn to experience not one but a variety of hatreds spread across a spectrum from the purple of vicious, destructive rage at the less mature end of these color bands, through the hot red of vengeful hatred, to the bright yellow of constructive hate at the other. Indeed, we can break free from captivity to simple reactive hatred, grow to experience a reflective moral contempt for evil, and ultimately arrive at the maturity of a just hate that includes hate for hate itself. This chapter will offer a fresh paradigm for understanding hatred, which provides a constructive language for speaking of the multiple types, goals, uses, and misuses of hate in individual and social relationships.

I carry a hatred that never leaves my heart," says Maria Nordin, a victim of Sweden's mid-twentieth-century pursuit of genetic perfection. As a teen, Maria was legally declared genetically inferior and sterilized. Now, a half century later, Sweden is confronting the anger of thousands who suffered at the hands of a state-sponsored program of sterilizing the "unfit."

In 1943, at the age of seventeen, Nordin had her ovaries removed on the recommendations of the headmistress and consulting physician at a reform school for girls. In the parlance of the time, she was said to suffer from "genetic inferiority that the Swedish welfare state did not desire passed on to offspring." Although described as "kind and obedient and nice in appearance," her family, doctors said, had a history of alcoholism, promiscuity, and mental illness. Considered "feebleminded" because of her poor academic performance, Maria's problem was later discovered to be primarily uncorrected nearsightedness. She could not see the blackboard. Like 62,888 others who were sterilized, from 1935 to 1975, Maria long concealed her agonizing secret and the silent rage it creates: "I have tried to let my hatred go, to melt it down. But it isn't possible for me."

In the 1960s, Nordin and her husband confronted the physician and the headmistress with the false diagnosis that was used to authorize her sterilization. "They are lies—'feebleminded' and all those other words they said about me—lies that ruined me." Neither person expressed remorse or admitted that Nordin's educational, vocational, and public service careers had proved them wrong. In 1996, Nordin at last went public with her story, and telling the world about her experience of injustice has brought the first signs of happiness. "The biggest relief," she said, "is that people finally understand that I am the one telling the truth about me" (Murphy 1997, 1, 8).

Truth telling, the moral validation of a life narrative, and the transformation of "retributive hatred" to what we might call "just hatred" are essential to her integrity. What are these varieties of hate? What is this passionate demand for moral justice?

The Multiple Faces of Hate

Hatred, like aggression, is commonly spoken of as a simple, single-cause response to frustration, or obedience to a drive. This, however, is reductionism. On sober reflection we see that both hatred and aggression are aggregates of diverse acts, with diverse origins, diverse motivations, and diverse goals. They are bound together by their impact on objects rather than by a common or unitary drive. Hatred, like aggression, may be motivated by anxiety, fear, anger, rage, loyalty, conformism, hunger, sexuality, dominance, weakness, loss, need, bigotry, prejudice—or by outrage at evil, passion for justice, concern for the inviolability of memory, compassion for the oppressed.

Hate is not a single, simple emotion or motivation—no matter how single-minded or simpleminded it often appears to us. Hatred is composed of a wide spectrum of reactions, from emotion, to sentiment, to behavior, to prejudice, to commitment to values. It may be intense, focused, and direct; or it may be impersonal, detached, instrumental, and indirect. Hate is a complex series of negative feelings-attitudes-sets-behaviors. Yet a single word is largely employed to cover the whole set. Just as Eskimo languages have words for a dozen types of snow—powder, sugar, crusty, wet, heavy, frozen—and those who live in the tropics have but one, so our preference for the warmth of love has stimulated the creation of a rich thesaurus of words for affection and our fear of the coldness of hate has frozen our languages to a paltry few.

In ancient Greece, for example, love had many names, among them, *eros* (sensual love), *philia* (friendship), *storge* (familial love), and *agape* (disinterested love). Hate, however, had minimal vocabulary, even though in classical Greek literature hatred was considered a "natural" quality of human experience, could be expressed in unbounded acts of cruelty and also be praised as a virtue to be emulated. In Homer's epic story, the mythical Achilles drags the corpse of his opponent Hector behind his chariot around the city of Troy to celebrate his victory by publicly dishonoring the defeated hero. Homer's myth became reality when Alexander, recapitulating the story of Achilles, had the feet of Baetis, the brave defender of Gaza, pierced, and tied him, alive, to his carriage, to drag him around the conquered city while his Greek soldiers mocked the dying leader of the enemy. The philosopher Nietzsche, commenting on Alexander's gross and heinous caricature of Homer, called it "revolting, offensive. It makes us shudder. Here we look into the abyss of hatred" (Nietzsche 1924, 33).

"The whole of Greek antiquity thinks differently from us about hatred and envy," Nietzsche observes. Such thinking calls a discord that leads to the annihilation of evil "virtuous"; it judges the eradication of a group or city of opponents "good." The Homeric world centered around the mortal contest as a work of art—competitive acts of violence justified themselves. Yet it also modeled unbridled malevolence in conflict that reveals "the terrifying savagery of hatred and lust to annihilate"—what Nietzsche called "the abyss of hatred" (Nietzsche 1924, 38).

Nietzsche was wrong. The ancient and the postmodern are not all that different. Two millennia later, Troy is reenacted again and again. Alexander rides once more in the rage of nations pursuing tribal, political, or economic wars. Myths of heroic violence score high at the box office and sell well at the bookstore. As a political tool for raising approval ratings, winning elections, and justifying budgets, threats and counterthreats of violence remain our most successful strategy. The capacity for enacting banal evil in obedience to authority or blind evil in solidarity with the group is an eternal human phenomenon.

The Banality of Evil

Gillian Slovo, the daughter of a white South African leader in the long fight against apartheid, lost her mother, Ruth First, when a buff-colored envelope bearing a false logo of the United Nations exploded and smeared the walls of her Mozambique office with parts of Ruth's body. That was in 1982. In the 1990s, in an attempt to confront the atrocities of apartheid, the daughter met with her mother's killer in a courtroom of the South African Truth and Reconciliation Commission to find an end for her own long pursuit of truth, if not justice. To bar the way against a national scourge of recriminations that the South African society could ill afford, the Truth and Reconciliation Commission allowed those implicated in political crimes to gain immunity if they recounted what they did in public confession.

Craig Williamson, a former secret police agent, evaded Slovo for weeks before agreeing to meet, but when they did, he talked for hours. A student informer who later became a full-time functionary, Craig explained the terrorist murder smoothly. "It was almost casual, it wasn't as though somebody was responsible for this kind of thing . . . it was almost the luck of the draw." Finally he offered his philosophic conclusion: "God help us . . . we must try and stop this thing so we can move upwards and not downwards."

Slovo, when the interview was over, wondered why she felt neither fury nor a lust for revenge. "Our meeting had been an exercise in dissociation from which I'd emerged in a stupor that had sent me into dreamless afternoon sleep." She found no answers to her mother's murder, only the tiresome banality of evil. Although her father survived to return from exile in triumph with Nelson Mandela, her mother had become one of the thousands of almost random victims of murder—in a campaign to eliminate visible representatives of those prominent among the hated majority (Slovo, 1997).

"An exercise in dissociation" is the metaphor Slovo finally selects to characterize the detached, unemotional atrocities carried out in allegiance to or obedience of group goals. For the functionary doing the final act, the motivation may be only banal conformity, shallow belonging, empty complicity. The malevolent decisions for murder, mutilation, or terrorism were made antiseptically somewhere up a sterile hierarchy of ideologically distanced and mentally dissociated functionaries, and delegated down a serial file of human dominoes.

> The *sine qua non* of bureaucratized violence is not hatred but cold, emotional detachment and robotic discipline. Indeed, efforts are routinely made to screen out through diagnostic tests those who in pre-modern times might have been celebrated as berserkers. But this observation applies only at the point of execution of state violence. Having lived in the twentieth century, we know that mass hatred is not only compatible with "cost effective" military violence. It is one of its preconditions. (Aho 1994, 199–220)

Institutionalized hate may be laundered of emotion in service of the military, the corporation, academia, or the state. Rarely does it seethe with rage or disgust. Conscious concern for order and efficiency cloak the strategies for limiting or eliminating human lives. Look not for the viciously intense but for the vacuously banal.

"The absence of hate in the killer is even worse than the hate. The members of the *Einsatzgruppen* massacred thousands and thousands of Jewish children they did not hate," Wiesel says (1995, 373), recalling the banality of evil in functionaries of the concentration camps. Evil, sterilized of emotion, is even more terrifying for its cold methodical precision; hate, enacted in obedience to orders, is nonetheless hate behavior; violence, inflicted with well-justified rationale, is still violence.

A Spectrum of Hate

No two hates, whether personal or social in sphere, are alike, yet all hate falls into patterns, into spectra of negative sentiments and behaviors. Exploring such a spectrum may offer us a better language with which to debate the crucial questions such as: "Is there such a thing as constructive hate?" "Is hate sometimes an acceptable, even valuable human emotion?" "Is hate essentially immoral?" "Must it be an impulse to harm or destroy?" "Can it be a resistance against that which harms you, endangers loved ones, or devalues all you hold dear?" "Is the hatred of evil a positive emotion or a negative emotion?" "Do hate, contempt, and the dissociated emotions of resentment, anger, envy, and even jealousy have a place in either enforcing or challenging a moral order?"

Sorting out the varieties of hate, and assembling a nomenclature that defines gradations of personal, social, moral, and political outrage, may provide a language for reconsidering questions that are implicit in any exploration of justice. Such explorations stretch from the proverbial dictums of Confucius, the legal codes of Hammurabi, the social rules of Solon, the communal laws of Moses, the philosophical categories of Aristotle, down through the ages to the contemporary debates of legal precedents and consistent rulings which, since justice is a journey not a destination, must be renewed in each generation.

The diverse forms that hatred takes confuse us, Jean Hampton notes, because "the word 'hatred' covers a *'family'* of negative emotional responses. For example, I can hate a person in the same way I hate cloudy weather or snow-mobiling or mosquitoes. . . . This is *simple hatred . . .* much less simple is the kind of hatred toward human beings which is experienced in many moral contexts" (Murphy and Hampton 1988, 61).

"Hate" describes a "family," a cluster, a nebula of responses that has many variations from a simple defensive reflex to a reasoned moral antipathy; the word "hate" may be used to name two very different feelings—disliking a person or despising an action. Although often "I hate you" is said to the perpetrator, "I resent what you did" is said of the action. Hate may be reserved for the actor, resentment for the action, but these two are not easily distinguished, since the despised act is a part of a complex pattern of toxic behavior, and such patterns become traits and traits combine to become the whole personality and personality is not easily distinguished from person. Dismay quickly becomes dislike and then disgust, followed by detesting and despising.

Among the varieties of anger, outrage, and hate, we can distinguish a multicolor linguistic spectrum (green envy—yellow fear—pink humiliation—red anger—purple resentment—blue funk—black rage—white hate) that, in a preliminary way, reaches across a great variety of emotions, sentiments, or attitudes. Table 1, "The Spectrum of Hates," provides an initial overview of the argument that follows. These concise definitions of the family of hates, charted for quick reference, may serve to clarify and visualize the concepts before they are discussed at length.

The continuum that progresses from simple hate to just hate moves

Table 1   The Spectrum of Hates

1. *"Simple hatred,"* or *Disgust:* dislike of the distasteful or disgusting, a mosquito in the night, a cell phone at a concert, a fingernail on a blackboard, a driver who hogs a lane

2. *"Spiteful hatred,"* or *Resentment:* simmering rage at an abuser, nursed grudge toward a bully, resentment of an unfair boss

3. *"Malicious hatred,"* or *Revenge:* the fervent desire to do unlimited injury to a perpetrator in retaliation, not "an eye for an eye" but eyes, ears, nose, and head

4. *"Retributive hatred,"* or *Retaliation:* the stubborn demand for full measure of equal justice in repayment; a "tooth for a tooth" demand for "a pound of flesh"

5. *"Principled hatred,"* or *Deliberative hatred:* a settled hostility constructing a coherent rationale to justify the antipathy or legitimize the retaliation being plotted

6. *"Moral hatred,"* or *Moral contempt:* despises both the abuse and the abuser, although it begins to separate the act from the actor, an aversion to someone immoral or evil

7. *"Just hatred,"* or *Just contempt:* hatred for deliberate injustice, intentional violence to or violation of persons or peoples. Act is clearly differentiated from the perpetrator

through revenge, retribution, and self-justification to a level of self-critique and moral caution. The range of such sentiments is charted in Table 2, "Visualizing a Spectrum of Hates." From one end of the continuum the object of contempt shifts from hated thing (or person seen as a thing) to hated person and/or group, to contempt for unjust action and oppressive social system. On the one end, little ambiguity is tolerated, issues are seen as simple, clear, absolute; on the other end, there is a toleration for high ambiguity and the issues are seen in their full and irreducible complexity. In the simple forms of hate, the person is obviously nothing more than that person's worst action, reduced to the crime or prime evil; in just hatred, the person is always more than any single action, no matter how heinous or indefensible that action. At one end thinking tends to be exclusively *either/or* in simplification of contested issues to we/they, good/bad, right/wrong categories; in the middle range, the thinker struggles to use *both/and* concepts which attempt relating, correlating, balancing polar opposites in compromise or collaboration; and at the far end thinking broadens to allow a *neither/nor* perspective, which recognizes that the complexity of the conflict requires that we seek a new category, a different vantage point that can include, redefine, and perhaps transform us both, so that the outcome will be neither my perspective nor yours, neither will I win and you lose nor will it be the reverse. A third option can be created, an alternate path discovered, that both affirm but neither claims as her victory or his resentment at his defeat.

This spectrum suggests a way of viewing the wide range of emotional

Table 2   Visualizing a Spectrum of Hates

1	2	3	4	5	6	7
Simple Hatred	Spiteful Hatred	Malicious Hatred	Retributive Hatred	Principled Hatred	Moral Hatred	Just Hatred

Hated thing or person as thing			Hated person or group		Hated actions or system	
(No ambiguity tolerated) Person is no more than the noxious act		⟵⟶			(High ambiguity tolerated) Person is always more than the worst act	
(In hates 1–3) *Either/or* thinking			(In hates 4–5) *Both/and* thinking		(In hates 6–7) *Neither/nor* thinking	
Splitting between self and other			Splitting between offender and offense		Refuses splitting and seeks an alternative solution/resolution	

and volitional responses of an individual or a group toward a hated object. The object is perceived very differently as one moves across the spectrum and the object of hatred moves from hated thing or person hated as a thing—to hated person—to despised behavior—to destructive process—to evil system. The progression is from simple disgust or spiteful hate (I hate "it") toward malicious or retaliatory hatred (I hate you) to principled hatred (I have every good reason to hate you), then undergoes a major shift as one arrives at moral hatred (I hate the act or injury) or just contempt (I hate evil itself, its corrupt, enslaving system).

Simple hatred reduces the other to an irritant, an object, a thing. An example is military rhetoric that redefines the opponent from human to target zone. Damage to innocent civilians adjoining the enemy becomes regrettable but unavoidable collateral damage. Only when the person in the crosshairs has become nonperson, when the human life has been reduced to an obstacle that must be removed, can one kill with impunity. In time of war, the higher forms of hatred are suspended, and their motivations are called in service of simpler forms of hate. Retaliation and revenge are co-opted; and spiteful, malicious, or retributive hatreds are employed to perceive the other as an offending foe deserving retaliation.

The movement toward moral or just hatreds requires a level of maturation that allows a person to hold mutually contradictory precepts and concepts in the mind at the same time. This ability to sustain ambiguity is a mark of cognitive maturation and a prerequisite for truly moral reflection.

The Spectrum Defined

Simple hatred (Disgust) is the dislike of objects or aversion to persons we experience as unpleasant. It is the fervent wish that the irritant be removed. This is the hatred of a person, place, or thing arising from disgust or distaste: "I hate rainy weather," "I despise mosquitoes," "I can't stand that woman, she is constantly interrupting." Such simple hatred is the polar opposite to "simple love," the attraction one feels for sunshine, chocolate, or intriguing people (Murphy and Hampton 1988, 60–61).

Spiteful hatred (Resentment) causes us to angrily despise the other as noxious or abhorrent, desire her ill fortune, brood on ways of inflicting injury, relish the satisfaction arising from her misfortune. It wishes to return pain for pain, injury for injury. It more often lodges in the memory as a grudge held, an old account unsettled, waiting the day when the other will receive a well-deserved comeuppance.

Malicious hatred (Revenge) is the antipathy one feels toward those who have personally harmed one; the act may or may not be a moral wrong, but an insult or injury has been received. Spite or malice is interpersonal. The hater feels horror toward the injury, but hatred toward the perpetrator. This personal animosity generates a competitive response to the wrongdoer (Murphy and Hampton 1988, 62). Thus, malicious hatred creates a wide range of covert strategies for bringing the other down in the hope that it, in some way, will lift the self up. It is by nature *strategic* hatred, bent on exacting revenge, fired by the hope of satisfaction, vindication, or retaliation. The spontaneous self-protective reflex turns into savage brooding. The human mind seems infinitely inventive of ingenious ways to get even. The greatest tragedies in literature are built on the deep urge for retribution; to cite two, we see Hamlet in search of revenge or Medea murdering her sons and hurling their corpses in the face of their father.

Retributive hatred (Retaliation) is a complex of "feelings that another person's current level of well-being is undeserved or ill-gotten (perhaps at one's own expense) and that a reduction in that well-being will simply represent his getting just deserves" (Murphy and Hampton 1988, 89). It leads one, not to seek personal retribution, but to instigate, to contribute to, to be gratified by the other's prosecution and punishment. It is supported by and proceeds from several common-law principles: (1) no one should be allowed to profit from his/her own wrongdoing; (2) justice requires a proper moral redistribution of whatever goods are in question; (3) retribution is appropriately directed to the wrongdoer and proportionate to the injury felt or done. Retributive hatred, such as might be felt by a rape victim who sees the rapist leading a life of freedom and contentment, or the defrauded who sees the fraudulent prospering, may be fueled by spiteful or malicious fires, but in time it becomes *principled hate* as one creates justifications for desiring to avenge the abuse, vindicate the wronged, or expose evil done.

Principled hatred (Reasoned rationale) is the hate that creates a case for the defense. It arises in the construction, by an individual or group, of a legitimate case for loathing, a prejudicial platform for despising the other that becomes a chronic disposition or a communal mind-set toward the outgroup, or a national policy of opposing some political entity or enemy. Its result may be as elaborate as a government's white paper supporting military action or as simple as a matched set of prejudices which enables one group to defend its hostility toward another group on the basis of past threat, atrocity, or race. The idea of "race" itself is an example of a "principled hate" construct that has no empirical base. Race continues to be used as a category even though we know that more variation exists within so-called racial groups than between them.

In the heat of principled hate, the person hating rapidly develops a rich matrix of beliefs that form a social location validating a "historical, social, moral, or legal case" for fearing, hating, or feeling contempt for the enemy. Principled hate forms the moral high ground for acts of justified aggression or retaliation for the individual, the clan, or the state. Retaliation is the health of the state, we may say with cynical accuracy. The tightness of the argument that a state can present and the compelling nature of the propaganda it can create to support it (rationale plus slogans) provide the mandate to carry out acts of violence in return for affront or injury perceived. Principled hate provides the philosophical basis not just for holy wars but for virtually all wars.

Principled hate may become the cultural "wisdom" that is held sacred as a definition of national sanctity and sovereignty. Cultures develop their own devices for transmitting their instructions for hatred and the ensuing acts of retaliation. With pervasive subtlety, prejudice sustains hatred from generation to generation; in cultures where retaliation is obligation, it assigns the task with specificity—like the southern Slav mother who lays her infant son to sleep each night covered by the bloodstained shirt of his murdered father. A life vocation is conferred on the child before he knows the feeling of obligation—he will exact revenge against the descendant of the murderer. One death will satisfy another, but this requires a further step in a principled blood feud that reverberates through generations of retaliation.

Moral hatred (Moral contempt) may despise both actor and action, but it begins the difficult move of separating actor and action. The hater now questions the previous practice of reducing the abuser to "nothing more than the evil act." It is the deep aversion one feels for Nazis such as Hitler, Eichmann, or Goebbels. When the person's evil life project is ultimately expressed in a heinous crime, separation of the perpetrator and the atrocity becomes difficult, even dubious. The horror of the holocaust demands profound repulsion from a moral conscience. Hampton introduced this category of moral hatred to define those situations where both the action and the person who performed the action deserve morally to be despised and hated. Moral hatred is indignation at and aversion to both the "insulter herself—her character, her habits, her disposition, or the whole components of her," since she is so fully identified with the evil cause. "Such aversion for her cause and to *her* is motivated by morality; it involves believing, by virtue of the insulter's association with the evil cause, that she has 'rotted' or 'gone bad' so that she now lacks some measure of goodness or moral health" (Murphy and Hampton 1988, 80).

Moral hatred can exist in degrees of intensity, with the strongest hatred felt for heinous criminals, mass murderers, persons like the Nazi Goebbels, who, by all known moral standards, are "irredeemably 'rotten' like a piece of meat that has been allowed to become full of maggots and decay" (80). Their moral condition goes beyond those who are cloaked in evil, or acting evilly but not wholly without some sign of cohumanity. We might measure the degree of moral hatred by the inclination to repudiate rather than reclaim or rehabilitate the person. Not to experience indignation at a flagrantly immoral action, or to feel hatred for the immoral cause on which the wrongdoer acted and yet not to feel the same aversion toward the wrongdoer himself if he totally identifies himself with that evil cause, appears to involve giving up one's commitment to the cause of morality.

Moral hatred may at first seem essentially impersonal since it focuses primarily on the lack of morality in the other's actions. But the person's evil behavior, public acts, and private choices get enmeshed in beliefs, personhood, and character like cancer cells invading healthy tissue. Hating the malignant but respecting the benign is difficult; distinguishing growth from the grower is a delicate demarcation. Tumor and tumorous organ sometimes eventually become one and the same. The common platitude "We must hate the sin, but love the sinner" is inadequate, says Lifton. "We must underscore the distinction between potential and actual evil," because, he argues, "once a man performs an evil deed, he has become part of that deed, and that deed a part of him" (Lifton 1986, 502).

Moral hatred is the basis of just war theory, although its use is more often as principled hate. Its proponents often present it as just hatred, but even the most persuasive and/or absolute arguments do not remove its ambiguity.

The preeminent danger of moral hatred is that it may blind us to the humane and decent elements within another. The temptation to ascend a righteous throne and pronounce absolute sentence lurks in all moral judgment. Our entitlement to the high ground seems self-evident when passion fires the mind. Truly moral thought can never dismiss the question "Is the person no more than the worst act committed, or is every individual more than the most noxious act?"

Just hatred (Just contempt) fully affirms one's moral hatred of the act, unhesitatingly defends the victim of the evil action, while stubbornly seeking justice for the actor as well. It is the negation of any form of deliberate injustice. It is grounded in a passion for fairness, a commitment to the just and equal rights of persons, groups, even nations. Just hatred is focused on existing inequality, discrimination, abuse, violence, or destruction; it demands that justice be seen, known, validated in experience and embodied in human relationships or social systems.

In just hatred, one has discovered that no person can be so decayed that the person loses the last trace of some decency, loyalty, or integrity, or so "rotted" as to have no remaining trace of goodness or residue of worth. The hated injustice is, although often painfully difficult to do, differentiated from the perpetrator(s) of the evil. Just hatred seeks an end to the evil and works diligently at inviting and facilitating appropriate repentance and restitution, so that justice may be seen to be done. Just hate recognizes that we must face not only the other group's evil but our own as well. It realizes that there is no reconciliation between groups until people talk about their own ethnic group's crimes as honestly as they point out those of others. Victors who claimed their cause as just must reflect repentantly on their own injustices as they address the war crimes of the defeated foe. Americans, for example, who seek deeper justice, know they dare speak of Nuremberg or the Hague only through the admission of Nagasaki, Vietnam, and Dresden.

Sorting Out Principled, Moral, and Just Hate

Sorting out the final three hates on the spectrum is a complex puzzle for the observer, a torturous task for the one hating. Principled critique of a wrongdoer, moral outrage at a wrong done, and just hate of wrongdoing are not easily differentiated. Confident in its own rightness, *principled hate* biases the process by laying down as its first two principles: "My retaliatory hate is unquestionably moral hate," and "My moral hatred is indubitably just hatred." Retaliatory hate can create instant justifications for action, and moral hatred is equally quick to generate rationales to defend itself. All three are defensive: all three pretend to be above challenge. This may explain why hatred is the most rationalized of all emotions. When confronted, the person expressing hate invariably defends himself by telling of injury, or loss, or wounded pride. The case for justifying a continued negative set toward another person or group is usually complexly textured with personal, moral, social, historical, political, and, above all, theological strands interwoven into an intricate rationale of principled hate.

In hating, there is a division between the self and the other known as "splitting," and the rule that seems puzzling at first becomes obvious on second thought: "A split between occurs when there is a split within." Conscience is split from emotion, and social interest from anger. Principled hate flows from the need to render the split within the self acceptable to the self; it is then given in a reasoned explanation for the split between self and other. The hater must live with the division between the natural concern for fellow humans and the vehement denial that the fellow human is worthy of any compassion or concern. This tension can be sustained only within a framework of justifications—principled arguments that vindicate the self for writing off another person or group. The framework may be quickly cobbled together from secondhand prejudices, familial myths, and social biases. But it is more often a sophisticated construction of wider social stereotypes and even moral values supported by admirable characteristics such as loyalty, corporate ambition, nationalism, belief in progress as evolutionary good, and other publicly approved opinions.

Principled hate is the attempt of retributive hate to justify or rationalize itself as moral hate. It is retributive hate in moral clothing. No more relevant example can be found than the principled matrix of hate that enabled Adolf Hitler to motivate a nation of the world's most religiously and philosophically sophisticated people to undertake the most pronouncedly focused hate project in recent history. The "principled" foundation of

Hitler's eloquent rhetoric (if we enter his thought world empathically) rested on five principles:

1. The cosmos and all human history were product and result of an impersonal fate, or destiny functioning by natural laws. He denied the existence of transcendent moral universals or any personal God.
2. The purpose of both individual and nation should lie in obeying nature's iron laws, since nothing exists beyond nature. Social Darwinism had convinced Hitler that life is a continuous struggle for existence, dominance, and progress through the survival of the fittest. The practice of eugenics and the extermination of inferior races was a necessary way to improve the human species and accelerate progress.
3. Evolution is the ultimate moral absolute. That which advances evolution is a moral good, that which hinders evolution is evil.
4. Expansion of the Aryan race is good—they are the most advanced race, the originators of civilization and higher culture. Limitation of Aryan world dominance is evil.
5. The evolution of humanity will advance through the achievement of this noble ideal of a purified race and a refined culture.

Thus, Hitler could and did conclude, his policies and decisions were good and beneficial. A universe without God, without a transcendent morality, without universal human rights but with a clear mandate for evolution of the fittest, will ultimately benefit the human race. The final solution—his principled doctrine of anti-Semitism—of eliminating the inferior who stop this inevitable march of progress was to produce a world that was *"Judenrein"* (pure of all Jews) and free to advance toward the development of a super race (Weikart 2001, 21).

Hitler was, in spite of his agnosticism, capable of using theological references to communicate his convictions. In *Mein Kampf*, he wrote: "I believe that I am acting in accordance with the will of the Almighty Creator: by defending myself against the Jew, I am fighting for the work of the Lord" (Hitler 1942, 84). The conviction that he was acting in accord with the Christian God, mythical though this god may be, summoned his followers—the vast majority of Nazis and German citizens who supported him were Christians—to see the Third Reich as a kingdom under God. Two thousand years of anti-Semitic Christian voices and vices culminated in the holocaust, revealing the extent to which cumulative hatred will go. His principled hate empowered him to rouse his countrymen to embrace war as a struggle for existence that would decide the destiny of humanity, a destiny inextricably bound up in the fulfillment of the Aryan evolution. To falter was to fail their glorious moment in history, to stumble in the forward march of providence, and to thwart the ultimate consummation of the goal of all human existence.

The Nazi construction of principled hate is not unique in history, although the holocaust stands unparalleled in its malevolent design. The defense ministry of virtually every nation perceives its world from a complex of self-justifying assumptions and weaves tight arguments from the egoistic ethical foundations it posits. Similarly, principled hate, in all its institutional social or individual forms, pursues its own reality doggedly, conceals itself in sacred causes with subtle philosophies, conscripts the support of religion, and constructs persuasive politics. It is present in some form in the thought of virtually every group or person in defense of its uniqueness and hegemony. It is a tendency in thought that may be anticipated in any argument for one's own rights, entitlements, or claims to the possession of truth. *Therefore we should view with suspicion and doubt any idea that makes suffering more understandable and less abhorrent or makes it easier to approve killing.*

Principled hate is grounded in both *attributive justice*, justice according to what may be attributed to those worthy and entitled, and *retributive justice*, justice that repays with equity what has been earned, is deserved, and must be rectified through retaliation. (See types of justice in chapter 9.) A just contempt of evil, what we call "just hate," begins from a radically differing ground, that of just and right human relationships grounded in *distributive* and *redemptive* justice. Just hate stands in critique of retributive and principled hate, in apposition to rationalized hate. Just hate refuses to accept answers that are grounded in equivalent repayment, or to gain satisfaction through returning morally principled evil for the original irresponsible unprincipled action. It seeks to move from retributive or attributive justice toward distributive, redemptive, and transformative justice. (There is a more complete discussion of these types of justice in the last chapter.)

Just Hate as Love of Good

Just hatred is a profound antipathy to all that works evil, that creates systems that impoverish, devalue, or destroy persons. The hate is focused on violations of objective moral values. It sets up the tension between virtues and vices. Vices are those actions which have external rewards achieved by exploiting others; virtues are those practices which are internally rewarding because of their essential goodness (MacIntyre 1981).

Just hatred, in its profound commitment to the good, is virtually synonymous with love. Seeking to be constructive in intent and objective in focus, it promotes the good of all persons in agape; it is the mature union of love and hate in creative synthesis. The desire for such synthesis resides within every maturing human being—to love the surrounding world *and* to feel contempt for its injustices and its threatening presence; to love humanity and to feel contempt for inhumanity. Contempt and compassion are not incompatible. The ability to feel accurate, genuine contempt toward threat while truly caring about the one who is threatening is an undeniable sign of maturity. Contempt may express this balance of affirmation and negation with just accuracy, but too easily it may be inaccurate and distorted by our own inner conflicts. In the latter event, the contempt is a vain attempt to add to the self by lessening something else, denigrating the other to elevate the self. As one moves toward just hate, the hate engenders compassion rather than mere disgust. It becomes a new vision of possibility, the possibility that love and hate can be reconciled, that candor and compassion allow one to be a keen and eminently fair critic without feeling or expressing contempt. When moral criticism is clouded with inadvertent contempt, hate corrupts the attempt to discern the truth about the other. The hunger for truth with the desire to critique is a human characteristic that facilitates the formation of identity, the clarification of selfhood, the development of relationship. The yearning for accurate, truthful criticism grows from a hope of identifying what is good in ourselves so we can increase and strengthen it; and learning what is unworthy and unjust so we can correct it. In our development and growth we fear and avoid criticism because it so often cloaks contempt, but when we encounter another who exhibits the knowledge and caring to criticize authentically and with consummate fairness we recognize an invitation to grow toward our full selfhood. It is a profound disappointment to live through stages of life without encountering such a mirroring friend who in goodwill is willing to risk authentic encounter without expressing crippling contempt. Experiencing just hate united with genuine compassion allows us to recognize the common finitude of all humanity, and to develop a measure of existential humility. We become reflective on the deeper sources of evil, those within ourselves as well as those in others. As the contemplative Thomas Merton writes: "Instead of hating the people you think are war-makers, hate the appetites and the disorder in your own soul, which are the causes of war" (Merton 1991, 82).

Just hate is akin to grief; it contains a deep sadness that injustice or brutality is part of the human situation. On the fiftieth anniversary of the January 27, 1945, liberation of Auschwitz, Jewish writer David Grossman observed, "Whenever I think back on the Holocaust the predominate feeling continues to be that of hurt. It is not anger or lust for revenge, it is not hatred, but a bitter, inconsolable hurt that such things were done to human beings" (Mueller-Fahrenholz 1996, 26).

Just hatred is a constituent element in what I have elsewhere called "forgrieving," that painful forgiveness in which the injury one has suffered is truly faced and fully felt, and the repulsion at evil borne is honestly recognized, even when there is no recognition or repentance by the offender (Augsburger 1996, 71). In forgrieving, one moves through anger with its retributive goals toward not simply resignation to reality but a courageous acceptance of redemptive and transformative goals. The passion about evil does not die; it is reborn in new forms of commitment to justice. Dietrich Bonhoeffer describes this movement in similar terms. "Forgiveness is a form of suffering—when I forgive I have not only suffered the offense but also released or suppressed the rightful claims of strict retributive justice in favor of a costly redemptive justice" (Bonhoeffer 1963, 100).

Contempt as a Moral Attitude

Releasing the claims on an eye for an eye opens the possibility of a kind of justice that protects both parties' eyes. Redemptive justice, springing from a hatred of all that is unjust and a hope that true justice can be done, seeks a new way of transforming the old cycles of retribution. To demonstrate this movement from retaliatory through principled to moral hate, consider the Letelier family story.

> " 'Do not let this teach you to hate,' were my mother's first words to us in the emergency room of George Washington Hospital. It was late September, 1976, my father, Orlando Letelier, and an American co-worker, Ronnie Moffitt, had been assassinated on the streets of Washington, D.C.," Letelier's son recalls. "A hit squad under orders from Chilean General Augusto Pinochet, working with paramilitary Cuban exiles, planted a remotely controlled bomb in his car and detonated it as he drove past the Chilean Embassy.
>
> "I remember being pulled from a high school classroom. Our car passed the bloody fragment strewn bombsite. There is an indelible image stored inside of me, of ambulances and firemen cleaning up Massachusetts Avenue, hosing blood away and searching for the dismembered remains of my father's body.

"Since that tragic day, my mother, Isabel Morel, and others, including my father's sister Fabiola Letelier, in Chile, have worked tirelessly for justice and to indict the men who authored the murder." Now, with the detainment of Pinochet in Britain, and the attempt to bring him to trial for war crimes, Letelier adds, "We are celebrating the truth which has always been ours, *'justice is real'*"(Letelier 1998, B7).

"Do not let this teach you to hate," the widow forbids. "Do not rage for revenge or retaliation." Yet for the rest of her life she will be directed by a passion for justice—until "justice is real."

The tension between the various forms of hate, the focused pursuit of moral hate and the repudiation of revenge as a motive are clear in her words. Perhaps also the pursuit of just hate, difficult as it is to express or maintain.

I have described moral and just hatred as forms of contempt. What can this mean? Contempt in its raw form is the source of every brutality, the basis of violent acts, the inner permission for all negativity. But when contempt is focused by moral virtues that prize and serve justice, the result is *just contempt*, a moral attitude of constructive, critical, and even caring response. Just contempt is disdain for what is less than human, disgust for all that dehumanizes. It negates all that negates humanity, all that denies justice and denigrates reverence for life.

The dynamics of contempt are distinct from those of hatred, as Wiesel illustrates in his novel *The Town behind the Wall.* Michael encounters the symbolic character, "the spectator" who simply watches moral evil being perpetuated and waits for it to pass, serving as a metaphor for all who want only to live in peace and quiet, whatever the price. Michael is astounded by this detachment.

> How can anyone remain a spectator indefinitely? How can one continue to embrace the woman he loves, to pray to God with fervor if not faith, to dream of a better tomorrow—after having seen that. . . . Between victims and executioners there is a mysterious bond; they belong to the same universe; one is the negation of the other. . . . The spectator is entirely beyond us. (Wiesel 1969, 161)

In his confrontation with the spectator, Michael clarifies the distinction between hate and contempt, and for him, contempt becomes a moral outrage that is beyond emotion, beyond all recognition of the other as human.

"No," I said, "I don't hate you." A pause, then: "I feel contempt for you. That's worse. The man who inspires hatred is still human; but not the man who inspires contempt. . . . Hatred implies humanity. . . . But contempt has only one implication: decadence." (Wiesel 1969, 170)

Michael's indictment of indifference and noninvolvement as utterly scandalous is an attempt to articulate a holy rage for justice in the face of a blind detachment from even seeing the pain of victims when it is right before one's eyes. The passion for justice in Michael's protest is a search for a deep morality that resides within contempt. Contempt, as a moral attitude, expresses a *just hatred* that unites concern for justice, mercy toward the offender, and humility in the pursuit of both. The prophet Micah embodied this attitude. One who "walk[s] humbly with . . . God," Micah concludes, does justice and loves mercy (Mic. 6:8). This is the central ethical maxim of both First and Second Testaments, the love of God and the inseparable equal esteem of neighbor. The inverse human position is arrogance toward God and injustice and cruelty (the opposite of mercy) to the other. Micah, who hates injustice, contemptuously condemns the arrogant cruelty done for cruelty's sake that he sees in the social and religious system. Micah's contempt for human cruelty identifies it as essential evil and rises to a moral attitude that demands constructive justice among his people.

> Listen, you leaders of Jacob, rulers of Israel,
> should you not know what is right?
>   You hate good and love evil,
> you flay men alive and tear the very flesh from their bones;
>   you devour the flesh of my people,
>   strip off their skin,
>   splinter their bones;
>   you shred them like flesh into a pot,
>   like meat into a cauldron.
>
>   (Micah 3:1–3)

> Listen to this, leaders of Jacob,
>   rulers of Israel,
> you who make justice hateful
> and wrest it from its straight course,
> . . . .
> [who] sell justice.
>   (Micah 3:9–11)

Micah's loathing of injustice erupts in mutilation metaphors as he expresses his horror at cruelty. Cruelty, the willful inflicting of physical or psychological pain on a weaker being in order to cause anguish, fear, or suffering, is evil done to one who has an equal claim to justice, the neighbor—and what is done to the neighbor is in reality done to God. It is supremely evil because it is a denial of goodness and of God. Ironically—need we point out?—some of the greatest cruelties in history have been done in the name of goodness and the service of God.

Hatred of evil, Micah teaches (in his trilogy of justice, mercy, and humility), even profound contempt for evil, can be expressed without employing cruelty. Such hate, "just hate" we are calling it here, is largely unconsidered, seldom explored, rarely tried in human affairs, because we have succeeded in splitting the two principles—doing justice and loving mercy. Micah's God is a God of both justice and mercy, who hates injustice and cruelty, prizes equity and compassion. God is also a God of vengeance, and "if hatred and vengeance are permissible for God," Jeffrie Murphy contends, "then there must be a sense in which these responses are *in principle* permissible" (Murphy and Hampton 1988, 98 n. 13). The nature of that vengeance—both merciful and just—remains for us to seek in following the way of a God of steadfast love.

In the Gospel of Matthew, Jesus' injunction against spiteful hate (Matt. 5:43) as destructive and murderous stands alongside his ability to demonstrate moral contempt in his stark confrontation of the endemic evils of religion become destructive and his forthright moral judgment of those who champion it (Matthew 23). In this decisive critique, Jesus uses the language of moral contempt that names both practices and people as rotted, "full of dead men's bones and all kinds of filth" (v. 27), as so far beyond hope they are "fit for hell" (v. 15). But in his final encounter with entrenched evil—the trial and crucifixion—he showed no evidence of either moral or just hatred, exhibiting radical enemy love. Like their master, the writers of the New Testament, except for the author of the Revelation of John, where dramatic hatred finds vivid expression alongside finally triumphant love, affirm the way of nonviolent love rather than moral hatred directed at persons. Recognizing that our knowledge is limited, our capacity to judge imperfect and flawed, they turn away from a moral hatred that reduces another to ultimate evil. In recognition of the call to love the enemy, Paul, for example, commands one to "loathe" evil (Rom. 12:9) but never to "pay back evil for evil" (12:17), instead, to refer hatred of the wrongdoer to a higher court (12:18–19) and act compassionately toward the enemy (12:20–21). Not hellfire but the healing fire of visible moral goodness—just hatred and love of justice—shall be given.

Excusing the Self—Accusing the Other

If we do allow ourselves to recognize our own hatred, it is the human tendency—even the norm—to excuse the self as justified, as acting out of rational motives, as carrying out an understandable course of action, while seeing the other as unjustified, acting with irrational motivation, and carrying out indefensible unacceptable behavior. Each disputant is tempted to see the self acting from the higher point of the scale and the other as one or more steps down the continuum. Hate, being competitive, sees self as justified, other as indefensible; self as ultimately benign, other as malevolent.

We human beings have an almost universal distaste for and an unwillingness to use "hate" to describe our own emotion, although we are much less hesitant to apply it to others, and not at all in ascribing it to the enemy. As psychoanalyst Reuben Fine observes: "To begin with, hatred is always rationalized. No one likes to be told that he has hateful feelings; if he is told that, he reacts with 'appropriate' rage" (Fine 1990, 650). We rationalize our own hate into invisibility, we equivocate over words in constructing our defense. Psychiatrist-theologian Paul Tournier, in writing of this wordplay of self-concealment that rejects the word "hate," questions use of the word "contempt" and prefers "disdain."

> The word "contempt" is rather strong. We ought to speak of "disdain." But perhaps even the shade of difference in meaning between the two words hides our need to justify ourselves. I speak of contempt because those we treat with disdain feel it as contempt. Contempt is the social problem *par excellence*. (Tournier 1979, 108)

No matter how "just" the motivation of one who speaks out of moral disdain, he or she will be heard by the object of criticism as contemptuous. "The one who throws a rock, soon forgets. The one who is struck never forgets" goes the Arab proverb. In all conflict, I discover, I judge my actions by my intentions—which are just and good—and the other's actions by their consequences—which are arbitrary and evil. I see the conflict from my consistent and coherent story and the other's actions as disruptive and dysfunctional. My motivations are higher on any moral spectrum of justice, the opponent's intentions are lower. As I excuse, I also accuse; as I exonerate myself, I may incriminate you. The language we employ betrays the way our judgments are made. "I am just, you are unjust, he is evil," or, "I am principled, you are confused, he is corrupt" are common ways of conjugating motivation. So we too easily conclude, "My hatred is just, yours is perhaps moral although questionable and unfortunately wrong, but hers is nothing more than retributive revenge."

Anger as Moral Passion

Moral hatred against evil is often defined as anger, but anger channeled toward constructive goals. Such hatred may be essential to moral passion, Elie Wiesel has argued, "and without hate we could not hope to obtain victory."

> Because my people have never known how to hate, their tragedy, throughout the centuries, has stemmed from their inability to hate those who have humiliated and from time to time exterminated them. Now our only chance lies in hating you, in learning the necessity and the art of hate. Otherwise . . . our future will only be an extension of the past, and the Messiah will wait indefinitely for his deliverance. (Wiesel 1999, 200)

The goal of life, Elie Wiesel concludes, is to transmute hatred into anger, and to turn anger to creative ends. This is the great achievement that he observed, almost as a gift of grace, among fellow holocaust survivors. After recalling all the killings, the tragic separations, the brutal trivialization of human life, he asks, "What do we do with these questions, these memories? What do we do with the anger? The great miracle of my generation is that somehow the anger was channeled to humanistic purposes" (Wiesel 1979, 36).

Elsewhere in Wiesel's writings, he offers clues to how such a transformation takes place. His portrait of Rebbe Barukh of Medzebozh reveals one who embodies such just anger: "He was angry? Naturally he was. He was angry because he cared, because he was concerned, because he was present to anyone in need of human presence" (Wiesel 1978a, 60).

To one of his students, Rebbe Barukh proposed:

> I know there are questions that have no answers; there is a suffering that has no name; there is injustice in God's creation—and there are

reasons enough for man to explode with rage. I know there are reasons for you to be angry. Good. Let us be angry. Together. (Wiesel 1978a, 60)

Anger, expressed by an individual, accountable only to one's own conscience, is in great danger of being self-serving. Anger that is tested with others, shared with others in community, can be changed from a solitary emotion to a shared communal concern. If it issues from a joint passion for justice, there is opportunity for correction, for clarifying its direction. When the anger is seen by others as a passion for justice that repudiates social indifference and rejects callous exploitation of fellow humans, it becomes a commitment to a moral community. "Love and anger are compatible," Rebbe Barukh teaches, "provided they are motivated by concern for [community]" (Wiesel 1978a, 61).

For Wiesel, the creative transformation of hatred is accomplished by repudiating hate and affirming anger, by refusing to mirror the perpetrators' hate with the identical attitude, and by choosing to care passionately about justice, work to ensure justice, cry out for recognition of injustices done. His perspective affirms moral and just hate expressed as anger, and rejects spiteful and malicious hate that seeks and justifies revenge. Since "anger is the experience of demands," as Frederick Perls defined the anger gestalt, this passionate anger is a demand for a new order, for new humanity, for renewed or re-created justice.

"No, of course I do not hate Muslim extremists," said Chinese Christian theologian David Santoso of Jakarta, Indonesia, reflecting on the six hundred churches burned and hundreds of people beaten, raped, killed in fundamentalist scapegoating of Chinese Christians. "To hate them is to be held captive, to continuously violate my own soul. No, I do not hate them. What I feel is a moral outrage that such acts are done. Contempt? Yes, contempt at the evil perpetrated by the whole tragic clash of cultures, contempt that life can be snuffed out without a second thought, contempt that the justice by which we live as a society can in a moment of social unrest be lightly tossed aside and neighbor takes actions of brutality and inhumanity against neighbor."

"Hate," he argued, "despises the person who is the perpetrator of evil, but contempt is somehow larger. It includes the clan that supports the violent action and the systems that first permit and then bless the racial-political crimes. Contempt feels horror at the evil which peoples can do—blindly and stupidly—against others who differ in some small way, but it is focused toward the system, on the structures, at the political powers that are the primary agents of this brutality and inhumanity" (Santoso 1998, Interview with author).

Out of the encounter with hatred—the concerted violence of fundamentalist groups, the attempted genocide of the Chinese who have lived in Java since the fifth century—rises a wisdom about hate. Chinese Christian leaders point people away from returning hate for hate and toward a disdain for the political injustices. This disdain, with its cry for justice, blends moral and just demands into a contempt for violence that goes unnamed. It embodies without naming this "just contempt," which deplores endemic violence, refuses cyclical retaliation, actively seeks out the little-used paths toward a more just society. It seeks for words to express motives for which we have such limited language. Perhaps the vocabulary in this chapter may provide more accurate names for these deep moral responses and offer words that enable cries for justice to find a more powerful voice.

Moving from Hatred to Compassion

It is possible simultaneously to experience multiple layers of hate. In fact, in times of injury, insult, or assault, the various voices of several hates regularly compete for attention. Within the inner courtroom, one voice calls for revenge, another insists that justice should be required in some visible way and presses the case with arguments in defense, a third insists that there must be a moral outcry, a rallying of support to condemn the wrongdoing. All three push and jostle for their place at the bench of your emotional trial. As the hearing progresses, revenge backs down, realizing that returning evil for evil turns bad to worse. Principled hate goes on presenting arguments, defending your rights, dwelling on how you have been wronged. Moral contempt wishes for some way to shame the shameless, consults with others on the rightness of its judgments, then sits back to take a longer view. At last the questions may turn in a new direction, from "Is there no way to gain satisfaction and retribution?" to "Is there no way to choose what is just even in the face of injustice?" From these new questions, new answers appear, suggesting the possibility of seeking and finding something constructive amid the loss. Eventually, the question of what is the truly *good* thing for all involved claims the attention of your inner judge. This is the moment when passion takes more into consideration than your needs and your concerns. Passion becomes com-passion. Concern for the whole situation, for offender and offended, comes to mind. One does not arrive at this point instantaneously. The case may drag on in your inner court for days, months, years, but when, finally, *just hate*, the contempt for evil that prizes the welfare of both the plaintiff and the defendant, takes the witness stand and speaks, both justice and mercy have found a voice.

Chapter Two

The Transforming Moment: Breakthrough to Empathy

I am so consumed with hate all the time,
how could I ever love anyone?

—Kip Kinkel

*(From a journal of the seventeen-year-old Oregon student
who killed his parents and two fellow students and wounded
twenty-five at Thorston High School in 1998.)*

One of the primary reasons people came to me for help,
was the enormous guilt they felt when they realized
how "abnormally" much they hated those they loved.
—Theodore Reik
(psychoanalyst and author)

In time we hate that which we often fear.
—Shakespeare, *Antony and Cleopatra*

Proposition for Chapter 2

Subjective hate (personal malice, desire for revenge) can be clearly differentiated from *objective hate* (realistic anger, rational contempt). Subjective hatred of an evil or an evildoer can be converted to an objective motivation that responds with constructive hatred (moral or just hate). Transforming moments of radical change occur when one moves from hate that is subjectively centered in personal satisfaction of grievances to a moral anger that is concerned for the welfare of both self and other. This chapter will explore these two sides of hate and trace the movement that results in a mysterious process of breaking down old barriers and breaking through to a willingness to risk again. Objective hate is, not surprisingly, closely akin to authentic love and, eventually, may mature to an authentic social concern for the neighbor.

The Bible, you have to understand, is a book of war, it's a book of hate, it's a book of separation," says Michael Teague, a white supremacist spokesperson. "It's hate the evil and love the good.". . . "All human history"—as white supremacists see it—"begins with the union between Eve and Satan that produced Cain—the 'hybrid, mongrel, bastard and soulless child'—and culminates in such signposts of the coming Armageddon as the 'fraudulent' United Nations and the U.S. Constitution," which has been "destroyed by Jewry influence of the Supreme Court" (K. Murphy 1999, A14).

The white supremacy message that Jews are descended from Satan, that blacks are soulless descendants of "mud people," that white women who marry outside their race should die, that white Aryan men are "Adam's pure blood seed-line," descendants of God through Adam, who alone shall inherit the earth, contains a worldview that grounds hate in biblical history blended with the mythology of racial self-idolatry.

There are about three hundred and fifty known white supremacist groups in the United States. Europe has its own varied range of extremists. It is estimated that about five thousand Americans are members of the Ku Klux Klan, and about seventeen thousand belong to other racist organizations such as Aryan Nations, Chicago White Vikings, Church of the Creator, National Association for the Advancement of White People, Identity, Bomber Boys, Youth for Hitler, Youth Defense League, White Youth League, United Aryan Youth, Separatists (also known as Nationalists), Third Position, Racial Survivalists, Interstate Congress for Equal Rights and Responsibilities, and Protect Americans' Rights and Resources.

All of these are *white* supremacist hate groups. Nonwhite hate groups, such as the Yahwehs, a black Hebrew Israelite organization that teaches blacks are the true descendants of the ancient Hebrew tribes, spread their own subjective doctrines of superiority and hostility. Supremacist groups—of whatever color or creed—thrive by uniting racism and prejudice as a group ethos, with individual reserves of hate and bigotry to create a common bond of antipathy that focuses on designated persons who represent the despised target. These groups have the avowed mission of fostering hate, feeding its growth, and following through on its goals. But they are not the only or the largest communities of organized hatred. Subjective structures of hate are present in the wide society in forms that, because of their invisibility, are more invidious and invincible.

Fringe and Elite Hatred

Polite middle-class society excludes hate mongers. In public conversation, we usually identify them—with a raised eyebrow and a knowing look—as lower-class whites, right-wing extremists, or nondominant culture groups. But those who advocate or promote hate are spread across the classes. Hate is an equal opportunity obsession. Elites who attribute racism to other social groups are failing to face or deal with the racism that the dominant class imposes and maintains. A decade of research by van Dijk on the social conflicts of the Netherlands demonstrates this. He shows that the dominance of the elite classes, though cloaked in the language of tolerance, institutionalizes the suppression of, discrimination against, and economic exploitation of the multiethnic components of society (van Dijk 1995, 2–25):

> It is not primarily "popular" racism, but elite racism that is particularly influential in the reproduction of racism. The media, educational, academic, social, corporate, and political elites, among others, control or have access to widely published types of text and talk and may thus preformulate, though often in mere "moderate" terms, the kind of modern racism that will then be taken up and be legitimized by large segments of the general population. . . . All of this elite text and talk is obsessed by the possible accusation of discrimination, bias or racism and emphatically denies it. The elites have the unshakable self-image of being specifically tolerant, unlike ordinary people. (van Dijk 1995, 24–25)

Elite thought constructs its own subjective culture from deep reserves of "inner truth" that confuse optimism with hope, privilege with entitlement, self-confidence with arrogance. When one stands at the top of the social ladder, it is not difficult to take it for granted. The justifications for one's right to be secure in a dominant position seem self-evident.

Eileen Gardner, writing for the Heritage Foundation, a conservative think tank, has stated, "There are no injustices in the universe. As unfair as it seems, a person's external circumstance fits his level of inner spiritual development" (Gardner 1983 in Shields 1986, 1). Gardner used this thesis to explain physical handicaps in a position paper that advocated cuts in funding for programs assisting the physically challenged. She was later hired as a consultant by the United States Department of Education; her external circumstances had become good indeed, but her inner spiritual development is unknown. Such hatred becomes all the more elusive and anonymous when its influence is concealed within systems, institutions, political structures, and the webs of commerce and collaboration that connect them all. Thomas Merton, a modern voice for spiritual awareness, writes incisively of the elaborate schema of elite and privileged violence pervading the webs of modern existence.

> The real problem of violence is not the individual with a *revolver but death and even genocide as big business*. But this big business of death is all the more innocent and effective because it involves a long chain of individuals, each of whom can feel himself absolved from responsibility, and each of whom can perhaps salve his conscience by contributing with a more *meticulous efficiency* to his part in the massive operation. (Merton 1961, 6)

The real crimes of war are committed not at the front, he argued, but in war offices and ministries of defense in which no one ever sees blood.

> Modern technological mass murder is not directly visible, like individual murder. It is abstract, corporate, business-like, cool, free of guilt-feeling and therefore, a thousand times more deadly and effective than the eruption of violence out of individual hate. (Merton 1961, 7)

Living as we do in systems that engender hate, profit from hate, simultaneously deny and yet devote themselves to manufacture, distribute, and defend the instruments of hate, who of us is fully aware of our complicity in the permeating effects of this passion?

Elite hatred—the systematic antipathy that shapes societal patterns in pervasive ways—is largely invisible. We rarely see our own hate with objectivity, and we loyally refuse to see that of those we value and emulate. Like pressing the mute button on our remote control, we join our society in subjectively silencing awareness of the negative side of self and of social context by seeing hate as "out there," not in here, as the problem of separatist or subversive subgroups, not our own group. We are united in turning a blind eye to its objective presence in the dominant culture. When hate is invisible, in oneself or in one's group, it functions even more powerfully as motivation or group sentiment, but its unseen face dons many masks—settled hostility pretending to be reasoned opinion or righteous conviction in political propaganda, editorials of all kinds, and, most openly, in letters to the editor.

When we deny our hate, we lose not only the awareness of our inner negativity, but the language for naming it, the pathways for processing it, the words for initiating change and healing. Owning hatred is humiliating, denying it is a matter of self-esteem. Asserting our rights is socially acceptable; coming to terms with how we resist the rights of others through discrimination or prejudice is definitely not. Claiming just entitlement for oneself is socially respectable; naming how we profit from the disadvantages of others, in tropical sweatshops or across town, is a social embarrassment. Seeing the offender as a fellow human is painful; despising the transgressor as a sinner is strangely comforting. Reestablishing one's moral high ground over the perpetrator is reassuring; realizing one harbors the some longing to annihilate another human being is threatening. Realizing that we feel the impulse to injure another is so dissonant to cognitive balance and conscientious harmony that only the deeply reflective dare entertain such self-knowledge. As a people, we allow our history of racism, prejudice, and discrimination to slide into the dim and distant past. Racial conflict in the past century is not easy to overlook. It includes such events as the Chicago riots, July 27 to August 2, 1919, in which thirty-eight people were killed, 537 hurt, a thousand left homeless by fires because four youths crossed an imaginary color line on the Lake Michigan beach (Chicago Commission 1922, 4–5). The Omaha Riot of September 28, 1919, ended in the lynching of a man named Will Brown and the attempted lynching of the mayor and the police commissioner. Since the Civil War there have been approximately five thousand documented lynchings across the country (Ginzburg 1969, 253). The civil rights struggles of the '60s included the bombing of the Sixteenth Street Baptist Church in Montgomery; the race riots in seven cities after the 1964 Civil Rights Act was passed; the Watts riot in Los Angeles, August 11, 1965, with thirty-four deaths, 1,032 injured, six hundred buildings burned; the 164 disturbances in the hot summer of '67. The '70s and '80s seemed more hopeful, but then on April 29, 1992, the South Central Los Angeles riot exploded—its toll, forty-five deaths, two thousand injured, twelve hundred businesses destroyed. The roots of hate run deep beneath us all.

How can these events, blocked from memory, so easily become invisible? The kinder, more gentle world promised in presidential speeches must include remembering the unkind and ungentle world, and must involve serious reflection on the nature of hate crimes and the way in which common social prejudices fuel the fires of hatred on our streets.

Hate Crimes as Atypical Violent Acts

Hate crimes, which are acts of domestic terrorism, more often rise not out of the pathological obsessions of deviant types in organized hate groups but out of the very mainstream of society (Levin and McDevitt 1993, xi). They are most often committed under ordinary circumstances by surprisingly unremarkable people—neighbors, a coworker, or a group of teens looking for a thrill. No matter who commits them, hate crimes show certain characteristics:

1. Hate crimes tend to be *excessively brutal.* They are much more likely to entail personal violence. In a study of forty-five hate crimes reported to the Boston police, fully half were assaults. Of all crimes reported nationwide, only 7 percent are assaults. Three-fourths of hate assaults resulted in personal injury to the victim; in contrast, only 29 percent of assault victims receive physical injury according to national figures (Levin and McDevitt 1993, 11).

2. Hate crimes are often apparently senseless or irrational crimes *perpetrated at random on total strangers.* In the Boston study, 85 percent of all hate crimes involved offenders whose identity was unknown to their victims. (National crime surveys report 61 percent of crimes of violence are committed by strangers.) The victims are "interchangeable"—any victim will do.

3. Hate crimes are usually perpetrated by *multiple offenders.* Only about 25 percent of all crimes of violence are committed by more than one offender, while, in contrast, 64 percent of hate crimes involve two or more perpetrators. Such group support encourages attacks against innocent and incidental victims and grants a certain degree of anonymity, blame is diluted, members incite one another to blatant bigotry and increasing levels of violence (Levin and McDevitt 1993, 16–17).

4. Hate crimes share similar *patterns of motivation,* which include (a) resentment for abuse, powerlessness, deprivation, or poverty which is displaced onto victim(s); (b) thrill-seeking exploitation of others, of nonselective, interchangeable violence; (c) reactive hate crime intended to "send a message," "even a score," "strike a blow against oppression," "stop the invasion of outsiders"; (d) a divine mission to "rid the world of evil," "dispose of subhuman people," "wipe out the enemy"; (e) a defense of heritage (my race) against any outside influence (any other ethnic group) that is protected by government interference (most often

meaning Jews or humanists or Catholics or other) that is ruining the lives of average citizens (white Anglo-Saxon Protestants); (f) war mentality that can create a national enemy.

The Everpresent Rage of Subjectivity

Who has not felt a flash of hate toward another human? And who does not prefer to call it by names other than hatred? Perhaps "hurt," "righteous indignation," "outrage," "offended dignity," even "disgust."

Evidence that subjective passions, angers, and hatred leap out of control appears in every newscast. Spouses behave abusively, parents ignore children, friends attack friends, strangers violate strangers because of race, ethnicity, religion. Opposing groups act negatively (and with stunning reciprocity) toward each other—Catholics and Protestants, Christians and Jews, Arabs and Israelis, Indians and Pakistanis. Cyclic chains of hate-triggering-hate-triggering-hate defy our attempts to break the bonds of hostility—Hispanic contempt for Anglos, Anglo fear of African Americans, African American ill-will toward Asian-Americans, Asian-American dislike of Hispanics—and crossover hostility between all the preceding. Each of these groups holds strong commitments to the inalienable rights of the individual, to the valuing of human dignity, to social theories of equality, to legal privileges of equal rights before the law, to democratic principles of egalitarian justice, to some form of the Golden Rule, to the valuing of human dignity and the ultimate worth of persons. One might expect any one of these values to inoculate us against the subjective bigotry and prejudice that remain common in human emotions and actions.

What is the reason for such subjectivity among rational beings? Is there a fatal human flaw that turns us against each other? Explanations include the philosophical, theological, biological, historical, and social. All offer varieties of determinism that seek to isolate the factors that promote, provoke, or precipitate prejudice, but the question still must be asked:

1. Perhaps we are born baby bigots? Is selective prejudice essential to humanness? The dominant philosophical view maintains that hostile tendencies are deeply rooted in human nature. Self-interested humans are intrinsically or essentially bent toward bigotry, inclined toward prejudice, twisted toward hatred.

2. Perhaps subjective stupidity is genetic and hereditary? We are wired for aggression. The biological-genetic perspective points to the inevitable and recurrent patterns of aggressive behavior that characterize humans and their defensive, aggressive, self-serving cerebral programming that

serves to protect the reproductive success of each group. The implacable laws of genetically fixed tendencies offer little hope for our human capacity to transcend xenophobia. The most we can hope for is a more enlightened understanding of our natural tendencies to protect our genetic pools and seek a more civil management of innate drives.

3. Perhaps the cause of subjective actions can be extracted from human history? We are trapped by the past. The social-historical view argues that we are limited by our "historical and social location." We function from partial perspectives inevitably biased by prejudice because we are finite, limited, historical creatures. These contingencies combine to create powerful destructive tendencies, but we are not shaped by a hard, unalterable determinism. Choice is possible in human history, deliberation about direction is necessary, alteration of destiny is a real hope.

4. Perhaps the negative dynamics are simply relational? We are socialized to be antisocial. The social-interactional view sees the deep roots of prejudice and suspicion planted in the basic human need to classify and categorize others. Our world is confusingly diverse, and one must learn labels and construct stereotypes in order to pattern and manage our interactions and relationships. Our need to simplify the complexity of human community leads us to construct prejudices as manageable patterns of perception, definition, and interaction. Although these offer the desired efficiency, they have an inevitable and unfortunate dark side. They create bigotry and multiply negative prejudices, which alienate us from each other (Baird and Rosenbaum 1999, 12–14).

5. Perhaps the problem lies in our moral inability? We are morally challenged. The theological-moral view sees humans as inevitably, but not necessarily, turned inward in self-seeking; turned against others who threaten self-security, turned downward in a moral law of entropy as evil follows evil. We are—when seen in the light of what is needed for us to live as a human society on this planet—all morally retarded. This condition is inevitable—it is the human condition, remember—but it is not necessary, since the familial-psychical-social-cultural determinism of evil is alterable through moral growth and/or transformation. By owning the evil within, accepting the possibility of change through grace and the discovery of new moral ability, persons and social units make actual change.

There is no agreement on "*Why* this inability?" The agreement comes when the question is changed to "*What* is the inability, and *how* can it be altered?" The philosophical and biological perspectives are strong on the *what* and offer little on the *how*, inferring little can be done. Both the genetic and the essentialist view protect us from naive optimism on the *what* and call us to a radical reexamination of the *how* of our destructive-ness. The social-psychological and the historical views describe in depth the *how* of economic, political, and religious institutions that shape us all. The social-interactionist view hopes for change through challenging encounters that contradict stereotypes and open new possibilities for rela-tionship with fewer side effects. The social-historical view hopes for social action to undermine the historical legacies of the past and challenge the results of centuries of xenophobia and rigid boundary construction. In both these latter, as well as in the moral theological position, the *how* emerges with hope. They agree that the tendency toward destructive behavior can be altered by objective and thoughtful social, historical, and moral reflection that results in the communal decision to create contexts that nurture character and foster more receptive, inclusive, tolerant pat-terns of behavior. Yet cyclical distaste, with no objective base but richly subjective rationale, reappears with dismaying reactivity.

Subjective and Objective Hatred

No matter how objective we may be in our personal behavior—closing an escrow or purchasing a compact car instead of a gas-guzzling SUV, for instance—subjectivity can take us by storm at unexpected moments when emotions flood us.

A terrified young father stands over his defiant two-year-old son, bites his lip, clenches his fists, and despises himself for wanting to smash the little boy: The stubborn anger in the little guy's eyes awakens the dad's childhood rage, which had been squashed by his explosive father. Now this son, whose birth and growth have elicited the dad's hated father—"Have you been hiding in me all these years just waiting to emerge?"—defiantly shows the hate that the dad never could and still will not recognize in him-self. Out of subjective depths, his personal demons rise to haunt him.

This is *subjective hate*—hate in the subject is being directed in a diffuse way toward substitute objects. It is unjustified, unrealistic, and utterly confusing to both giver and receiver. Subjective hatred is a complex moti-vation that ties together multiple pieces of emotional stuff from one's past into a pastiche of twitchy, reflex reactions that involve little or no thought. In contrast, a father may feel objective hate when defied by the child. Such feelings of anger are focused on the actual behavior, in a realistic and responsible way.

Subjective hatred is expansive; it knows few limits. It easily becomes obsessive, dominating both thought and affect; it is subtly possessive, seizing control of thought, values, goals, and the means of achieving these ends. It can expand to fill the cosmos.

Objective hatred, in contrast, is limited, contained, focused on a rational goal, directed toward a more principled end. However, while it too is invasive of thoughts and feelings, capable of arousing profound passion, it remains subordinate to rational process, directed by moral consciousness. It is not flooded by the overwhelming impulse of its subjective brother.

Donald Winnicott, the British founder of object-relations thought, was the first to distinguish between subjective and objective hate. His particular focus was on the counseling and treatment of psychotic or antisocial individuals, but his thought applies to all adversarial relationships. Subjective hate, he observed, is associated with unresolved issues from the personal past, while objective hate is a response to an actual event or person and is based on objective observation and reflection.

Winnicott and his wife took a disturbed orphan boy into their home for a brief period and sought in the daily life of the family to support his growth from isolation to affiliation. The boy, like many abandoned persons, had a deep need to induce hate by ventilating intense rage upon parental figures. Winnicott saw this as a motivational process to be channeled, not a behavior to be eradicated. In order to move the rage/hate process forward, Winnicott reasoned that both he and the boy needed to recognize, name, and deal with the hate.

"If the patient seeks objective or justified hate, he must be able to reach it, else he cannot feel he can reach objective love," Winnicott concluded (1976, 199). To be totally accepting, loving, and kind to a child who is inducing hate is an error, because the child knows it is a lie. "Should the analyst show love, he will surely at the same moment kill the patient," he said in hyperbole that is psychologically true (199).

To deal with the hate with objective clarity, Winnicott responded to the explosive temper tantrums by taking the boy "by bodily strength" and putting him outside the front door—no matter the weather or time of day or night. A special bell was placed for the boy to ring which, he understood, would give him immediate readmittance and full acceptance with nothing said about the preceding fit. Each time Winnicott put the boy outside, he said, "I hate you for what you have just done." By doing this, he modeled objective hate toward the action as well as toward the boy; thus the boy evoked the authentic feeling he was seeking to induce. It was easy to say, Winnicott observed wryly, because it was true, and it enabled him to continue working with the child "without losing temper and without every hour and again murdering him" (Winnicott 1976, 200).

The availability of the bell taught the boy that he had the power to induce acceptance, respect, and love, and enabled him to move to a maturing relationship of equality with the other as a separate object who responds fairly and with just reciprocity. His unacceptable feelings were validated, but their logical consequences—exile outside ended by ringing the bell—were required in a way that he could internalize as a request for inclusion, which as it matures grows into a conscious need for loving affiliation.

The danger in returning hate for hate, Winnicott explained, is that the counselor may unconsciously add his/her unknown and unowned hatred to the counselee's hate, pouring infection into injury. The therapist must be able to deal with the hate that exists in the self before attempting to deal with the hate encountered in a patient. The patient can only come to "appreciate in the analyst what he himself (i.e., the analyst) is capable of feeling and 'above all' he [the analyst] must not deny hate that really exists in himself" (Winnicott 1976, 200).

The basic premise of therapy—love heals—is true only when it is fully defined. It is the relationship that heals, and the relationship is composed of both love and hate. The therapist who trusts solely in positive bonding—loving and being loved—to be the curative dynamic while avoiding the negative issues provides the context for only superficial healing. "No negative transference, no growth," my supervisors often reminded me in training to do psychotherapy. Not only love heals; so does dealing with hate. (In classic psychoanalysis, patients who hated their therapists were not only unpopular, but generally discharged from treatment as incurable.)

The client brings to the therapeutic encounter as much hurt and hate, disappointment and anger, as there was in the original relationships of infancy and early childhood. Those who felt loved as children will be more comfortable with close emotional contact and be cooperative in self-exploration. These are popular patients but are also in less need of therapy. Those who take offense at suggestions, who refuse help offered, who react with anger or withdraw into depression are those who received the least love and offer even less to the therapist. Instead of "How grateful I am for our work this past year," they say, "I've been seeing you for a year and things are only worse."

The therapist may be tempted to return the client's negative feelings in hidden, denied, or subtly superior ways. But instead welcoming the expression of hate is the necessary movement toward growth. Expressing and recognizing its meaning is what heals. As Winnicott discovered, unexpressed hate is the main factor that attaches the patient to old destructive patterns. The hate serves as doorkeeper to love. When unowned and unexpressed, hate locks up the capacity to love. Only when it has been faced, dealt with, disempowered is the person able to love freely.

The Good-Bad Balance

Winnicott, in the case of a disturbed mute child, reports that the child's initial communication consisted of biting Winnicott's knuckles, which he permitted, then of throwing objects on the floor, also accepted, so that the message given was "I can take anything you give me, no matter how intense your rage or hate. It will not destroy me or my love for you." This takes the destructive aspect out of the hate, diffuses its danger, and moves the person to accept his or her own destructive and self-destructive impulses. Just as a child needs to experience acceptance of both its bad and its good sides—its lovable and its stinky self—so the adult also needs to recognize, own, and redefine feelings attached to all the issues of hate so that self-disgust is transformed to self-acceptance. Mature self-functioning embraces both the light and the dark of one's inner world, and moves the focus of hateful feelings from the general to the specific, from the personal to the principled, from subjective exaggeration to objective clarification, from the retaliatory to the constructive, from powerlessness to capability, from spitefulness to justice:

> It is probable that our need in babyhood to project our dangerous painful states of anger out of us into someone else and identify someone else with them, and ourselves only with our good states, is one of the main stimuli towards recognizing other people's existence at all. In other words, our whole interest in the outer world and other people is ultimately founded on our need of them; and we need them for two purposes. One is the obvious one of getting satisfactions from them, both for our self-preservative and pleasure needs. The other purpose for which we need them is to hate them so that we may expel and discharge our own badness, with its danger, out of ourselves on to them. (Klein and Riviere 1962, 42)

We learn to discharge our badness, first on persons, then on ourselves, then in ways that harm neither self or other. In more deeply disturbed children or adults, the need to discharge hate can take precedence over the yearning for love; in fact, it seems that only through hating can they reach the emotion of love. They do not wish to hate, nor do they want to be hated, but they experience profound hunger to have the experience of their hate being recognized, received, tolerated, and survived; they are equally driven to test safety and security—to know firsthand that they survived after risking the expression of hatred toward parents, authority figures, or their therapist. They equally demand evidence that the other has survived their ventilated rage to assure them of the safety of risking such deep feeling.

Winnicott suggests that the same process is inherent in healthy parenting. Mothers both love and hate their infants. Objective reasons for hate—a negative complex of issues including the danger to the mother's body in pregnancy; the peril and pain of childbirth; the ruthless control that enslaves the caregiver; the need for unconditional love for both clean and dirty, pleasant and unpleasant; the child's arbitrary affection which gives love until the child has gotten its own way; the excitation of emotional, spiritual, sexual feelings without reciprocity—all these elicit both compassion and resentment, affection and irritation. The mother's authenticity in giving objective negation alongside an unquestionable affirmation of the child offers a model that allows it to develop and mature through the vicissitudes of loving and hating its caregiver, as Winnicott acknowledged:

> It seems to me doubtful whether a human child as he develops is capable of tolerating the full extent of his own hate in a sentimental environment. He needs hate to hate. (Winnicott 1949, 202)

The adult goal is to be capable of experiencing and accepting a full range of emotions; of making clear distinctions between subjective and objective feelings of love and hate; of being able to express these in ways that create bonding alliances and resolve conflicts productively. Sentimentality about totally unconditional love is appropriate for the first weeks of life, when an infant can receive love without hate. After the psychological birth of the infant at three months, love and firmness become necessary. The child's emotions now run warm and cold, loving and hating. Without parental recognition, parental limits, and parental direction, the child feels abandoned to the darker impulses that terrify her with their suddenness and intensity.

Healthy adult love and hate, if maturation has been successful, are more disinterested (self-transcendent) than controlled by self-interest (self-absorbed). The lover actually meets and comes to love the world she encounters. She comes to value something beyond the self for its own sake, to care for its own development and growth. She becomes capable of hating that which is abhorrent apart from self-centered criteria.

Objective and Subjective Love

The central development in the realization of love is moving from a *subjective orientation* toward the other to an *objective appreciation* of that person. Love itself, however, may be subjective (I see in another what I choose to see), emotional (I experience the other according to my feelings about her or him), and intentional (I perceive the other out of my own needs, constructs, and values). Love may be objective (I see the other as *other*, a distinct, unique, and separate individual), rational (I can be reflective and aware), extentional (I see what is there, I perceive with little "reading in" or "reading out").

The contrast between these two loves—subjective and objective—has been likened by Erich Fromm to the contrast between immature narcissism and mature adulthood.

> The main condition for the achievement of love is the *overcoming* of one's *narcissism*. The narcissistic orientation is one in which one experiences as real only that which exists within oneself, while the phenomena in the outside world have no reality in themselves, but are experienced only from the viewpoint of their being useful or dangerous to one. The opposite pole to narcissism is objectivity; it is the faculty to see people and things *as they are*, objectively, and to be able to separate this *objective* picture from a picture which is formed by one's desires and fears. (Fromm 1956, 118)

Since the seminal work of Heinz Kohut, we view narcissism as a lifelong developmental process that moves progressively from an infantile state of egocentric subjectivity toward full maturity by means of a gradually increasing capacity for objective relating. It is the bondage to infantile narcissism that Fromm addresses as he links subjective, or narcissistic, love to the dreams of omnipotence and omniscience all children have during infancy. Narcissistic persons sustain such illusions throughout life.

> The insane person or the dreamer fails completely in having an objective view of the world outside; but all of us are more or less

insane, or more or less asleep; all of us have an unobjective view of the world, one which is distorted by our narcissistic orientation. (Fromm 1956, 100)

As examples of subjective love, Fromm points to parents who perceive their children as extensions of themselves, who experience their behavior in terms of how it reflects on them, whose central concern is the pleasure they derive from the child's obedience, achievement, or success, husbands who perceive their wives as domineering because, still negatively attached to their mothers, they cannot differentiate spouse from parent, or wives who describe their spouses as weak because they fall short of a father, or boring because they do not fulfill childhood fantasies of Prince Charming.

Objective love, in contrast, is shown by the parent who attends accurately to what the child feels and thinks; by the husband or wife who relates to the spouse as distinct from all those in one's past, as a unique self, uncontaminated by projected fantasies.

Objective love is reasonable, humble, realistic: "To be objective, to use one's reason, is possible only if one has achieved an attitude of humility, if one has emerged from the dreams of omniscience and omnipotence which one has as a child" (Fromm 1956, 119). Objective loving becomes possible as one can relate to the world with accuracy, clarity, and justice. This includes the entire spectrum of relationships between the individual and the environment, things within it—people, groups, community, nation.

Persons have varying capacities for objective loving. The ability to actually love ranges from the attached psychotic love's utter inability to establish tender relations or genital intimacy with another human, to moderately narcissistic love characterized by exploitive control or sexual promiscuity, to borderline love with a primitive idealization of the love object, a clinging infantile dependency on it and some capacity for genital gratification, to neurotic love with the ability to establish stable and deep object relations but without the capacity for full sexual union and gratification, to mature love with the capacity for tenderness, mutual sexuality, and a stable, deep relation to another as a separate and respected person (Kernberg 1995, 186).

What is clear from these analyses of subjective and objective love and hate is that they are inextricably interwoven in the person and must be balanced constructively in the mature personality. It is not a matter of either-or, but clearly the both-and of integration, and ultimately, we shall observe, the neither-nor of transformation to the higher forms of just and merciful empathy, compassion, and agape love. Gandhi, for instance, confronted the massive Indian hate of the British—created by long colonial domination—by calling for a transformation from hatred to objective respect for the opponent:

> When his followers began to have strong feelings of hostility toward the British, Gandhi would always say: "stop until you have gotten over this feeling of hostility. We won't go on until you have. It is only when you cease to hate the British that we can afford to go on opposing them." His goal was to end British rule without lasting hostility between the Indians and the British and he achieved it by pressing for objective not subjective opposition. (Toynbee 1971, 59)

"Hatred remains blind by its very nature," argues Martin Buber. If it were not blind, it would be able to see the whole person and thus be incapable of hating. In hating "one can see only a part of a being. Who ever sees a whole being and must reject it, is no longer in the dominion of hatred" (Buber 1970, 68). Instead, the person is caught in the common human struggle to see the other person with accurate vision, either affirmatively or negatively. Either is respect—either sees the other as a "You," not an "It." "Whoever hates directly is closer to a relation than those who are without love and hate," Buber concludes. Antipathy is closer to encounter than is apathy.

In anger or hate, the You becomes an It. "Every You in the world is doomed by its nature to become a thing or at least to enter into thinghood again and again. In the language of objects: every thing in the world can—either before or after it becomes a thing—appear to some I as its You. . . . the It is the chrysalis, the You is the butterfly" (Buber 1970, 69). The promise, the hope, that Buber constantly reveals is the possibility of transformation—hate can return to love, *things* can be seen again as *persons*, the *It* can become *You.*

The Transforming Moment

The breakthrough from subjective to objective vision of the hated other is an encounter with truth, a radical shift in perspective, a transforming moment. It is better illustrated by actual cases, stories, individual experiences:

Christmas Eve, 1914, on the front lines of World War I, time stopped for an hour when the two opposing armies came out of their trenches and met in the midst of "no-man's-land." Christmas carols sung on one side were answered by the soldiers on the other. Then, the men rose and advanced to meet each other without their weapons. The English sang "Christians Awake," and the Christian within them awoke; the Germans broke into song in response. They were no longer German or English to each other, but simply fellow men. As one British participant wrote of that moment:

> It happened as if it were a change of weather, the sun coming out after a storm; and when it happened it seemed more natural even than wonderful. *What was unnatural was the former state of war in which men had been to each other not men but targets: and now they had come to life for each other,* and in a moment they were friends. (Clutton-Brock 1985)

One peaceful evening in Portland, Oregon, Mulugeta Seraw, an Ethiopian exchange student, was returning to his apartment with several African friends. A passing carload of skinheads skidded to a stop, honked their horn, and yelled racist threats. One of Seraw's friends responded with an obscene gesture; the skinheads replied by leaping out and breaking car windows with a baseball bat. A fight broke out, and the skinhead with the bat began the fatal beating of Seraw.

At the trial, one of the skinheads, Steve Strasser, described how Seraw, knocked to the ground and seeing the bat swung back for the fatal blow, began "a really freaky kind of yelling. . . . It was like crying death. It's something you'd never forget." Then the man with the bat, Ken Mieske, clubbed him to silence (Blue and Naden 1994, 6).

As the white Western man heard the Ethiopian crying out with the keening of one mourning his own death, the humanity of this man from another race and culture pierced his soul. Cold, closed subjective hatred began to break open.

Mark Twain, in *The Adventures of Huckleberry Finn*, tells of such a transforming moment in the relationship between the runaway Huck and the fugitive slave, Jim. The two are floating down the Mississippi River on a raft, with Huck aiding in the slave's escape. Huck awakes at daybreak, finding that Jim has let him sleep through his watch, and discovers the older man in tears.

When I waked up just at daybreak he was sitting there with his head down betwixt his knees, moaning and mourning to himself. I didn't take notice nor let on. I knowed what it was about. He was thinking about his wife and his children, away up yonder, and he was low and homesick; because he hadn't ever been away from home before in his life; and I do believe he cared just as much for his people as white folks does for their'n. It don't seem natural, but I reckon it's so. (Twain [Clemens] 1960, 198)

Such moments of encounter with another reality—the perspective of the other, if entered, result in a reorganization of worldview. Twain's words, simple and transparent, have often been called the most perfect account of radical transformation. In the encounter with the tears of a father, Huck sees what is invisible in his culture, the equal humanness of the oppressed. The son of slaveholding society realizes the equal humanity of the slave. Later, when he finally writes the letter of betrayal informing on the runaway in order to be free of the guilt of complicity, "I felt good and all washed clean of sin for the first time I had ever felt so in my life, and I knowed I could pray now." But he recalls the earlier event, and all the good Jim has done for him, and conventional moral obedience becomes intolerable. "I was a-trembling, because I'd got to decide, forever, betwixt two things, and I knowed it. I studied a minute, sort of holding my breath, and then says to myself: 'All right, then, I'll *go* to hell'—and tore it up" (263–64).

In his *Humanity: A Moral History of the Twentieth Century*, Jonathan Glover describes this as what he terms "emotional breakthrough"—the startling recognition of shared humanity, common nationality, similar parenthood, or other parallels that remind the unfeeling torturer or soon-to-be-killer of why it is not possible to go on with the torture or execution. "Sometimes the breakthrough is a simple emotional response, triggered by the visible reminder of someone's family: by the family letters and photographs of girlfriends found by soldiers in the pockets of those on the other side" (Glover 2000, 409). This is a recovery of moral identity rooted in the response of the human.

Then Glover speaks to the most dismaying moral dilemma of the last century, the silence of the onlookers at Nazi death trains, camps, gas chambers. "Sometimes the crust of hardness cracks and ordinary human sympathy breaks through. The physical presence of victims makes break-through more likely. Being present as a spectator at the Nazi mass shootings could have an impact even on those most responsible for them. . . . Our inclination to show this respect (for another human) and our disgust at someone's humiliation, is a powerful restraint on barbarism. Human responses to other people, the responses of respect and sympathy, are the heart of our humanity" (345).

Glover notes, however, that rarely did such breakthroughs among Nazi functionaries lead them to waver from their oppressive roles. Almost never did the waverer go beyond a private revulsion to make an act of public revolution that challenged the system brutalizing both the oppressed and the oppressor. More often the person opted out of the participation and let others carry out the acts of cruelty that no longer could be stomached: "The fact that 80 percent did not . . . is grim testimony to the power of psychological mechanisms of adjustment. . . . The Nazis coerced people with moral dilemmas. Critics had a terrible moral choice. They could acquiesce in genocide or they could speak out, but this might add their own family to the victims while saving no one else" (345–46).

Yet transforming "emotional breakthroughs" did and do occur with the flash of insight into the cohumanity of the enemy. Central to moral imagination is seeing what is humanly important. When not just empathy, but when this moral intuition of understanding and identifying with another is stimulated, the result is an emotional breakthrough of human responses. A general in his field office, a politician ordering bombing strikes does not see the human toll of the act, deadened as they are by such things as distance, political theory, racism, tribalism, or ideology. But the emotional eruption of compassion that can occur when the truly human in one touches the authentically human in another checks conformity, questions authority, and ends blind obedience, bringing to the fore what matters humanly rather than the current norm or the official policy.

Moments of transforming significance occur when one springs or is catapulted from an old reality to a new. James Loder has traced how ordinary modes of apprehending reality can be suspended by the intrusion of a convincing insight that arrives with convictional force and transformational power. All our life perspectives are built on basic assumptions, whether in the arts, the sciences, philosophy, theology, personal spirituality, or the assembling of a human self throughout the developmental process. When these assumptions are challenged by alternate ways of seeing reality, the result can be a transformational moment of new vision and a resultant revision of the self. This transformation is a process, Loder argued, with a five-part sequence: (1) conflict-in-context; (2) interlude for scanning; (3) insight felt with intuitive force; (4) release and openness; (5) interpretation and verification. These steps exist in all revolutionary human shifts, in routine stages of growth, in the process of psychotherapy, in mystical or spiritual breakthrough, in the artistic creative moment, in scientific discovery (Loder 1989, 100ff.).

The transforming moment, when a hater reassesses the hated object, is an encounter with an alternate reality that is radically unsettling. For the first time, the hated object appears to the hater as, in some way, similar to himself, as possessing common humanity. The concrete split between we and they, the absolute contrast between self and other, the total judgments that created the ideology for the splitting all begin to weaken and crumble. Self and other appear to be composed of familiar stuff, long for the same things, pursue like goals, share common needs. So the imperative to hate is revealed as false; it must be questioned. In that questioning, the absolute certainty of the hate-position cracks, uncertainty threatens its foundations. The structure of the self, its infrastructure of beliefs, its superstructure of total commitments comes apart. Viewed on the spectrum of hatreds, the breakthrough happens most frequently when the rationale justifying revenge, retaliation, and resentment is finally questioned. The person realizes that moral reflection demands a wider vision of the other, no matter how passionate the feelings of hatred may be. The movement to moral hatred is an emotional breakthrough as well as a spiritual one; a moral awakening as well as a renewal of social conscience. The old subjective feelings, which empowered the rationale, are tempered by objective questions and a new realism is born.

Table 3   **Transformation in the Spectrum of Hate(s)**

1	2	3	4	5	6	7
Simple Hatred	Spiteful Hatred	Malicious Hatred	Retributive Hatred	Principled Hatred	Moral Hatred	Just Hatred

                                                ^

                                                ^

The transforming moment when principled hate breaks open and moral thought restores perceptions of humanity (the cohumanity of the other becomes visible again)

The transforming moment is not unlike a religious conversion (although a religious conversion can also reinforce old hatreds, offer an alternative hate object, or kindle new fires of prejudice). As a positive conversion experience, it is a radical reordering of the inner life that results in outer change in direction and action. The transformation of hate from subjective to objective sentiment is an essential growth process by which we move toward maturity. By owning our darker passion, by encompassing the chaotic, by finding a place for the negative, and through gradually tolerating ambivalence we slowly transform hate. The development of resilience where we once were frozen, adaptability at the point we were stuck, creates a willingness to adjust to reality and adapt to collaboration with those who are different.

South African journalist Nicky Arden tells such a story of her shocking encounter with the "other":

> "As an administrator for a large social service agency, I had gone to New York, to a conference on alternate dispute resolution. During the opening remarks in the elegant, chandeliered dining room, the speaker noted that participants had come from far and wide—one even from as far away as South Africa. And he, the one from South Africa, stood so that the audience could see this square, squat Africaner who had come all the way to New York.
>
> "An Africaner! The oppressor race. But I walked over to where he stood and introduced myself, saying that I, too, was from South Africa. We talked briefly. The hated accent grated on my ears and opened an ache in my heart. He said he would look out for me that evening. I went late, walking alone through the dark New York streets.
>
> "He came over when he saw me, his round 'predicant' or preacher face breaking into a smile. We talked, first small talk about this and that, and then, as the discussion intensified, I about being an expatriate, he about being a pariah.
>
> "We left the dinner and walked the cold city streets, heads down, arms wrapped into our jackets. On and on we talked: I blamed, he absorbed; I made assumptions, he proved them wrong; I grew angry, suddenly ranting, railing against the loss. And with each block covered, as each hour passed, the layers around my soul peeled back, until at last we came to the place where our roots twined together in the African earth, and we stood and wept for our lost fatherland" (Arden 1996).

Transforming Identity—The Process

The emotional breakthrough we have just discussed can lead to a transformation of identity. Negating-distancing identity leaps the relational divide to become an affirming-relating identity, as in the case of Nicky Arden just cited. In the crisis of self-doubt, the person's previous sense of selfhood is challenged, identifications with significant others are questioned, and the identity that stands on both of these is up for grabs. The person, for a moment, is free-floating until the new reality of being and belonging forms. This unfreezing-change-refreezing process requires an encounter with an alternate truth that disconfirms the old self-center, allows a withdrawal time for objective reflection and reorganization, and then reconfirms the central commitments that define the self. This is not a new or foreign process; it has happened previously in the normal developmental process of the teen years. Identity forms through exploratory identifications with those whom we know and admire and who teach us to know ourselves. A youth may identify with a parent, teacher, model, or mentor. Gradually these patchwork identifications unify to define who the person is becoming and knit together a coherent pattern of images that form the self. Then these formative identifications with admired persons are split off and internalized within this new solidifying self to become an internal spine—the personality structure of the individual.

For the person who fails to find positive mentors or models for attachment, negative identifications serve the identical function. A hated object can define a self through negation of the despised as a means of self-affirmation. ("I hate the alcoholism of my father; I will not be addicted to anything.") Negation may seek to replace the vice with an inverse virtue—the abused child may become a superparent in antithesis. The son of a bigot may be a crusader for civil rights—compassion may be chosen in a refusal to be controlled by contempt.

Reaction may also be the purest form of imitation (mimesis). That which one resents, often one repeats; what one abhors, one may replicate; hate evokes hate; disgust elicits disgust. The moment of discovery, when one sees the hated other present within oneself, is identity-shattering. The moment may fade as one turns away in denial. Or it may free the discoverer to make new attachments as the old fabric of prejudices, fears, and negations disintegrates, and the self may form anew around a less defensive center. A self previously organized around victimhood, for example, may give up simply repeating the protests of unfairness and turn outward, looking beyond itself, to articulate larger questions of justice and injustice, equity and inequity. The moment of moral discovery and ethical questioning can signal a transforming shift in categories, moral contempt becoming a passion for justice, just contempt.

At this point, one moves beyond seeking what is "good for me" to seeking what is truly "good"; beyond "what I hate" to what is worthy of resentment. Bowen's description is of the discarding of pseudoself and the forming of solid self. Pseudoself is composed of secondhand values absorbed from others and changed readily to gain approval or provide security. Solid self forms when inherited values get masticated and digested until firsthand conviction and commitment emerge. Solid self is formed from values, virtues, and beliefs chosen slowly, not in reaction to pressures from without, but in response to wisdom and wit within. Solid self is constructed from balanced commitments to stay firmly connected with others in loyalty while at the same time maintaining one's separateness with integrity. The mature person lives in solidarity with others and at the same time with distinct individual, moral, intellectual clarity (Bowen 1978, 153).

When pseudoself is high, the person has limited ability to tolerate ambiguity within the self or between self and other. Maturity is characterized by a higher degree of solid self, which is capable of embracing one's whole self (positive and negative sides) in integration and of bridging the distance between self and other with objectivity and compassion. Solid self is able to respect those who disagree, to enter an opponent's perspective with empathy, to visualize a mutually satisfactory solution to differences even while holding to one's own perspective firmly, to listen to both parties in an altercation and seek common ground in pursuit of reconciliation. Solid self has a firm grip on reality, having come to the understanding, perhaps possible only in hindsight, that in any dispute both sides have a perspective that deserves to be heard, that neither side is totally right—each possesses a partial perspective. Both sides are flawed and fragmented; neither possesses absolute truth. Each of us brings our humanness and fallibility to even the most one-sided situation of offense. Neither of us can claim that the right to justice is totally our own; both of us are in need of creating a more just future. Each of us needs to rediscover that justice for all must move beyond the either-or of retributive justice and discover a goal of transformative justice if we are to go beyond just settling a dispute to actually restore or rebuild human relationship.

In 1999, a devastating earthquake struck Turkey. Thirty thousand people lost their lives, hundreds were trapped in the rubble, holding on to life in hope of rescue. The first aid came from nearby Greece, which sent its trained emergency crews. The hostility between the Greeks and Turks, centuries old, has continued the bitter enmity of the Ottoman Empire battles. The television coverage of Greeks clearing fallen houses and rescuing wounded Turks softened feelings on both sides of the Bosporus. Only weeks later—ironic twist of fate along the fault lines—an earthquake struck Greece. Turks returned the emergency aid in Athens. The *New York Times* reported:

> The day after Athens was struck by its most serious earthquake in decades, millions of television viewers throughout Greece watched in awe as Turkish rescue workers pulled a Greek child from under a pile of rubble. Announcers struggled to control their emotion. "It's the Turks!" one of them shouted as his voice began to crack. "They've got the little boy. They've saved him. And now the Turkish guy is drinking from a bottle of water. It's the same bottle the Greek rescuers just drank from. This is love. It's so beautiful." (Kinzer 1999, 1)

Signs of the Transforming Moment: Empathy and Compassion

The moment of emotional breakthrough, when subjective outrage begins to ask tentative objective questions, marks the return of empathy. Choosing to see it with double vision—exploring the other's perspective while being true to one's own—does not condone, will not excuse what has been done. But in seeing it from the other's side, we may rediscover the other's humanness, and on further thought the other's cohumanity. The love that results is compassion, sharing for a moment or forever after the discovery of our common passions.

> Compassion is the name of that form of love which is based on our knowing and understanding each other. Compassion is the awareness that we are all in the same boat and that we all shall either sink or swim together. (May 1972, 51)

In the movie *Dead Man Walking*, Sister Helen Prejean, in her final conversation with the man about to be executed, tells him to fix his eyes on her face as the lethal injection is taking place. "That way the last thing you will see before you die will be the face of someone who loves you." Genuine presence can transform bitterness to shared compassion. Compassion is not something we create, not something we can force from our soul, not something we just *do*. Compassion is something we *discover.* We discover it when we realize, with some painful objectivity, that we are not totally unlike those who have hurt us, that we are more than a little similar, that the other's evil action is mirrored in my answering evil impulse—justified as it may be—and the good that is in my longing for justice may, in some way, be present in the offender too.

It is compassion that allows us to realize the cohumanity of another and the humility to affirm our cofallibility with her; it is compassion that frees us from standing over another in condescension and frees us to judge or approve without condemnation. Pity and mercy suggest a power differential, a superior-to-inferior relationship. Compassion is feeling with, suffering with, struggling with an equal, not reaching down but reaching out in some level of solidarity. Nothing human is alien to me, Henri Nouwen concludes in his thesis on compassion:

> Through compassion it is possible to recognize that the craving for love that men feel resides in our own hearts, that the cruelty that the world knows all too well is also rooted in our own impulses.
>
> Through compassion we also sense our hope for forgiveness in our friends' eyes and our hatred in their bitter mouths.
>
> For a compassionate person nothing human is alien: no joy, no sorrow, no way of living and no way of dying. (Nouwen 1972, 41)

We are all flawed and finite persons; none of us is exclusively good; none is solely evil. We each are made of good and evil together, and even the evil may contain distorted good. Sorting ourselves out is terribly difficult. Within our best may be the love of a worthy end, yet we reach for it in a less-than-worthy way. Within our worst there may be an end misused, or a means distorted, or both become destructive. If it's so difficult to sort out our own motive and action, sorting out the other's is no simple matter. In the transforming moment, one sees the possibility of objective love and cares for the other for its own sake; one discovers the possibility of objective hate, and cares about justice for both the offended and the offender. This is the transforming moment when the capacity for compassion is touched by the discovery of the greater good. Good is the love of neighbor, even when the neighbor acts out of contempt. Good is the striving for justice, even when it seems an elusive destination.

"Good and evil are not each other's opposites like right and left. The evil approaches us as a whirlwind, the good as a direction" (Buber 1970, 114). In compassion, we turn from the whirlwind of cyclical violence to seek the *good;* we see that the *good* is not a state to be achieved and defended, but a virtue lived in the long and arduous journey of neighbor love.

Chapter Three

Learning to Hate:
Hate Taught and Caught

I once heard a boy say, after learning that the class bully was in fact
a victim of child abuse, "That takes all the fun out of hating her."
—Jeffrie G. Murphy

The mistreatment, humiliation and exploitation of children is the
same world wide, as is the means of avoiding the memory of it.
Individuals who do not want to know their own truth collude in
denial with society as a whole, looking for a common "enemy" on
whom to act out their repressed rage.

—Alice Miller

Proposition for Chapter 3

We are born bilingual—wired for both love and hate. As we grow to become persons we learn
constructive and destructive ways of both loving and hating. We may learn to love in confused
and controlling ways or, instead, in clean and healthy ways. We may learn how to hate in either
vicious reactions or in vital responses to injury or pain. We can unlearn and relearn early ways
of thinking, feeling, and relating badly. Objective hate, as described in chapter 2, can be modeled for children, taught to adults, learned as a constructive passion for empathy, mature into
an understanding of others, and become a commitment to do and to seek justice.

On April 20, 1999, two students, armed with an arsenal of explosives
and guns and consumed by rage, opened fire on their classmates at
Columbine High School, Littleton, Colorado. It was the worst school
massacre in U.S. history. Fifteen people died, including the gunmen;
twenty-three were hospitalized. The predictions of the two shooters, Eric
Harris and Dylan Klebold, were that 250 people would die. The ninety-five

explosive devices they had planted failed to go off because of a simple electronic failure. There were three sets of bombs—one placed a few miles away to distract police; the second in the school cafeteria to kill classmates and trigger a mass exit into their line of fire; a third in their cars in the parking lot to create chaos when police and paramedics arrived.

Videotapes in which Harris and Klebold explained their rationales made it clear that they had nurtured hatred toward tormentors for months. To keep it alive as they planned the horrendous deeds, they fueled each other's hate. "More rage, more rage! Keep building it on!" Harris says on camera. The boys' hatred did not develop in a vacuum. A context of youth culture and a hierarchy of cliques surrounded their tragic strategies of revenge. One of the athletes interviewed, a member of the football team (the top of the hierarchy), said of them:

> Columbine is a good clean place, except for those rejects. Most kids didn't want them there. They were into witchcraft. They were into voodoo. Sure we teased them. But what can you expect with kids who come to school with weird hairdos and horns on their hats? It's not just jocks; the whole school's disgusted with them. They're a bunch of homos, grabbing each other's private parts. If you want to get rid of someone, usually you tease 'em. So the whole school would call them homos, and when they did something sick, we'd tell them, "you're sick and that's wrong." (Gibbs and Roche 1999a, 154)

Hate speech from peers became hate mirrored; hate grew into monstrous fantasy; two hated and hate-obsessed boys created a strategy for violent revenge; the language and plot of a video game became a heinous reality. The context of toxic competitive cliques, common on campuses across the nation, creates a hostile environment for the majority—the losers, that is—the winners comprising a much smaller group than we would like to think possible.

Littleton is not an isolated instance. In Santa Cruz, California, the hierarchy is: the jocks, the preppies, the surfers, the ramers, the nerds, the Goths, the dirts. In Scottsdale, Arizona, the levels are: the jocks, the student government/drama clique, the technology twerps, the in-between crowd, and, at the bottom, the Church Step Dirties, who meet across the street in front of a church to smoke. The groups are clear and inviolable, with lunchtime geography demonstrating winners and losers in each set. "Precisely where a student falls on the clique hierarchy determines his or her level of stress or degree of happiness" (Gibbs and Roche 1999a, 17).

The feelings of being ostracized by others in childhood can have long-term effects on the development of relational abilities and self-esteem. As Goleman concludes: "How popular a child was in third grade has been shown to be a better predictor of mental health problems at age 18 than anything else—teacher's and nurse's ratings, school performance and IQ, even scores on psychological tests" (Goleman 1995).

The unpopular child feels the rejection as hate, finds multiple models of hate, and may soon mirror the hate.

Learning How to Hate

The proper question is not "*How* do we learn to hate?" but rather "Where and when do we *learn* how to hate?" The capacity to hate is prewired, innate, but how we experience it, when we express it, where we focus it, what we allow to trigger it are learned behaviors that can be unlearned and relearned. No one has improved on Karl Menninger's basic proposition: "The real fact seems to be that the child does not learn to hate; it comes into the world equipped with it, for better or for worse, and learns to use it, wisely or unwisely according to experiences. Under proper tutelage and with what we may call normal experience he gradually becomes more and more able to distinguish between those objects which are properly to be feared, hated and fought against, and those which may be more promptly accepted, utilized and loved" (Menninger 1942, 10).

In the July 1, 1939, *New Yorker*, the following song, written by a four-year-old boy and sung each night in the bathtub, was published as "one of the handsomest literary efforts of the year, as well as proof that children are the really pure artists, with complete access to their thoughts and no foolish reticence." The young mother who copied it down reports it is sung "entirely on one note, except the voice drops at the end of every line." Seldom has the vision of any heart's desire been put down so explicitly.

> He will just do nothing at all,
> He will just sit there in the noonday sun.
> And when they speak to him,
> He will not answer them,
> Because he does not care to.
> He will stick them with spears
> and put them in the garbage.

When they tell him to eat his dinner,
He will just laugh at them,
And he will not take his nap,
Because he does not care to.
He will not talk to them,
he will not say nothing,
He will just sit there in the noonday sun,
He will go away and play with the Panda.
He will not speak to nobody
because he doesn't have to.
And when they come to look for him
they will not find him,
Because he will not be there.
He will put spikes in their eyes
and put them in the garbage,
And put the cover on.
He will not go out in the fresh air
or eat his vegetables
Or make wee-wee for them,
and he will get thin as a marble.
He will not do nothing at all.
He will just sit there in the noonday sun.
                (originally appeared in
                the *New Yorker*, July 1, 1939)

What person does not become four years old again, reading the chant aloud?

Can a child be raised without hate? Wide differences in capacity to hate exist in children, as in adults. How would one raise a child with minimal hate? Karl Menninger hypothesized such a situation as follows:

> If we can imagine a parent sufficiently skillful to replace each satisfaction of which the child is deprived by another satisfaction which the child could accept as approximately equivalent, without disloyalty to the requirements of reality, we should expect to see in the progeny of such a parent an ideal person, not one without aggression but one without a sense of being thwarted in the adventures and misadventures of life, and without hate for anything except those things which would be hated and fought against in defense of his own ideals and best interests. (Menninger 1942, 11)

Such hypothetical parenting is useful as a model, but perfect parenting may also be destructive. When the parent is all good and the child, in the normal "all or nothing" thinking of childhood, feels all bad, it is a crazy-making situation. Not perfection but "good enough" parenting is most desirable for balanced healthy child development. Any account of how parents go about teaching either the constructive art of managing angry impulses or the destructive part that turns to hate must begin at the beginning. The metaphor that Jungian writer poet Robert Bly uses to picture how a child learns is a helpful starting point:

"When we were one or two years old we had what we might visualize as a 360-degree personality. Energy radiated out from all parts of our body and all parts of our psyche. A child running is a living globe of energy. We had a ball of energy, all right; but one day we noticed that our parents didn't like certain parts of that ball" (Bly 1988, 7).

Like a navel orange, the little child's soul is peeled and divided; parts of the self—hate, anger, rebellion—get split off. The sphere of wholeness is sliced away, pip by pip. By the time identity is formed, at sixteen or twenty, only a wedge remains of the child that once was. Bly says, "So I maintain that out of a round globe of energy the twenty-year-old ends up with a slice. We'll imagine a man who has a thin slice left, and we'll imagine that he meets a woman: let's say they are both twenty-four. She has a thin, elegant slice left. They join each other in a ceremony, and this union of two slices is called marriage. Even together the two do not make up one person!" (1988, 7). True, the 360-degree personality gets sectioned, and parts that are not approved are pulled away. They disappear from sight, but beneath the surface the child still learns to hate, although in secret ways.

Hate Formation

How and why can an innocent infant hate? Initially, the baby is bathed in a kaleidoscope of sensations: warmth, touch, light, wetness, closeness, and aloneness. Some of these are pleasing, comforting, and desirable, others are distressing and undesirable. The world outside the womb is not easy; it is both hot and cold, embracing and abandoning, satisfying and frustrating.

Melanie Klein, Margaret Mahler, Michael Balint, Donald Winnicott, and others have offered the most widely trusted maps of early development patterns in infancy. Central among them are the signs of negative feelings—hate—in the infant. In what follows, I offer an introductory theory, as a composite picture of emotional development, followed by a brief discussion of the thought of Klein, its most important explorer:

1. Childhood begins with hope, the hope that comforting touch, enveloping warmth, satisfying food, the physical-emotional breast will return. Early patterns of sensation coalesce in the baby to form expectations of certain experiences, the first being the feeding experience. Among the sensations of touch, sound, and warmth, the most important is the experience of *the mother as breast*. The first relationship is to a part, not the whole. For the infant, the mother is the breast. Any disruption between baby and breast is experienced as catastrophic. When the expectation arising from need is not met, the baby responds with alarm.

2. But the parent always fails the infant's expectations. There is no future, only *now*. The expectation of the breast will lead the baby to *search* for it, and failing to discover it, to cry in *distress*, eventually to *scream* and show distress in the whole body. *Anger*, if not rage, is exhibited. If the mother reappears, the baby may *reject* her, attack her, continue in the anger state. The mother may need to persist in reestablishing contact and comforting the child.

3. From this comes the first dilemma—the good and bad mother: The "good mother" who comforts, feeds, and gives warmth has become a "bad mother," who in going away abandons the child. It is impossible for the baby to reconcile these two intense and "total" feelings. How can the infant both love and hate the very person who is necessary for survival?

4. Good gets split from bad. The baby solves the dilemma by splitting good from bad, by keeping the two contradictory sets of feelings for the mother separated. It gets rid of the bad mother (whom it hates) to protect its attachment to the good mother (whom it craves). Its angry, hateful feelings are split off from its warm, needy, loving feelings.

5. In splitting the mother, the baby splits itself. That baby will not experience the mother as a separate being for some time. The infant's identity is merged with the mother, so it is actually splitting its bad experiences from its good experiences, and its hatred of the bad mother/breast is also experienced as hatred of those parts of the self that are identified with the bad.

6. The split-off parts are expelled in projection. The unacceptable parts, once split away, are expelled through projection onto a person, a part person, usually the frustrating or "bad" mother. The mystery of the baby's experience, still undifferentiated between self and mother and between the good and bad parts of the self (the comforting and the threatening), suggests that in the fantasy life wishes and fact are one, impulse and action are the same, so love and hate inevitably coexist.

7. So hate is born. The sequence is most likely like this: The mother/breast inevitably frustrates the baby. If there are good reparative experiences to intervene, the frustration is expressed as anger and comforted. If the mother is cold or punitive to the angry infant, the frustration turns to anger and then to hate. This part of the self which feels hate is then expelled and projected onto others.

8. However, projecting is depleting and requires giving up important parts of the self. Although splitting and expelling get rid of bad experiences, there is a loss of power, of inner experience, of one's own domain.

9. The mother becomes monster. The fantasy of the bad mother turns her into a terrifying giant, witch, ogre, familiar to us in fairy tales. Getting rid of the persecutor within the baby sets up an evil threat without.

10. But the good experiences of mother, in normal relationships, outweigh the bad mother experiences. So the child internalizes the good experiences (introjects the good mothering) to form a loving inner harmony, so that its fears of persecution and threat are lessened, its need to keep projecting fears is reduced, and the unacceptable parts of the self—the rage and hate—are hidden.

When the child's rush of emotion is more intense than its immature ego controls can manage, a flood of frustrated feelings may pour out. This intense rage may elicit parental rage in response. (The actual child calls out the inner child of the parent; the adult-child is hooked by the child-child.) The parent may then express anger, which the child interprets as being the same emotion that it is feeling, since it feels very much the same to the child. Whether actual hate is modeled or not, a model of hate may be taught by the parent, caught by the child—the infantile rage of the child invites, the immaturity in the parent reacts; the situation models, and the child learns. This repetitive drama can continue, episode on episode, throughout the stages—school age, youth, young adult. The child seeks out, finds, and hooks the hate hidden in the parent and the two begin a dance of hate with the beloved. The mistrust of the other's love: "You say you love me, but how can it be true?" is expressed in self-negation, but is primarily an act of suspicion, seeking to get behind the mask of hate. The fear of suspected hate will precipitate the next cyclical test of human bonding.

The Deeper Layers of Animosity

Expelled from an Eden of safety at birth, the child, losing the sense of oneness with the mother in the womb, is thrust into the new separateness. This is a total change of worlds, a crazy-making detachment, and the child is inevitably schizoid. The longing for return to union and the reality of separation will, in time, form the emotions of love and hate that are the opposed poles of all developing impulses. This is the focus of the pioneering work of Melanie Klein, which explores the deeper strata of hate—beneath the adult floor of depressive feelings lie these two further layers, the paranoid layer of blaming others and the schizoid layer of isolating oneself from the world. These three layers of early childhood experience are at our core, laid down in the three stages of early management of loss and fear. Samuel Beckett wrote, "We are all born crazy, some remain so." These stages reveal how and why—how they are laid down on the floor of the soul, why they surface in hard times:

Stage 1, the *schizoid level*, maintains the unity of the womb in cosmic continuity with the mother and therefore with the whole world. As a budding person who has no emotional skin, no boundaries, the observer and the observed are one. At one with the mother before birth, an infant's cosmic sense of omnipotent control, of oceanic connectedness to the environment, of unbroken solidarity with the mother continues for the first three months. This period, called schizoid by Klein, is boundaryless, seamless, and given the presence of a constant mothering figure it is a time of secure bliss. This provides a calm of unity and cradle of security. The schizoid layer develops with potential both for extreme terror and loss of self and for exquisite unification of self in love, transcendence, and spirituality. If abandoned with little or no contact, ambivalently ignored and smothered, or abused by a parent, the splitting from the external world continues into the next stage. As life offers threat and pain, we protect ourselves by creating boundaries as a first line of defense. Keep out. No admission. The good and pleasurable are welcomed within our domain; the evil or painful get walled out. The split between inside and outside allows us to divide good and evil safely and sustains security.

Stage 2, the *paranoid level*, lasts from four months to well into the second year. The infant responds to threat with paranoid process. Paranoia in its earliest stages is a state of confusion about what is inside the self and outside in the world. The transition when the child emerges from the schizoid stage at about four months to enter the paranoid stage, is what Klein termed the psychological birth. Now the child is alone; the mother is not a continuous (though disappearing and reappearing magically) extension of the self. The mother is other, split off from the self, sometimes good and nourishing (a good milk-filled breast), and at other times bad and withholding (a bad, dry breast). Growth into this stage is necessary for the child to move toward socially shared reality.

When there are injurious relationships too severe to be assimilated, the indigestible violation is internalized (swallowed whole like a mouse in a snake). The lump, called an "introject," is composed of love and hate mixed into a contradictory mass capable of intense fission of explosive feelings. Instead of the essential love needed to sustain life and growth, acute injury has been received. This internalized chunk of pain, which can be neither absorbed or excreted, is felt as a foreign object within, as something "other," something separate from the self, an autonomous parasite traveling along within the psyche. Early experiences of injury, striking in the paranoid period of development, and later experiences that push us back to the paranoid layer of our psyche, are likely to be projected outward to cast fearsome images on the screen of the world outside. These projections, created by the projector (not unlike the movie machine of the same name), are thrown on the screen of the external world in living color and with intricate plot. The more primitive the organization of the personality (or stuck in the second stage), the more frequently the picture within will be projected onto the world without. Images once pushed down the psychic throat, and therefore not incorporated into the self, remain indigestible. They are always "other," forever foreign, and finally must be regurgitated. Until that ejection they are subject to projection.

> The more frightening the inner world, the greater the need for boundaries, as walls, to shut out all that scares us as outside, as not in here, but out there. This automatic defense against hateful and fearsome experiences is to split—to split off from the threat. All adults remain paranoid to some degree or another. Even the most efficacious nurturing, combined with the most fortunate temperament, will leave some significant residue of the paranoid position in the adult psyche.
>
> One could construct a scale from one to ten or from one to a hundred on which every human being could be graded as to the degree to which paranoid response and action determine existence. . . . One could do the same for every human society, past or present. Every society is paranoid. . . . Furthermore, the degree of the paranoid position can differ profoundly within a society from one decade to the next, even from one year to the next. (Segal 1973, 15)

Stage 3 of development, the *depressive period*, dawns at about twelve to eighteen months. Instead of splitting the good (within) and the bad (without), the child begins to experience both within the self. This is made possible by the discovery that the mother is a whole being, both giving and withholding, both present and absent. The child can now begin to grieve the loss, make reparations for its rage and rejections, and reconnect with the mother across permeable boundaries where both giving and receiving take place. These permeable boundaries increasingly accept what is within, without projecting, and respect what is without, without blaming.

The child's growing awareness that the loved parent is the same person as the hated parent results in the capacity to feel guilt and its consequent urge to make amends for, to do repair work for, the effects of one's destructive urges. It is the recognition of, rather than the denial of, the capacity for hatred, envy, greed, and rage that produces the reparative impulse in the developing child. The conflict and ambivalence that characterize all human relationships must be faced and dealt with, not denied, before compassion, concern for others, and a striving for justice in the social order can be experienced and expressed. When we bring the two sides of our inner conflicts into proximity, love tends to work a change in the contents of the soul.

When one feels helplessly dependent, feelings of hate are stirred, separated from love, allowed to metastasize. With these feelings we reassure ourselves that those persons who are neglecting us, not we ourselves, are bad. Though they are important to us, we cannot but suspect that they do not love us, so we reassure ourselves that we can do without their love, no matter how important to us they may be. Dependence is intolerable, especially despondent, helpless dependence. To be at another's mercy is humiliating; to await necessary care according to another's pleasure or whim is denigrating. To find one's rights compromised, one's freedom determined by another with the power to control it or curtail it, is demeaning. Hate is a barrier against such primitive feelings of dependence. This archaic childhood state remains with us, and our capacity to hate functions as a seawall to protect us from flooding with feelings of abhorrent helplessness. "The barrier of hatred is a necessary emotional component of separation, a not-too-expensive guardian of our maturity, preventing us from sliding back into the archaic object-world, into the infantile dependence" (Balint 1952, 149).

Hatred has, thus, two sequential forms, primitive hatred and mature hatred. "The more mature an individual the less is his/her need for barriers against regression into primitive forms of object-love, and so less is the need for hatred" (Balint 1952, 150). The mature person, when facing these situations of oppression by some outside force, possesses a "barrier of hatred" which serves as "the guardian of our maturity" and blocks regression to primitive feelings. This allows the person to weigh the contradictory feelings within—the ambivalence of love and hate—and connect with the person who is the object of these negative feelings. With a firm barrier within, one can have permeable barriers without, between self and other. In contrast, the person who regresses back to primitive hatred has only permeable barriers within and so creates rigid, impermeable boundaries between self and the hated other. To fill out this picture of learning to hate, we look now at the theories of a moral philosopher who provides an interpersonal paradigm for the emergence of love, fear, and hate.

Hatred and Primary Relationships

Two basic motives, *love* and *fear*, create relationships, argues John Macmurray, Scottish moral philosopher. Love creates the "you and I"; fear defends the "I" against disappointment. To understand his argument one must start at the beginning of the developmental process. "The thesis we have to expound and to sustain is that the Self is constituted by its relation to the Other; that it has being *in its relationship*; and that this relationship is necessarily personal" (Macmurray 1961, 17). "Persons, therefore, are constituted by their mutual relation to one another. 'I' exist only as one element in the complex 'you and I'" (Macmurray 1961, 73). The self is not an isolated identity; it is one of two or more agents in personal relationships. "The idea of an isolated agent is self-contradictory. Any agent is necessarily in relation to the Other. Apart from this essential relation one does not exist."

To understand the nature of personal relationship, Macmurray contends, we must begin with the most elemental form of relationship: the bond between mother and child. The mother-child relationship can be empirically observed as authentically relational. The child is not determined by "instincts"—we are born with none. "All purposive human behavior has to be learned. To begin with, our responses to stimulus are, without exception, biologically random" (Macmurray 1961, 74).

> In the human infant—and this is the heart of the matter—the impulse to communication is its sole adaptation to the world into which it is born. Implicit and unconscious it may be, yet it is sufficient to constitute the mother-child relation as the basic form of human existence, as a personal mutuality, as a "You and I" with a common life. For this reason the infant is born a person and not an

animal. . . . Human experience is, in principle, shared experience; human life, even in its most individual elements, is a common life; and human behavior carries always, in its inherent structure, a reference to the personal Other. (Macmurray 1961, 75)

The essential motivations of the infant—the positive and negative poles of bipolar motivation—are the germinal forms of love and fear. Discomfort expressed in the cry, the call for mother, is implicitly the fear of isolation; comfort is found in being cared for and expressed in delight as a germinal form of love. Love and fear as primary motivations refer not to erotic impulse and panic terror, but to motives that connect one to a personal Other. Personal motives press one toward *communication*. Communicating is expressed in fondling, caressing, crooning, playing, which has no biological significance but a personal relational delight which banishes loneliness and celebrates delight in relationship. The needs that love and fear express can be satisfied only by another person's active response.

Love is positive and direct, fear is negative and indirect. Love is love for the other; fear is fear for oneself and of the other. The primary fear is that the Other will not respond to my need and I will be abandoned or swallowed up. Fear presupposes love and is secondary to it.

Hatred—the third original motivation—is derived from the interrelation of love and fear as positive and negative motives clash. Hatred is an original motivation since, like love and fear, it is "a universal component in the relation of persons inherent in the personal situation in all its forms. . . . [Yet it is] derivative because it presupposes love and fear as operative motives. It originates in the frustration of love by fear" (Macmurray 1961, 73).

Love requires a response for its completion, is fulfilled only when it is reciprocated. When a response is refused, love's motive and action are frustrated, mutuality is refused, personal existence is threatened in an absolute fashion, and the child fears for its own personal existence, resents negation, and the resentment becomes hatred. Hatred, as an original motive, is inevitable in personal relations. It is impossible that any parent or partner should always be able to respond to all needs according to all expectations. Hatred, as a component of complex motivations, is always present, although not necessarily dominant.

Mutuality and reciprocity of hatred is the negative side of relationships. Insofar as I threaten your personal fulfillment, I invite your reciprocal threat to mine. Mutual negation of a person relationship can accelerate to conflict, assault, murder. "For this reason we contrast love and hatred as opposites rather than love and fear. Both have a direct reference to the

Other. . . . Yet the opposition of love and fear as contraries is more fundamental" (Macmurray 1961, 74).

The positive relation of persons always contains and subordinates a negative element; a negative relationship inverts this motivation so hate is dominant and love subordinated. In hate, one rejects the relation of "You and I," but the "You" is necessary for any truly personal existence. In rejecting "You," I negate both "You" and "I." "Hatred," Macmurray concludes, "is perhaps what is referred to by theology as original sin. . . . The distinction between a positive and a negative relation of persons is the origin of the distinction between good and evil" (Macmurray 1961, 75).

Rhythm of Withdrawal and Return

The mother-child relationship establishes a pattern that becomes paradigmatic for all relations—withdrawal and return is the process of establishing aloneness and self-sustaining independence vis-à-vis togetherness and nurturing dependence. One learns to wait, expect, and subordinate the negative motive and to imagine, expect, and await the satisfaction with anticipatory pleasure. Regularity and consistency of care lead to the creation of a motivation system that subordinates the negative disappointments to the positive satisfactions. Isolation, abandonment, and betrayal of regular satisfactions lead to dominance by the negative pole. The rhythm of withdrawal and return finally establishes a balance of reparation and reunion after distance and separation. "The overcoming of the negative always remains problematical" (Macmurray 1961, 90). But the rhythm is the full dynamic of the personal—a positive is constituted by and subordinates its own negative. Love is enhanced as it shines above its own fears that are incorporated as protection of both self and other. The negative (fear) has meaning only in reference to the positive (love). Hate exists for love's sake, protects its integrity.

Both withdrawal and return are phases of relationship—isolation does not annul the relation, it refuses it. The refusal intends annulment, but since both persons are constituted by the relationship, to annul it is to annul oneself. The most we can do is achieve a *symbolic* annulment—the appearance but not the reality. Just as we cannot *not* communicate— silence and avoidance are also communication—and we cannot not behave since frozen or immobile behavior is also behavior, so we cannot not relate. If we are formed as persons by being in relationship, we cannot annul, we can only refuse. Macmurray offers as illustration the following situation:

An only son has publicly disgraced his family. The father, bitterly affected, publicly disowns him, disinherits him, erases him from the family record, cuts him dead if they meet by accident. When someone speaks to him of his son he says, "I have no son." But he knows, the other knows, and both know that he knows that he has. His son cannot not exist, although he intends this, but the intention is impossible. He may wish the boy dead, wish he had never been born, but he cannot annul his son's future, his son's past, or his own past. (Macmurray 1961, 94)

The father's *withdrawal* breaks the rhythm and refuses the *return*. But the relation has not been annulled, although the rhythm between reference to the self and reference to the other is interrupted. "We need the Other in order to be ourselves. But in any relation, the focus of attention and interest may become centered upon the self rather than on the Other" (Macmurray 1961, 94). When withdrawal has been abusive, as in the case of Hal, which we examine next, paranoid fear with cyclical resentment and ambivalent hate may serve as the kernel of identity formation, and the person clings to it fiercely since his psychic life depends on it. This case, of one who needs hate to stay alive, and cannot stop hating—one of the many varieties of personality constructed around a core of hate—is a not unusual story.

The Case of Hal

The firstborn of parents who were locked in a marriage gone morbid, Hal was welcomed at birth into four interlocking toxic triangles. The father was a passive, withdrawn clergyman; the mother a negativistic critic; the grandmother an unwelcome guest turned inexperienced nanny. The mother, who administered the family business, was unavailable to child, spouse, and grandmother. The grandmother, an equally ineffective parent, dealt with the infant as a demanding tiny adult. A multigenerational pattern of delegating parenting to the grandparent, with parent ignoring the child, led to the disappearance of Hal's mother; the vanishing male in the paternal system produced a father who was aloof, ineffectual, and invisible.

Hal's early experiences of intense maternal anger and coldness and his grandmother's stern contingent reward system were internalized into high mistrust, a despair of gaining warmth, self-doubt, and shame. The birth in his second year of a sister who quickly became the favorite of both mother and grandmother reduced his already minimal care to physical maintenance and emotional deprivation.

As Hal grew toward school age, he found intermittent warmth in play with his father, but it was inconsistent and rejecting. The father's terror of his predominately homosexual orientation led him to withdraw to protect the child. Desire for his mother and hate for her coldness; longing for his father and rage at his abandonment; dependence on his grandmother and anger at her rigid controls and emotional unavailability; and sibling rivalry toward the sister who had displaced him all clustered like a virus. Hal developed a punitive conscience and managed the rage turned against himself by focusing hatred outward toward all the hapless people in his world.

His school years were marked by high achievement, in a driven search for adequacy, competency, and acceptance. There was no particular crisis as he formed an identity, but he struggled with intense internal conflicts. After several halfhearted attempts in other directions, Hal enrolled in seminary, to follow his father into ministry.

His courtships were short, intense, intricately involved. He had an insatiable hunger for being loved that was periodically overwhelmed by a need to hate, which took over when he began to get close to another. Hatred served as a test of each partner's loyalty and love. Hal at last found a nurse, a victim of sexual abuse, who was familiar with the drama of love that runs hot and cold. His cycles of intense closeness were followed by attack and rejection, then finally rewarded with his ultimate compliment: "Now I know that you really love me—but how can you love someone like me?" For Hal to love, there had to be episodes of hate that repeated the story of life with his parents. Hal's unconscious demand for his hatred to be recognized, received, and tolerated became welded to his drive for survival. The necessity of this cycle to his security as a person required this monthly test of his partner's love being greater than his hateful resistance. Each experience of rage, rejection, regret, and readmission gave evidence that he was truly alive; each reconciliation proved that the partner was truly there for him.

Hal's ambivalence between love and hate, Melanie Klein would point out, is not the experience of *mixed* feelings, but of *contradictory* feelings. Emotions and impulses exist side by side as positive and negative components forever in opposition. Ambivalence need not be, however, a static state. The polarity of love and hate remains constant, but it can be mitigated by love in a gradual process of integration. Gradually love can become predominant, but a full and permanent integration is never possible (Klein 1940, 351). Even in adulthood, when a counselor seeks to interpret the collected grievances of inner hate in a new light, a counselee like Hal will feel as though his central life issues are being devalued. "Any such attempt is felt as a threat of taking away their justification for existence; they really feel that they have nothing else to live for" (183). The grievances, and the basic fault in the personality that demands one cling to them desperately, must be accepted with patient empathy, and a period of mourning will run its course over a long period of time. It cannot be hurried; it must be witnessed; ultimately the patient becomes willing to accept the previously unacceptable objects, even though this person seems to be, as we shall see in the perspective we are about to discuss, "one who cannot stop hating."

Three Types of Hating

For clinical purposes, psychoanalyst Richard Galdston has grouped people into three categories with regard to their "competence to hate" (Galdston 1987, 372). He defines these three groups as follows:

1. *Those unable to hate.* Some persons who cannot direct their lives purposefully flow alongside others by functioning as part objects in search of a whole entity, living dependently, reacting passively, feeling superficially. Others unwittingly become their advocates, assume the task of protecting and defending them, even do their hating for them.

2. *Those unable to get over hating.* Chronic, extended hating occurs in at least two major forms: (1) First are those who know they hate, find a scapegoat, and use it as a prosthetic device to support the weakness of a divided and weakened ego structure. The splitting of love and hate feelings, the projection of the hate on a chosen enemy, spares the individual from the need to acknowledge and address the ambivalence. (2) Then there are those who deny that they hate and repress the emotion. This sustained repression of hatred is a perpetually carried burden that has two effects: it depletes the assertive energy available for attacking the problems of life, and it internalizes (swallows whole, "introjects") the hated object, making forgiveness impossible. So bad debts of rage and resentment cannot be written off, and the energy required to contain them is unavailable for further growth or new commitments. Chronically repressed hatred is a major cause of marital failure, a significant block to intimacy, a barrier to necessary grieving, and, as is the case with all that we deny, is projected onto the next generation by trickling down onto the children.

3. *Those who learn how to hate and how to get over hatred.* Such personalities allow both positive and negative feelings to flow into awareness and are capable of love and hate. They recognize both affection and antipathy, and when disappointed or disillusioned they can work it through, get over it, and get on with new goals and new commitments (Galdston 1987, 372–73).

Learning to get over hateful feelings begins very early—infantile dependency must be resolved, self and mother/other separated with increasing clarity, and the sense of object constancy achieved (the discovery that life, people, and events go on in reality even when I wish for them to be annihilated), so that the need to destroy the other in fantasy is overcome, and joy in the object's survival and continuing usefulness is discovered. When the child declares, "Mommy, I hate you," the mother replies without judgment or repressing, "That's all right, you'll get over it," and so offers the child confidence that the experience of hate can be contained and resolved in constant, enduring, trustworthy relationships—what we call "a context of enduring object relations."

Those who cannot hate did not learn this art; their fragile, unsafe environment threatened relationships so severely that they could not sustain negative feelings; they could not express hateful impulses with the confidence that both child and parent would safely survive. The fear of self-destruction or annihilation of the other was too great, and the only answer was repression—choke back the impulse, block out the hate, black out the memory that it ever existed.

Suppression, not repression, allows one to feel hate and get over it. Learning the skills of suppression (self-awareness, inner self-management, and cognitive control) allows the ego to feel outraged and to be certain of getting over it. The need to punish and yet preserve the person or thing hated empowers both anger at the other and a yearning to be reunited with the other.

Suppression of hatred is necessary for a person to "get over it." Temporarily, the child can hate as the child experiences the pain of disappointment, accommodates to the frustrating situation, and regains hope. Suppression of the impulse to act out the hateful feelings helps the person remove the destructive intent from the negative feelings and achieve the ego strength to love and to hate in a way that is acceptable to the superego and permissible in the family and social context. Hate thus becomes an intermediate step that moves the person toward acceptance, reconciliation, and forgiveness. The contrast between these three learned attitudes toward hate can be visualized as in Table 4. Seeing it in table form allows contrast and comparison in your further creative thought about the management of the impulse to hate.

Table 4	Developmental Contrasts		
	Those Who Cannot Hate	**Those Who Cannot Quit**	**Those Who Hate and Get over It**
Infant	Symbiosis continues unresolved. Dependency, passivity, high attachment, and inhibited relations with mother and others	Symbiosis is not resolved. Self is not separated from external objects. Hates self and others.	Symbiosis resolved, in a rudimentary sense of separateness of self from external objects, i.e., mother and others.
Toddler	Low aggression, little curiosity, limited learning from experience	High aggression with destructive intent. The object is destroyed in fantasy.	Parents accept high aggressive drives and intrusion into others' worlds without censure.
Child	No safety for hateful feelings. Relationships do not offer a sense of object constancy sufficient to allow hating. Few transitional objects, restricted play, inhibited feeling	Instinctual impulse of hatred is felt; child holds onto it to protect the self. Cannot get over it and mend relationships. Fantasies of hatred are magical in their destructive potential.	Object constancy, joy in the object's survival of aggressive attack; can express intense feelings and "get over them." Aggressive play becomes a way to assess and separate fact vs. fantasy.
Adolescent	Aggression and hatred repressed in dependence on institutions, on community or religious systems, to order one's emotional life passively without integration.	Overwhelming drives provoke keen disappointment and intense hatred directed at parents, authorities, institutions, enemies, without clear boundaries or limits.	Intensification of drives brings a heightened ability for disappointment, frustration, and hatred; these are keenly felt, clearly named, and cleanly expressed.

Compassion as Raging for Justice

"My sister confirms every memory I retell, and her story is virtually identical with mine—intimidation mixed with seduction in early childhood; then continuing violation rewarded by special privileges throughout my primary school years; and when I reach puberty, a father who is a perpetrator at night and a public hero in the community by day.

"Now he is dead. And I hate him. I cannot get past the rage that haunts me. My daughter, who was also abused by him while I was still in denial of my past, has forgiven him.

"I cannot.

"I am constantly flooded by waves of resentment. He died without a word of recognition of the abuse or apology for the evil done. When confronted, he responded with 'Just blame, go ahead and blame me—everyone blames me—I'm the cause of all the family's problems, but I don't remember any of it.' I not only lose the argument, and fail in the confrontation, I am treated as the guilty one while he continues his elusive moves.

"My daughter can get past the hate, I cannot. Is it perhaps, in part, because I, her mother, could at last, at very least, name the incest, call it what it was, tell the truth? My mother denied it sweetly, blamed her daughters for complaining, and made us feel crazy.

"I hate him. I hate his trapping, blaming, sneaking, lying ways. I hate what he did to me, to my sister, and most of all to my daughter. I hate all the guilt I feel because I let it happen again by denying it had happened to me. I hate the power he still had to throw it all in a black hole of denial, to rewrite our family history, to destroy us. I don't know what to do with all the hate I feel. I can't find a place for it. I can't quit hating."

Rage at such exploitation, and at one's own complicity as a silent bystander, does not go away. Finally one must find a place for it somewhere in the archives of memory. If the place found is a victim treadmill where the pain is renewed in each visit, there is little healing possible. If the place is in a vigilante armory where revenge is reviewed even against one long dead, the powerlessness grows even greater.

But if the rage is kept on file along with all the commitments to seek and find justice, then a transformation can occur. The urge to violence can become a drive for courageous action against—constructive intervention in and healing concern for—abuse. These are the qualities that create compassion. Psychologist Rollo May concludes on this point:

Compassion occupies a position opposite to violence; as violence projects hostile images of the opponent, compassion gives us the basis for judging someone without condemning him. Although

loving one's enemies requires grace, compassion for one's enemies is
a human possibility. (May 1972, 252)

Compassion for the enemy is not just a human possibility, it is the result
of our remembering our cohumanity and seeing once more that the other
is made of the same stuff as we. Loving one's enemies requires *grace*—an
inbreaking of the long-long-vision of a greater love, higher justice, and
deeper acceptance beyond deserving. Compassion does not remove the
rage or silence the outrage; it gives it a prophetic voice of hope. The hope
that justice, if not obtained for oneself, can be guaranteed for those who
follow and that gives strength to continue the struggle, meaning to transform pain, courage even in suffering.

Hate and love, combined, balanced, clarified, create the stubborn realistic compassion of the social worker who faces daily situations of abuse,
the therapist who intervenes in relationships that are cyclical and trapping, the pastor who walks with people who cannot break their compulsion to addictions. In realistic open-eyed compassion, concern for the
other as a person, driven by sadness at what troubles or limits the other
and shaped by moral disgust at what injures or violates that person, produces intense caring. Compassion also connects the two emotions of love
and hate when they are felt for the perpetrator causing hurt, the offender
acting in violation of another. The inner pole of hate is disgust and contempt at one who injures or violates another; the opposite pole of love is
awe and surprise at the mystery of another; and the two poles unite in
compassion, which remembers that somewhere within, we too have both
sides, we both need compassion, neither of us is all good or all evil. Nothing in another is foreign to me, nothing completely alien to human nature,
nothing beyond some essential level of understanding—although sometimes genuine disgust so permeates the empathic picture it must be consciously suspended for the moment to permit reaching out for rapport and
initiating conversation. So in compassion we can affirm:

Hate is the certainty that the other is without worth, positive potential, enduring value; love is the certainty that the other has potential, possibility, irreducible value; compassion is the certain and steadfast concern
about wasted potential and the unshakable hope that this potential can
be realized.

Hate is ignoring, dominating, or violating another to block potential;
love is listening, supporting, confronting, and joining in bidding another
to grow; compassion is recognizing that in growth we need each other.

Hate is the unwillingness to risk anything with another; love is the willingness to offer a part of oneself in trust; compassion is the willingness to trust and risk in small, growing increments of caring.

Hate is treating a person as a thing, using another as a means, exploiting another as a resource, commodity, or tool; love is seeing others as an end in themselves, prizing them for their own sake; compassion is nurturing another's growth even when it may be against my hopes, freeing them to take responsibility and privilege even when we cannot predict the outcome.

Hate is maintaining one's safety and security at the expense of the other; love is willingness to be vulnerable, to open a relationship to future possibilities even when it is costly; compassion is the willingness to risk even when it hurts.

Chapter Four

Hate and Memory:
Living out of the Past

Forgetting prolongs captivity;
remembering is the secret of redemption.
—Jewish Proverb

Dear family:
I admonish you always to remember—Be good haters.
—John Brown

Now hatred is by far the longest pleasure;
Men love in haste, but they detest at leisure.
—Lord Byron, "Don Juan"

Proposition for Chapter 4

Hate and memory have an integrated and interdependent relationship. Hate finds a place in memory, a home where it awaits review and demands satisfaction. Memory has a special tendency to retain experiences of pain, so it is uniquely hospitable to hatred. In this chapter we will explore the dynamics of memory, its captivity to anger and hostility, and the strong link forged by resentments. Understanding how we store painful stories for later use in protecting us from their repetition and how these narratives can be rewritten can help us discover ways to move from memories that demand "retributive hate" toward those that seek a "moral hate" or even a "just hate" and ultimately seek the redemption of both the hater and the hated.

A Bosnian Muslim woman reports:
"I am a Muslim, and I am thirty-five years old. To my second son who was just born, I gave the name 'Jihad' [Holy War], so he would

72

not forget the testament of his mother—revenge. The first time I put my baby at my breast I told him, 'May this milk choke you if you forget.' So be it.

"The Serbs taught me to hate. For the last two months there was nothing in me, no pain, no bitterness, only hatred.

"I taught these children to love. I did. I am a teacher of literature. I was born in Ilijas, and I almost died there. My student Zoran, the only son of my neighbor, urinated into my mouth. As the bearded hooligans standing around laughed, he told me: 'You are good for nothing else, you stinking Muslim woman.' . . .

"I did not know whether I first heard the cry or felt the blow. My former colleague, a teacher of physics, was yelling like mad, 'Ustasha, ustasha . . .' And kept hitting me. Wherever he could.

"I have become insensitive to pain. But my soul? It hurts. I taught them all to love and all the while they were making preparations to destroy everything that is not of the Orthodox faith. Jihad—war. This is the only way" (Vukovic 1993, 134).

The Serbian journalist Zeljiko Vukovic, having recorded this story, asks: "How many mothers in Bosnia have sworn to teach their children hate and revenge! How many little Muslims, Serbs, and Croats will grow up listening to such stories and learning such lessons?" (Vukovic 1993, 134).

Memory is long and hate is multigenerational in an honor-based social order such as the culture of Bosnia. Ledgers of retributive justice and injustice require the repeated recording of new entries—acts of retaliation and revenge. How shall we comprehend the willingness of a Serb to kill a Muslim neighbor as an act of revenge for ancestors who fought the battle of Kosovo against the Turks on the Field of Blackbirds in 1389? How is it that the mere numbers 1389 painted as graffiti on a wall in Serbia can evoke immediate memories of hate? The long shadows of resentment—six hundred years of hate—are not unique to the Balkans. Every nation has citizens and groups that hold deep strata of prejudice and resentment against descendants of other groups. The sins of the ancestors haunt the children and evoke hate in the progeny of ancestral victims—sons of slaves vs. sons of slaveholders; daughters of the kitchen vs. daughters of the manor.

In a foreword to *The Tenth Circle of Hell*, a memoir of life in the death camps of Bosnia, Elie Wiesel writes of ancestral hatred that is always present in some cultures and erupts between neighbors:

These are men who know each other well, neighbors who greet each other in the street, friends of many years standing who suddenly, poisoned by patriotic and ethnic fanaticism, become fierce and bitter enemies.

How to explain such cruelty, such sadism among people who only yesterday lived in brotherhood with their victims of today?

Why, among them, such a thirst to hurt, to injure, to humiliate human beings whose only wrong—whose only "crime"—is to believe in Mohammed rather than in Jesus? (Wiesel, in Hukanovic 1996, vii)

Thirst, hunger, gang rapes, exhaustion, filth, blows, insults, skulls shattered, sexual organs torn out, stomachs ripped open, these only begin the list of ways soldiers dehumanized their prisoners who were former neighbors. Photos of atrocities in process show torturers with facial expressions described as "gleeful, sneering." The emotion of hate, the belief systems that demand revenge, the motivation to retaliate, and the permission to wreak vengeance may lie dormant in peoples forced to live side by side such as those in the Balkan states compressed into the former Yugoslavia, then erupt with seething fury after a half century or more of deceptive quiet.

Milovan Djilas, vice president of Yugoslavia, wrote of his perpetually feuding Montenegrin clan:

Vengeance—this is a breath of life one shares from the cradle with one's fellow clansman, in both good fortune and bad, vengeance from eternity. Vengeance was the debt we paid for the love and sacrifice our forebears and fellow clansmen bore for us. It was the defense of our honor and good name, and the guarantee of our maidens. It was our pride before others; our blood was not water that anyone could spill. It was, moreover, our pastures and springs more beautiful than anyone else's—our family feasts and births. It was the glow in our eyes, the flame in our cheeks, the pounding in our temples, the word that turned to stone in our throats on our hearing that our blood had been shed. It was the sacred task transmitted in the hour of death to those who had just been conceived in our blood. It was centuries of manly pride and heroism, survival, a mother's milk and a sister's vow, bereaved parents and children in black, joy and songs turned into silence and wailing. Generation after generation, the blood chain was not broken, the inherited fear and hatred of feuding clans was mightier than fear and hatred of the enemy, the Turks. (Djilas 1958, 8)

Hatred may be preserved, hidden under ice. But in its own time and under opportune circumstances, the ice cracks, and old passions spring to life once more. Satisfaction delayed, and the myths of history often retold, may endow hatreds with authority and empower them with ferocity—like the ethnic cleansing in the Balkans, where religious beliefs serve as markers. A long history of homicidal feuds between Serbs, Croats, and Turks has maintained a subterranean stream of self-renewing hatred. Yet these Balkan peoples lived together in amity from 1878 to 1918 under the Austro-Hungarian Empire, and from 1945 to 1990 as the nation of Yugoslavia. Is the amity superficial, like the "conscious," and the hatred a latent reality, like the "unconscious," as Freudian thought proposes? Or do amity and enmity, both equally real, exist side by side, one or the other coming to the fore through political manipulation?

The truth, in all likelihood, lies "somewhere in between," argues Peter Berger. Archaic hatreds do live on "below" the surface, and yet they can be put aside when a leader emerges and proposes actions that call old enemies to become friends, rather than incite good neighbors to become mass murderers (Berger 1994, 142). When the leader summons memories of past atrocities and reawakens hatred, history may claim the identity of a new generation of subjects and offer them a mandate of obligations to rectify the reified past. On the other hand, a leader may point to an identity grounded in history yet also offer a challenge to claim a new freedom from the rage and irrationality of old violations. Historical memories, held sacred by a community, have the power to tell us who we are. Re-membering, in its root meaning, is to reconnect member pieces of data, fact, fragmented story into a coherent account. In deep re-membering, members of a community or group that have been dis-membered are re-membered. The severed is reunited, the broken made whole. Historical memory can continue to dis-member. "Remember the Alamo" can shape U.S.-Mexican relations; "Remember Pearl Harbor/Remember Hiroshima" can define Japanese-American counteridentities. "Historical memory . . . has to do with recovering not only the sense of one's own identity and the pride of belonging to a people but also a reliance on a tradition and a culture, and above all, with rescuing those aspects of identity which served yesterday, and will serve today, for liberation" (Martin-Baro, 1994).

The crucial element in identity is the cluster of memories, which defines who we are to be as individuals-in-community. We are our memories. Personal memories instruct us from our firsthand experiences of past successes and failures; familial memories may command us with past ledgers of family honor that function as emotional mortgages. Ethnic or tribal memories may obligate us to act, feel, think in solidarity with our group of origin; national memories may rally in times of threat or competition to demand allegiance or sacrifice for the good of the nation-state. Identity is a web of identifications, with their multilayered loyalties, which may offer a freeing sense of privileged selfhood or delegate a binding duty to "hate those we are supposed to hate." We may allow ourselves to inherit the memory legacies of those who have gone before us, or cut ourselves off from our predecessors. When the inheritance they bequeath to us is filled with unresolved injustices and unpaid emotional debts, the debit lists may be long, the debts deep. We may also collect our own individual log of entries in memory ledgers that record our own personal histories of injustices suffered, or we can censor the items that trigger hate and trust our unconscious to do the record keeping.

Ego as Memory's Censor

Our memories are censored. The human self possesses a dictatorial censor called the "ego" that filters, selects, eliminates, re-creates, reframes, rewrites memories, indeed, in situations of great threat or ambiguity, may create false memories out of whole cloth.

1. The human self, argues Anthony Greenwald, is a "totalitarian ego" that organizes its knowledge, screens its perceptions, and selects which memories to retain in predictably biased ways that are designed, like totalitarian governments, to protect its own safety and security (Greenwald 1980).

2. The ego is also a "self-justifying historian" that retains the information that supports its central ideas about the self and rewrites history in a way necessary to maintain its inner consistency. For example, the average American recalls the "founding fathers" as people who prized religious liberty, indeed, willingly gave their lives to defend it. This memory serves to justify current points of view for our corporate ego. We rarely recall that the Massachusetts Bay charter, in 1647, prohibited all Catholics from settling in Massachusetts Bay Colony, and called for the execution of any Jesuit who, once having been ousted, should return (Cobb 1902, 177).

3. Indeed, the ego is a "cultic librarian" that organizes information and knowledge into an elaborate internal library. Our rapid retrieval system is a network of linking and interlocking biases. Our commitment to a par-

ticular cataloging system (liberal political bias, conservative ideology, a religious framework of beliefs) requires that we spend more time maintaining the system than revising it. Our biases persist because they serve us well. They sustain identity, preserve self-confidence, and maintain mental organization. To illustrate how this prejudicial system edits experiences and produces stereotypes that betray hidden hate, consider what Teddy Roosevelt, who is ranked as one of our wiser presidents, once remarked about Native Americans: "I don't go so far as to think that the only good Indians are dead Indians, but I believe that nine out of every ten are, and I shouldn't like to inquire too closely into the case of the tenth" (Hagedorn 1921, 355).

4. In fact, the ego is a "brusque policeman." The flash of anger we feel when threatened with conflicting information is the mind's way of policing its boundaries. The assertion that "I know my own mind," when in reality we are refusing to be challenged, protects us from uncertainty, anxiety, indecisiveness, and the confusion that always accompanies the change process.

5. Finally, the ego is "an inflated self" which, when healthy, sustains itself with illusions of "overly positive self-evaluations, exaggerated perceptions of control or mastery, and unrealistic optimism" (Taylor and Brown 1988, 193). These illusions appear to be both normal and necessary for the usual criteria of good mental health, criteria that include the ability to care about others, to respect the self, to accept diversity, to deal with confrontation, to work productively. In fact, people who score highest on measures of self-deception such as "denies threatening but universal feelings such as guilt" score lowest on measures of depression or psychopathology.

A Home for Hate in Memory

Hate finds a home in memory. Memory, as host, nourishes the residues of anger and keeps the feelings, fears, and values alive, but not well, in the soul. Memory houses many secrets, and among them are self-determinations and self-evaluations that shape personal identity. Alongside them we store grievances, losses, injuries, angers, and hates within our inner archives. When the pain surrounding an experience is very sharp, we may encapsulate the wound and conceal the memory from ourselves. Hate is often the guardian against the loss of important memories that might otherwise be written off, their facts rewritten, or the truth lost forever. Memories denied are not erased; they go inward, but they do not go away. In time, they return from the unconscious to cry out for fairness and justice.

Exploring our memories requires courage. Fear of memory in its most acute form is amnesia, in its more common form, denial. Refusal to remember functions at a level we are unaware of in the automatic erasure of the past we call repression. When our attention turns inward, we cannot access the buried memory. Instead we may see: (1) the exact opposite: concern substituted for anger; admiration for resentment, empathy for hate; (2) exactly nothing: the absence of any emotion or feeling about the situation; or (3) exact projection: the anger or hate we cannot own is projected onto some other person. These three, called (1) reaction formation, (2) denial, (3) projection, serve us well in eliminating troubling memories without our realizing that editing and censorship are taking place.

Memory is not a camera that takes intricate and objective photographs, or a computer that creates accurate files for future use or reproduces past events unaltered or unretouched. Memory is not a mirror of reality, an accurate historian, or a safe storage vault. Rather it is a novelist, constantly refining the events of the past into a narrative acceptable and accessible to the self. At its most subjective, memory functions like a kaleidoscope, recalling past events dynamically, partially, in edited form, creating a mythology of one's life to protect an ideal self or to protest in behalf of an angry self. Since our memory can hold only a minuscule fraction of our experience, we must constantly forget in order to remember, and the reality we recall is made up of bits and pieces, fragments of conversations and fractured narratives that are accidental, unreliable, always evolving, forever shifting beneath our mental feet. But this kaleidoscope is what constitutes the "self" that I bring to this moment.

The median metaphor—between camera and kaleidoscope—is memory as compass and gyroscope. Like a compass, memory offers direction; like a gyroscope, balance. The selected recollections of the past preserve the economy and harmony of the psyche. Memory operates under the censorship of the ego and according to the guidelines set by the ideal self and the superego. Experiences that were deeply disturbing to our self-image, or dangerously threatening to our pride system, get blunted, excluded, or repressed. As Nietzsche said, "Memory and Pride were fighting. Memory said, 'It was like this' and Pride said, 'It couldn't have been like this'—and Memory gives in" (Perls 1969, 42).

Nothing changes more constantly than the past—although we assume it to be unchangeable. The personal past that influences our lives does not consist of what actually took place, but of what we believe occurred. Our yesterdays follow us to offer guidance, character, and meaning to the present; or, when full of unresolved pain, they prompt us to repeat the drama and perpetuate the evil done to us. Hate and anger serve as guardians of the truth, refusing to let go of an injury unrecognized, suffering unobserved, and pain unexpressed. They continue to demand validation of the insult or injury and to seek the healing that comes only through the truth being remembered, recovered, reintegrated into a life so that there is no need of such protectors. These twin guards, anger and hate, are frequently forbidden from doing their task by parental figures or teachers, and are thus silenced by external forces—forces that are then internalized—to keep the truth of what happened from coming to light. As child psychoanalyst Alice Miller writes:

> The normal reactions to injury should be anger and pain; since children in a hurtful kind of environment, however, are forbidden to express their anger and since it would be unbearable to experience their pain all alone, they are compelled to suppress their feelings, repress all memory of the trauma, and idealize those guilty of abuse. Later they will have no memory of what was done to them. Disassociated from the original cause, their feelings of anger, helplessness, despair, longing, anxiety, and pain will find expression in destructive acts against others [criminal behavior, mass murder] or against themselves [drug addiction, alcoholism, prostitution, psychic disorders, suicide]. (Miller 1986, 142)

We do not have a natural mechanism for coping with mistreatment. We cannot erase it from our bodies. We cannot empty our cells of the information about our past suffering. We have only the ability to anesthetize ourselves through repression and denial. The ability to own, grieve, express, release, and redirect our lives must be learned. Memory needs the nudge of anger to allow the truth to be told—the truth that is in the cells, the soul, the inner self.

Storing Hate—Short and Long-Term Memory

The word " remember" is ambiguous—it can mean putting something into memory, as in "I will certainly remember what you did to me," or it can mean getting something out, as "I see you and immediately I remember how you hurt me." The working memory, often called *short-term memory*, is where we put things for a brief time—directions, simple instructions, or the previous sentence that helps us get to the next one we are reading. Short-term memory is limited in capacity and duration. Without concentration and rehearsal we lose the information; otherwise the mind would be clogged by the mass of details encountered hourly. This short-term holding process provides continuous purging of the mind and voluntary selectivity for intentional retention of certain data into *long-term memory*, which is memory proper, synonymous with learning, growth, accommodation to events, and assimilation of their meaning. Its contents last as long as the brain persists and survives.

Knowledge and understanding enter short-term memory through repetition, rehearsal, and sustained attention, and access to the data is direct and immediate. Long-term memory, in contrast, assimilates, envelops, attaches that data to a structure that already exists in the mind, and makes it a part of our network of experience. We learn what we like to learn; we retain what we find necessary to retain; we internalize what we desire as well as what we fear. We learn so efficiently that even data that is not useful or adaptable may stay firmly in place. We are actually quite bad at forgetting—the harder we try to forget, the more fixed a piece of information may become. Some suggest that there is no forgetting from long-term memory, just suspending of contact with a particular part of the network until the appropriate stimulus occurs.

We cannot access memory directly, like going to a file or checking an index. Long-term memory is a network of associations, and we must look for a point of entry to find how and where the items are related to each other. If a piece of information is placed in a rich and current network of interests, it springs back almost instantly, but as it is overlaid with other data it becomes difficult to retrieve, until that particular neural network is caught by a relevant association and the data appears "in a surprising flash."

After a five-day trip, I can recall exactly where my car is parked in the airport lot. But a week later the location is lost—unless, when I returned to it, I found it broken into and the radio stolen. This alarm signal adds a second significance. The image of location, bits of glass, and an empty place in the dash may be retained, and that parking spot avoided in future visits. Routine is quickly forgotten, the unusual or unpredicted more easily retained.

Recall your frustration on writing a word, looking at its odd appearance, and deciding it is misspelled. You try to verify the spelling by direct search of long-term memory (the normal way to access short-term memory), but it is not possible. You pull up a variety of spellings, but none of them look right. Long-term memory responds more efficiently to relaxation and nonanxious scanning of memory traces. When you end the direct search process, and relax the mental scanners, soon the correct memory comes into focus. Releasing the demands for instant retrieval allows the networks to function normally, and within minutes the correct data often surfaces.

Long-term memory contains many layers of data from life experiences—the recalled, the recallable, the unrecalled, and the repressed. Whole networks—such as those holding memories from years one to five—may be inaccessible. Yet they send signals of their existence through emotions that erupt, and what is essentially a two-year-old toddler's tantrum of anger, unaltered by the years, can be displaced onto parallel targets thirty years later.

Memory and hatred have a long, intimate relationship. We have all forgotten much more than we remember, and the selection of memory items is not under our conscious control. Experiences attached to our mental networks of long-term identifications define the self-identities that we form: *"I am"* is formed from *"I have been"* (memory) as well as *"I will be."* Both those whom I have loved and those who have loved me become a part of my inner identity-forming recollections, as well as those I have hated and those who have hated me. These networks of love and hate web throughout the many pathways of interconnecting memories, linking many bits on many levels, in coherent and incoherent ways.

As is the case with other long-term memories, direct access to love and hate memory networks is not consciously available; we cannot force them by power of will, but indirect processes can alter memories. New perspectives on a hated event can move the memory from the network of fear arousal to a network of responsible self-protection. The memory network of multiple facts and feelings of tragic loss can be relocated into a new location of injury forgiven and loss grieved to completion. Hate of a person can be reframed into contempt for an act, and the memory shifts from grievance file to agenda for action. The old traces are not erased—some may be altered by new memories, or the two memories—injury and healing—remain accessible side by side.

Freud, in his *Interpretation of Dreams*, referred to dream as the "day's residues," that is, the events of the previous day and the meanings attached to them remain with us in the memory structure where they were embedded. Among these residues are savored love and smoldering anger and chilly hate. Negative memories are the residue of the day's stress and pain that we revisit to do grievance work (planning to address the issue or redress the injury) or to do grief-work (letting go and feeling the loss).

Hate, then, may be construed as the residue of the unfinished or unresolved part of the interpersonal injury, a definition derived from Murray Bowen's insight on grief. Grief, he observed, is the residue of the unfinished portion of a relationship, and we can therefore quantify the varied amounts of grief-work siblings will face on the death of a parent; the one still in conflict is admitting by that conflict that he or she is still a child and thus has much to finish. The mature adult, with few parts of the relationship still unresolved, will have much less residue to clear away in grief.

Hate, as a parallel function, is the brooding-work that allows a person to revisit, review and rework the unfinished portion of a painful relationship. The more incomprehensible the action of the offender, the more unjust the injury received, then the greater the amount of emotion and cognition one must digest and assimilate. The legacy of pain demands that an injury be either resented and revenged or reframed and redirected. As "residue" it is the emotional and cognitive stuff that cannot be ingested, so it is swallowed whole. Once forced down, it lies indigestible, beyond assimilation, like a toxic lump leaching pollution from the floor of the unconscious.

The cumulative residues of hate, settling in layered resentments that solidify into stony antipathy, lie heavy on the soul. Resentful brooding is an attempt to dissolve these deposits. Our return to them is often cyclical, in a spiral of descending emotions, cognitions, and actions that tend downward toward the repository of remembered garbage, rather than upward toward a goal of transcendence. The collected remembrances of pain serve to renew the outrage rather than release the rage. But the resentment contains the longing to find a way through the detritus to release and freedom.

Hate, Hope, and Memory

The most powerful writing on the relationship between memory and hate has been done by holocaust survivor Elie Wiesel, who after being set free from a concentration camp was silent for a decade of meditation and recovery. Then, at last, he wrote his story in *Night*, the encounter of a boy and his father with the horror of Auschwitz.

> Never shall I forget that night, the first night in camp, which has turned my life into one long night, seven times cursed and seven times sealed. Never shall I forget the faces of the children, whose bodies I saw turned into wreaths of smoke beneath a silent-blue sky. Never shall I forget those flames which consumed my faith forever. Never shall I forget that nocturnal silence which deprived me, for all

eternity, of the desire to live. Never shall I forget those moments which murdered my god and my soul and turned my dream to dust. Never shall I forget these things, even if I am condemned to live as long as God Himself. Never. (Wiesel 1960, 7)

Wiesel, knowing the fear of forgetting, commits himself. He shall remember, shall hold the memory forever, lest it, and with it the meaning of all this suffering, be forgotten. This fear is the ineradicable obsession of all survivors who passed through the universe of the damned. The enemy counted on people's utter disbelief to engender a kind of unconsciously irresistible reactive forgetfulness. The Nazi plot of committing gross genocide in concentration camps built right down the street from churches, blocks from the schools and meeting places of normal community, placed great faith in the public's short and fickle memory and in the inability of people to continue thinking the unthinkable. Their plot hung on the inevitability of memory fatigue and clung to the hope of being somehow covered and blessed in the annals of history, construed as a "final solution" necessary to the progress of evolution. History, indeed the social memory of humankind, would be rewritten by the victors, since history becomes the property of the winning generals.

How can we foil this plot? *By remembering.* When memory refuses to join in the collusion, the plot will fail. The memory must be kept alive by retelling the story, reawakening the emotions, rekindling the fires of horror and contempt.

"Isn't there a danger that memory may perpetuate hatred?" Elie Wiesel asks. "No, there is no such danger. Memory and hatred are incompatible; memory may serve as a powerful remedy against hatred" (Wiesel 1990, 201). Remembering forces one to find a place in the memory for the atrocity, no matter how abhorrent, and integrate it into the mission of one's life. There is no guarantee that memory will enrich empathy or connect the severed capacities to trust and risk. But the soul, when remembering, goes on wrestling with the meaning of suffering. With the transformation of suffering comes the mystery of soul-making. We sometimes speak of a *great soul* in recognition of the depth and breadth of a person's character, or of a *puny soul* to describe another's stunted growth of character. The size of one's ultimate character, of one's soul, can be measured by the accumulated wisdom, the learned humanity, perhaps from the amount of suffering assimilated into soulfulness—that depth awareness of the preciousness of life, of the irreducible value of persons and of human community.

In reading the diaries of Etty Hillesum, a young Jewish woman schooled in law, psychology, and languages, one listens in on her final two years before her death on November 30, 1943, at Auschwitz. "I would like to feel the contours of these times with my fingertips," she wrote, and as she attended to the suffering of others she mapped the terrain of pain so honestly she unsettles readers' souls. Awaiting inevitable arrest and death in a concentration camp, she attempted to describe how suffering can be felt deeply and yet not destroy the feeler.

> Does that mean I am never sad, that I never rebel, always acquiesce, and always love life no matter what the circumstances? No, far from it. I believe that I know and share the many sorrows and sad circumstances that a human being can experience, but I do not cling to them, I do not prolong such moments of agony. They pass through me, like life itself, as a broad, eternal stream, they become part of that stream, and life continues. And as a result all my strength is preserved, does not become tagged on to futile sorrow or rebelliousness.
>
> And finally: ought we not, from time to time, open ourselves up to cosmic sadness? . . . You must be able to bear your sorrow; even if it seems to crush you, you are able to stand up again, for human beings are so strong, and your sorrow must become an integral part of yourself, part of your body and soul, you must not run away from it, but bear it like an adult. Do not relieve your feelings through hatred, do not seek to be avenged on all German mothers, for they, too, sorrow at this very moment for their slain and murdered sons. Give your sorrow all the space and shelter in yourself that is its due, for if everyone bears his grief honestly and courageously, the sorrow that now fills the world will abate. (Hillesum 1981, 100)

Remembering the suffering she encountered that very day, she sought to assimilate the memories into a two-tiered understanding: (1) the transcendent hope that sorrow shared with millions of sufferers takes into itself a moral power that offers meaning in the face of incomprehensible inhumanity; and (2) the personal, immanent hope that making space for sorrow in the soul leaves no room for vengeful hatred. She concludes:

> But if you do not clear a decent shelter for your sorrow, and instead reserve most of the space inside you for hatred and thoughts of revenge—from which new sorrows will be born for others—then sorrow will never cease in this world and will multiply. And if you have given sorrow the space its gentle origins demand, then you may

truly say: Life is beautiful and so rich. So beautiful and so rich that it makes you want to believe in God. (Hillesum 1981, 100)

Throughout her journal Hillesum returns repeatedly to this idea of unity among all sufferers, out of which comes a refusal of retributive retaliatory hate and a deafening, heaven-shaking cry for justice and compassion. Her gentle grieving/brooding/mourning/remembering on each day's sadness reveals the virtue of memory transformed into glimpses of cosmic empathy. Her discovering hope in the midst of despair, courage in the face of undeniable genocide, is a feat of incredible wisdom tempered by profound faith that turns unthinkable suffering into the stuff of soul-making. Out of her anticipatory grief—mourning her and her people's approaching death—she creates words to express the just contempt for evil as a kind of mourning, a lament of the righteous for the banal stupidity of iniquity.

Brooding as Mourning

As we noted above, brooding is to hate as mourning is to grief. Griefwork, with the classic stages of "protest, disorganization, reorganization" as Sir John Bowlby described it, is parallel to the brooding as a search for healing of hatred through the protest of rage, the disorganization of resentful rumination, the reorganization of memories (Bowlby 1982, 25). Both are forms of psychic work, and either of these may follow loss, disappointment, injury, or deep disillusionment.

"Brooding" is a unique kind of emotional/mental work, with multiple parts. Within the psyche, analytic theory suggests, the *ego* reacts with disappointment, the *ego ideal* with disillusionment, the *superego* with judgment and condemnation, and the *libido* empowers the impulse to revenge. The struggle between these four impulses, all pulling simultaneously in four directions, creates painful division in the self. Or, in more understandable words, the responsible self recognizes the reality of being wronged, the ideal self is appalled at the fact of the wrongdoing, the moral self sits in judgment on the wrongdoer, and the irrational self plots retaliation by avenging the wrong. This complex of thoughts and feelings of brooding, resenting, and wishful plotting combines to form normal hatred. How it is directed depends on the person's ability to stand back and look at the situation with some objectivity or to be overwhelmed by it in the emotional flooding of subjectivity.

Hatred, experienced objectively, can become a constructive personality function. The work of brooding can move us toward doing the hard work of communicating with the offender that leads to forgiveness. It may reorder our inner priorities and result in a new passion for justice. It may refocus one's life from just surviving to investing one's influence toward rebuilding the systems that turned a blind eye to those in need, or ignored or denied the existence of destructive relationships. In contrast, hatred experienced subjectively can turn remembering into resenting, recalling into a call for revenge, review into a desire for retaliation.

The stages of "hate-work"—working through hate—are similar to, yet distinct from, "grief-work." The process of working through has three steps: (1) *recognition of rage*—one's deep antipathy is acknowledged; (2) *responsibility for one's own feelings*—one stops pretending that the other is responsible for the feeling boiling in me; (3) *resentful rumination*—reliving the pain-event and reviewing the injury; (4) *reassessing its impact* and importance by reexperiencing the anger and sadness; (5) *release and reconstruction*—letting go of the hurt, not holding on to the old feelings and renewing their intensity when reviewing the injury. This is a process of reclaiming what can be learned from the pain experience, of finding a place for it that limits its ability to color or contaminate the future.

Healing and freedom come through recovery of our personal story, of our past and its injuries, our childhood and its pain. In order to become whole, one must discover the unique personal truth about past injustices and injuries, a truth that often causes pain before it releases us into a new sphere of freedom. "People who discover their past . . . will no longer be compelled to displace their hatred onto innocents in order to protect those who have in fact earned this hatred. They will be capable of hating what is hateful and of loving what deserves love" (Miller 1986, 126). Miller, whose personal story of abuse illuminates her work, writes with anger sometimes flowing beneath the printed lines. Hatred for abuse can be "clarified" as she argues, but is resolved only as far as insight can carry one. She is dismissive of any possibility of forgiving (Miller 1986, 13–16, 21, 100–101). Because she defines forgiveness as acceptance and unconditional release in acquiescence to parental "shoulds," she, in Freudian fashion, stresses instead the healing of truth (insight and authentic contact with reality), while dismissing the healing of grace. Her perspective on forgiveness offers a much-needed critique of those cheap and easy varieties of pardon that require no repentance or consideration of restitution.

Miller's position, consistent with the tradition of Freud's psychoanalysis, which she also critiques sharply, stresses the healing power of encountering reality (the truth) and coming to terms with the full experience of past pain. Those who dare to see who injured them in early abuse, and come to understand how it was done, will no longer act blindly and unconsciously out of hidden hate or rage. "They will no longer behave like the mistreated children they were, children who must protect their parents and who therefore need a scapegoat for the buried emotions that torment them" (Miller 1986, 126).

Miller draws two conclusions: (1) Consciously experiencing our legitimate hate is liberating because it opens our eyes to reality (both past and present) and frees us from lies and illusions; (2) But illegitimate hatred never disappears—it cannot be appeased, it only switches scapegoats, it continues its destructive course (Miller 1986, 127).

Illegitimate hatred poisons the soul and remains frozen and locked in the organs and musculature of the body. A history of horror can be driven into the unconscious, then later reemerge. Frequently this illegitimate hatred is placed on innocent persons in a vain attempt to act out a resolution by reenacting the offense. Parents may exploit children, the strong profit from the weak, society may select "a common enemy" on whom to project and through whom to act out its repressed rage (Miller 1986, 128).

"It is a great mistake to imagine that one can resolve traumas in a symbolic fashion. If that was possible, poets, painters and other artists would be able to resolve their pain through creativity. This is not the case, however. Creativity helps us channel the pain of trauma into symbolic acts; it doesn't help us resolve it. If symbolic revenge for maltreatment received in childhood were effective, then dictators would eventually stop humiliating and torturing their fellow human beings. As long as they choose to deceive themselves about who really deserves their hatred, however, and as long as they go on feeding that hatred in symbolic form instead of experiencing and resolving it within the context of their own childhood, their hunger for revenge will remain insatiable" (Miller 1986, 22).

Resentment as a Cry for Justice

In a fascinating set of fifteen sermons published in 1726, Bishop Joseph Butler included two titled "Upon Resentment" and "Upon Forgiveness of Injuries." The capacity to resent, Butler observes, is essential to humanness, a good part of our mental and emotional constitution—theologically, it is grounded in creation, not in the sinfulness of humanity. Bitterness and hatred are evil only when they are out of proportion to the injustice of the injury received, or are used as justification for revenge: "The indignation raised by cruelty and injustice, and the desire of having it punished . . . is by no means malice. No, it is resentment against vice and wickedness; it is one of the common bonds by which society is held together; a fellow-feeling which each individual has in behalf of the whole species, as well as oneself" (Butler 1726, 141). One can love one's enemies by also encountering them with "a due natural sense of the injury, and no more" (160). His distinction between illegitimate and disproportional rage and legitimate and proportionate anger holds true after almost three hundred years of psychological examination of the human personality and society. Anger and resentment need not be obstacles to forgiving. We may often accept an apology and restore relationship, yet know that we must find a place within ourselves for our hate of the injustice in question. This "just hate" calls us to work to see that such injustice not be repeated by us or against us, by or against our neighbor.

Resentment is an important dynamic in the psyche and the soul, and its demand for justice and equity is essential to reconciliation. Resentment is "God's good gift, protecting us in an injurious world from greater harms and inciting us to secure a justice we might otherwise be too placid or too compassionate to enforce," wrote ethicist James McClendon (1986, 225).

Resentment as a form of moral protest can express respect both for the wrongdoer and for the victim. As Murphy and Hampton argue, resentment can be a just desire for respect—even self-respect:

> If I count morally as much as anyone else (as surely I do), a failure to resent moral injuries done to me is a failure to care about the moral value incarnate in my own person (that I am, in Kantian language, an end in myself) and thus a failure to care about the very rules of morality.

If it is proper to feel *indignation* when I see third parties morally wronged, must it not be equally proper to feel resentment when I experience the moral wrong done to myself? Morality is not simply something to be believed in; it is something to be *cared* about. This caring includes concern about those persons (including myself) who are the proper objects of moral attention (Murphy and Hampton 1988, 18).

Finding a Place for Pain and Resentment

The most compelling and helpful metaphor for the internal process of dealing with loss was offered by Sigmund Freud to his colleague Ludwig Binswanger, after the death of Binswanger's son. "We find a place for what we lose. Although we know that after such a loss the acute stage of mourning will subside, we also know that we shall remain inconsolable and will never find a substitute. No matter what may fill the gap, even if it be filled completely, it nevertheless remains something else" (Freud 1960, 386). We can find a place for grief, rage, resentment—in memory. Whether the place found is in the inner, private chambers of grief and lament, or the courtroom of constructive just hate, or the logical library of reason and reality, or the inner chapel of forgiveness, or the inner fellowship hall of understanding and acceptance, wherever it is kept, it will be treasured, visited, and its meaning reassessed as long as one can remember. We find a place in memory for the injuries, but the choice of place, in spiteful brooding, vengeful plotting, retributive reckoning, or just reflection on redemptive change, alters the nature of the "resentment on reserve."

Just contempt for evil, with its passion for transforming the useless into something useful, can break the hopeless chains of retaliation and reenvision a future of stubborn hope. The hope lies neither in a perfect understanding, nor in finally forgetting, nor in blindly ignoring. We must commit an act of generosity that deliberately overlooks what has been done in order to remove the obstacle to our relationship and possible friendship. This does not mean that we approve or ignore the evil that has been done, but simply that we refuse to make the offensive action the basis of our future. All this begins in a memory suffused with moral judgment.

An Angolan proverb says, "The one who throws the stone soon forgets; the one who is hit remembers forever." Reconciliation requires remembering together; without this mutual, joint recalling, there is nothing authentic about the relationship. The way into the future lies through our past. Forgiveness begins with a remembering and a reaffirming of a moral judgment of a wrong, an injury, an injustice. The one who has suffered the wrong remembers in the act of reaching out to the wrongdoer; the offender remembers the wrong in the act of repentance that is constituent to both forgiveness and reconciliation. We may forgive and forget, but first we must remember together, resolve the pain together. Then we may agree to forget together. As in the healing process of therapy, the patient is permitted to recover the pain accumulated in the development of personality and the traumas and injuries endured, so what is true for personhood is also true for peoplehood. People need to remember their story, tell it with historical accuracy, recall the injuries given and received, and do reparative work or they are very likely to repeat it in painful detail. Simple forgetting, repressing of memories, substituting disinformation holds a group hostage to its past.

Are Memories Invaluable?

"Why is memory important?" Elie Wiesel asks. His answers include:

> To remember is to relive a past, to say no to forgetfulness, no to death.
>
> To remember is to allow the past to move into the future and shape its course.
>
> To remember is to reconcile justice to dignity, to acknowledge that time leaves traces and scars on the surface of history.
>
> To remember is to live in more than one world, more than one time.
>
> To remember is to make possible science and poetry, drama and philosophy, religion and fiction, art and ethics.
>
> To remember is to recognize the existence of the Law and its accessibility.
>
> To remember is to know and to be known—to open oneself to someone else's image of oneself, to respect the other's right to remember. (Dictators impose their memory on their subjects; the right to memory is a part of a universal charter for human rights.)
>
> To remember is to be sensitive to me and you. Remember and you will be sensitive to my words and my tales; forget and you will not even be sensitive to our own; to forget my past will inevitably lead me to forget yours. To remember is to build a bridge that brings people together. The one word that defines the fragility, vulnerability but also invincibility of the human condition is memory. A person without memory is still human; but he or she is no longer a person. Amnesia is a curse; Alzheimer's disease is cancer of identity, of being.
>
> To remember is to be—I am what I remember—memory and identity feed each other. Humanity is measured and judged by one's attitude toward memory—toward the other's memory—respecting the other's right to remember. (Condensed from Wiesel 1997, 11–28)

On June 2, 1987, Elie Wiesel was invited to give testimony at the trial of Klaus Barbie, in Lyon, France. He said:

> Your Honor, gentlemen of the bench. . . . May I say immediately that I feel no hatred toward the accused? I have never met him; our paths have never crossed. But I have met killers who, like him, along with

him, chose to be enemies of my people and of humanity. . . . Within the kingdom of malediction created by the accused and his comrades, all Jewish prisoners, all Jews, had the same face, the same eyes; all shared the same fate. Sometimes one has the impression the same Jew was being killed by the enemy everywhere six million times over.

No, there is no hatred in me: there never was any. There is no question of hatred here—only justice, and memory. We are trying to do justice to our memory. . . . It is for the dead, but also for the survivors, and even more for their children—and yours—that this trial is important: it will weigh on the future. In the name of justice? In the name of memory. Justice without memory is an incomplete justice, false and unjust. To forget would be an absolute injustice in the same way that Auschwitz was the absolute crime. To forget would be the enemy's final triumph. (Wiesel 1990, 179–180, 187)

Salvation as Forgetting

In contrast to Elie Wiesel's conviction that "salvation can be found only in memory," Miroslav Volf, a Croatian theologian reflecting on the tragedy of human violence, argues that it must be found in forgetting. "No final reconciliation will take place without the redemption of the past, and the redemption of the past is unthinkable without forgetting. Indeed, only those who are willing ultimately to forget will be capable of remembering rightly" (Volf 1996b, 12). Insisting that forgetting is not only possible but necessary, he argues:

> After we have repented of hatred and forgiven our enemies, after we have made space in ourselves for them and left the door open, our will to embrace them must allow the one final, and perhaps the most difficult, act to take place if the process of reconciliation is to be complete. It is the task of forgetting, I hasten to add—a forgetting that assumes that the matters of "truth" and "justice" have been taken care of, that perpetrators have been named, judged, and (one hopes) transformed, that victims are safe and their wounds healed, a forgetting that can therefore ultimately take place only together with the creation of "all things new." (Volf 1996a, 131)

Recognizing that victims have excellent reasons for never forgetting the injustices they suffered and that forgetting is more easily done by perpetrators who have everything to gain in putting aside the memory of their atrocities through both private and public repression of them, Volf insists that we have an obligation to know and remember what took place. We must remember rightly, so that the memory will forestall future inhumanities; the perpetrators need to remember rightly as well, if the guilty past is to be restored and a more hopeful future grow from the soil of old tragedies. Yet beyond this, he argues, we must let go of the memories. "Remembering" and "nonremembering" are two intertwined ways of reconstructing our past and forging our identities. We have the right to decide for ourselves what to forget and what to remember, and when to do so. The repeated incursions of the unredeemed past into the redeemed present through the door of memory must be stopped.

Volf's attempt to link human forgiveness to the metaphor of God's forgetting the past when we have repented of our evil acts makes an incredible demand on the human will. In speaking to the way in which a community comes to the recognition of its need to stop repeating old charges, reassessing blame and beginning to forget the past, his most persuasive argument is to "background" the offense, so that it no longer is the primary figure in a victim's perceptual field. Although, as a Croatian, he clearly recalls the atrocities done against the Croatians by neighboring ethnic groups, he calls for forgetting. In reframing the stories through enemy love, in the resulting change of meaning through pardon, and in seeking authentic forgiveness we can learn to let go of our hoarded memories of injustice, and "forget." The power of memory is pivotal, central, perhaps utterly basic in defining moral discernment, self-understanding and understanding of others, the emotional coloring of experience, and, above and beyond all else, our ability or inability to love and forgive. Forgiveness is not a matter of finally capitulating to "memory fatigue," or eventually (as is commonly said in popular parlance) deciding to "put it behind in *closure*" by evicting the event and refusing to be held hostage by memory or resentment in order to "get on with life."

Forgiveness is remembering in a new way, a broader way. In forgiving one chooses to remember the event in its complete context—remembering that the other is another human being, in spite of a terrible past, a despicable act, a culpable transgression; remembering that the offense happened in a given set of circumstances, a vulnerable period in both sets of lives, and that this occurred in the past—it is not happening *now* but happened *then*; remembering that all persons have inherent value—the moral status of an offender may remain in question, but this does not reduce the other's inherent worth as a human being. Remembering in this different light is also a kind of deliberate and decisive forgetting. What shall we continue to recall about one another, how shall we construe it, what will remain associated with or attached to every remembrance of your name?

The step of remembering—in actuality re-remembering—in constructive visualization of our shared humanity is a crucial means of moving remembered hate to a moral place in the personality where it can be assimilated into the center of enduring values we call *soul*. Such memory work is a part of both grief-work and hate-work. It is the work of seeking deep-level forgiveness. Forgiveness, when complete, is not unilateral, but possesses some degree of mutuality with both sides recognizing, owning, moving, changing, releasing, healing, redeeming the past, renewing the present, reopening the future to a more just relationship. When memories are reconstructed, repeated anew to the following generation, become the basis of reconciliation and collaboration, then we are living toward a new world.

Chapter Five

Hate and the Shadow:
Exploring the Soul

There is somebody who's living my life
And I know nothing about him.
> —Luigi Pirandello

The Insanity Prayer
God grant me
The clarity
To see good and evil
In pure form
On opposing sides;
The certainty
That we are good
And they are evil;
And the temerity
To resist all doubt.
> —David Augsburger (After 9/11/2001)

Proposition for Chapter 5

Every person has a shadow side that contains parts of the self that have been refused, rejected, repressed. As each person becomes her true self, the self that steps forward into the light throws a long shadow behind. The good face we present to the public world hides a darker aspect that we keep private, cloaked from others and largely concealed from ourselves. In this chapter we will explore the nature of the shadow, particularly as the negative side of the self, that like a black hole may collect hate into unrecognized and unknown reserves and unconsciously await the opportunity for retaliation, revenge, or retribution. From the shadow come prejudice, racism, and discrimination. In coming to know and own the shadow, we may recover many lost parts of ourselves and no longer need to provide cover for them, recognizing many unworthy parts of our hates and fears and no longer needing to repeat them.

In her troubling novel of sisterly rivalry become hatred, *The Game*, A. S. Byatt plumbs the dark labyrinth of two interlocking minds living out of their separate unconscious processes (Byatt 1967). The two sisters, one a more bohemian author, the other a conventional professor in Oxford, have been long estranged. The younger, having convinced herself that she is acting out of hope for reconciliation, writes a novel of radical honesty, in truth a trenchant analysis and scathing exposure of her older sister's troubled life as an Oxford don. The novel, instead of conveying her intimate understanding of her older sister, as she supposed, is taken as a devastating betrayal of trust that triggers her sister's suicide.

For the second child, the elder sister has been her mirror of identity, which she has used to observe the reflected effects of her actions. The other's reactions provided proof of, in fact validation of, her own existence. By testing herself against the rock of her sister she defines her own codependent personhood. In hating her sister she hates herself. In destroying her sister she destroys herself. Each embodies the other's shadow, each acts out of the other's projections in this enmeshed game of reciprocal manipulation.

Stripped emotionally naked by her sister's "novel," the professor, fatally exposed, takes her own life. In this act of suicide the elder is indicting the younger as murderess. In grieving her sister's death the younger is both hated and hater, both accused and accuser, both subject and object of the destructive rage that has consumed them.

Hate, hidden behind the public choreography of sisterly love, is a deadly dance that diminishes them each and both. It is as though each were saying to the other: "I am not what you are; you are what I am not. I despise what you have become; I deliberately become what you despise. Yet I am jealous of who you are; I resent your imitation of me. I must escape the despicable self I have become; I will do it by exposing the empty self you are. I will tell the utter and unflattering truth about you; in doing so, I may find the truth in me."

The Dark Side of the Soul

"Every man is a moon and has a dark side which he never shows to anybody." These are not the words of Jekyll or Hyde, Robert Louis Stevenson, or Carl Jung. They are the insight of Mark Twain (Kaplan 1966). Dark side of the moon, shadow, hidden face, disowned self, mysterious stranger, habitation of dragons, the threatening twin, the double, the sleeping monster—there are many names for the polar side of the soul where we play hide-and-seek with the face, form, and feelings that emerge in crisis, conflict, or inexplicable impulsivity.

Hide-and-seek is the childhood game we learn from the crib. Peeka-boo is its early form in English-speaking homes; *fort-da* (not here—here) in German; *inai-inai-bah* (now gone-now gone-here now!) in Japanese. As we grow older the game is played between one or more who hide and one who tries to find them. The game of hide-and-seek involves two activities, the creation of secrets and discovery, and requires the capacity for lying—innocent lying for the sake of preserving one's separate self. A child playing the game before she is old enough to lie will announce herself from the hiding place, still playing the appearing-disappearing game. Once identity has formed and casts a significant shadow, the secrets are kept under wraps in the soul, secret even from the self. These hidden bits of self-doubt, fear, and shame betray our attempts to be comfortable when alone or congruent when we are with others (Doi 1976, 273–75).

Hide-and-seek, played with those who think they know us, protects the core self from being fully known or embarrassingly disclosed. Being *found*, in its best moments, may be like falling in love or finding genuine friendship. Being *found out* is the frightening reverse. Any experience of discovering and self-disclosing parts of the shadow causes both fear and relief. Being uncloaked by our own outbursts or unmasked by another's criticism means being found wanting. When secrets that we fear to face are exposed, we lose face before both self and other—internal and external face. Playing this existential game of hide-and-seek is a trust and risk venture that requires uncommon courage and a sense of security. Secrecy and mystery are essential to personhood, and respect for the right to privacy is essential to any appreciation of the worth and dignity of the individual. To voluntarily risk exposure is to make the vulnerable movement toward intimacy; risking is a gift of trust. Hide-and-seek as a competitive game of storming the castle, and driving another out of hiding is rarely useful. When one's shadow is rich with tender longing and a will to empathy, the venture into the light is experienced as joy; when the shadow harbors a malignant mass, the toxicity may erupt in an attack on whatever is near, but sooner or later, if one is to be human, one must be found and come to terms with his own depths.

To set this concept into story, Robert Louis Stevenson created *The Strange Case of Dr. Jekyll and Mr. Hyde*, in which the personalities of the elegant Jekyll and the violent Hyde alternate in one troubled man. The dualism liberates Jekyll's ego from the painful burden of recognizing its own frightening and heinous impulses; frees Hyde to act out the rage Jekyll denies. The split, facilitated by Jekyll's chemical formula, alters mind and body, enabling the ego to disavow its own destructive hostility. It no longer needs the intricate web of rationalizations normally employed to conceal the darkness within from coming to light. The unbridled Hyde rages against annoyances that pass unnoticed before the social skills of Dr. Jekyll.

Jekyll is a "large, well-made, smooth-faced man of fifty, with something of a slyish cast perhaps, but every mark of capacity and kindness." Yet, we later learn, he "concealed his pleasures," and "stood committed to a profound duplicity of life," recognizing that "man is not truly one, but truly two." Hyde is young, full of hellish energy, small, and somehow deformed, a "juggernaut," a person who evoked hatred in others at the very sight of him. After Jekyll has been transformed by the drug into Hyde, he confesses: "I knew myself . . . to be more wicked, tenfold more wicked, sold a slave to my original evil." Personal evil has united with archetypical evil, as Jekyll concludes, "He alone among men is pure evil." Jekyll flees him by cutting off the chemical, turning toward religion and good deeds, but this attempt to escape the tension of opposites within him, the inner tug-of-war that makes us truly human, fails, and ultimately evil triumphs and then destroys itself (Stevenson 1952).

The Secret, the Shadow

Everything with substance casts a shadow when it stands before the light. When the ego possesses size and substance, it throws a long shadow. The larger the ego—that is, the bigger the "I"—the longer the shadow lurking behind the enlarged sense of self or the ego-engorged personality. The child has no shadow until the ego forms. As the self gradually stands up and steps forward, the shadow follows it to contain the hidden or denied parts that are incongruent with the "I"—the *I* that I present as the *me* worthy of love and respect.

Jung noted that each of us intuitively understands what is meant by "the *shadow*" or "the *other*." "And if he has forgotten, his memory can easily be refreshed by a Sunday sermon, his wife, or the tax collector. By the shadow I mean the 'negative' side of the personality, the sum of all those unpleasant qualities we like to hide, together with the insufficiently developed functions and the content of the personal unconscious" (Jung 1969b, 76). The thoughts, feelings, and behaviors that are unacceptable to ourselves, or to parents, peers, the culture whom we seek to please, are denied and then split off. The shadow, most simply, is the sum of all the things a person has no wish to be. Hate is the first of these things split off and dropped into the denial disposal. Splitting, a phenomenon of early-childhood ego formation around the age of three, begins as the child splits its own ego from its continuity with the mother's ego and forms a sense of "I-ness." This is followed by a splitting between what is "I" and what is "not-I." The undesirable parts of the ego are relegated to the unconscious. Nothing is ever completely lost; somewhere a trace resides in the shadow. "Unfortunately there is no doubt about the fact that one is, as a whole, less good than one imagines the self or wants to be. Everyone carries a shadow, and the less it is embodied in the individual's conscious life, the blacker and denser it is" (Jung 1969b, 36).

Wishes, impulses, desires, angers, hates are all referred to the shadow by the simple process of denial, the most automatic of all our defenses. A suicidal thought, a wish for another's annihilation, a recurring grudge can be blocked out as soon as it flashes on the mental screen. R.D. Laing described the denial reflex in one of his *Knots* as simply failing to notice that we fail to notice crucial things in our lives. There is little we can do about it, little we can change until we finally notice how failing to notice shapes all our thoughts and deeds (Laing 1970). Negative feelings, pressed from awareness but still possessing their own fearsome and perplexing powers, do not lose their emotional charge simply because they are on hold within the shadow, and when something connects with them, they spark to the surface.

In *The Little Book on the Human Shadow*, poet Robert Bly calls the shadow "a long bag we drag behind us" that contains our unacceptable parts. "Behind us we have an invisible bag, and the part of us our parents don't like, we, to keep our parents' love, put into the bag. By the time we go to school the bag is quite large. Then our teachers have their say: 'Good children don't get angry over such little things.' So we take our anger and put it in the bag. . . . Then we do a lot of bag stuffing in high school. This time it's no longer the evil grownups that pressure us, but people our own age. . . . We spend our life until we're twenty deciding what parts of our self to put into the bag, and we spend the rest of our lives trying to get them out again" (Bly 1988, 8).

The shadow personality—when its head comes out of the bag—usually appears in dreams, or in our repulsion and attraction to a character in a novel or an actor in a drama. It is more often a same-gender figure (unless contaminated by denied anima/animus or rejected mother/father images). It may appear in different guises, human or less than human (primitive, animalistic, crippled, deformed, or mutilated). When it appears in a dream, the dreamer will immediately disown, judge, or disassociate from the figure.

In *The Madman*, Kahlil Gibran told a story of a mother and daughter who were both sleepwalkers. One night, the two somnambulants met in the garden. The mother spoke first: "At last, my enemy. You have destroyed my youth, and built your life on the ruins of mine! I want to kill you!" The daughter replied, "Hateful, selfish decrepit old woman. You want me to be an empty echo of your faded life. I wish you were dead." At that moment, a cock crowed and both awoke. "Is that you, my treasure?" "Yes, dearest mother, it is me" (Gibran 1925, 15).

In the trance state of denial, feared feelings concealed from others are hidden from ourselves, and are totally disowned when they inadvertently appear onstage in any slip, eruption, dream, or projection. The most frequent channel for such emergence from the bag is *projection onto another*. The defensive denial "I am not self-centered!" is immediately transformed to the accusation "You are so self-centered." "What do you mean *I'm* lazy? *You're* lazy." The disowned part that we had gunnysacked returns to confront us; the split-off reappears in others who threaten us; the ostracized elements of our personalities are encountered in the adversary. "True believers," who in rigid self-righteousness brook no criticism of their crusades against "evil," are too often mounting a crusade to attack the contours and contents of their own shadows. Projection requires a great deal of energy—the psychic energy of defensiveness, hypervigilance, suspicion—to maintain a dissociated state of nonreflective unawareness. Each of us employs a significant measure of mental and emotional energy policing our shadow storehouse, screening the windows to awareness, the doors to self-reflection, and the gates into the public arena of relationships. A clear picture of the person we dislike most offers a revealing portrait of the shadow we repress. A common exercise in Jungian psychology asks us to select the villain from literature or film that we dislike most, and then reflect on how the monster is the reverse of our public persona, the characterization of the shadow we conceal.

A chief component of the shadow is hate. No one cares to own hate. Hate is covered by the instructions "Do not pass ego. Go directly to shadow." The hate I deny is the hate I hold in reserve; the hate I own, I can release. If I choose, I can negotiate my hostility with whoever is party to this intense negative relationship, or I can cancel the hate in acceptance of the other's humanity; either way, the hate disappears from shadow and soul.

Hate held in unconscious reserves is not truly hidden. It appears not only in surprising eruptions of anger, fear, disgust, and suspicion, but in the perceptions we hold and the judgments we make about the other. The shadow, the hidden "film noir" that I write in my unconscious musings, is projected onto the disliked other. The projection process is its own justification. It flows something like this: "See how hateful she is? How can I not hate her when she is so hateful!" Or it may be expressed as, "See how he despises others? How can I not despise him and his constant despising?" I choose that other person to play this role because some part of the person reminds me of the conflict within, and the drama I am creating through denial is then flashed on the screen in living color by my internal projector. When I can pronounce the drama I see being enacted by my opponent as totally evil, then I can construe my own reactions as perfectly normal, certainly justified in comparison. The intolerable internal turmoil is disowned in my self and discovered in the other. My hidden hostile drives can be externalized in this mental evacuation process. By depositing the rage that is in here into the other who is out there, I feel the relief of righteous cleanliness.

The Eruption of the Shadow

Flannery O'Connor, the greatest of writers from the American South, has written a tale of hate encountered in the story "Revelation" (O'Connor 1956, 405–24). I shall paraphrase it in condensed form to show how she reveals the shadow side in both its constructive and transformative aspects.

Mrs. Turpin, a southern woman with a white supremacist worldview, sits with her son in a doctor's waiting room, looking with disdain at the other patients and whispering a thank-you to Jesus that he had not made her a nigger or white trash or ugly. She recalls her familiar nighttime reverie of revenge on those inferior people who prosper, lower classes rising to undeserved wealth. In fantasy, she sees them finally jammed into a boxcar, being carted off to gas ovens. Across from her, a waiting patient, a surly college student, looks up from her book to glare hostilely as Mrs. Turpin carries on a bigoted conversation with other women patients. When Mrs. Turpin erupts in a passionate "Thank you, Jesus" that she is not one of those people that she hates, and exudes self-congratulations, the silent girl, exploding in fury, hurls her book in Mrs. Turpin's face, throws herself across the table, and clamps her fingers around Mrs. Turpin's throat.

When nurses have pulled the assailant off and the doctor has sedated her, Mrs. Turpin leans into the young girl's face, demanding some word of explanation of what the attack might mean. The girl's words are a revelation erupting from her unconscious shadow, telling her to go back to hell, calling her a warthog. Her sense of self is fractured, her world fragments. Is she virtuous and blessed by Jesus or is she, God forbid, one of them?

That evening, torn apart by irreconcilable contradiction, she walks out into the sunset and begins to interrogate God, demanding an explanation for the girl's message. Why? What does it mean? How can I be a hog and good woman at the same time? Her anger overwhelms her and erupts at the blood-red setting sun. A wave of fury at the Almighty sweeps over her, and she roars at the sky, "Who do you think you are?" Her bellowed question carries over the cotton field and returns as an echo, "*Who do you think you are?*" The answer is a true moment of revelation: Who *does* she think she is?

The fiery sunset appears, at last, not as a stairway to heaven reserved for her and her kind, but as a great bridge suspended from the earth to the sky, over which a vast throng of souls stumbles heavenward—white trash, freaks, lunatics, tribes of all colors, and her own bringing up the rear. In the red fire of the sunset, their pride and arrogant virtues are being burned away. The vision transforms her. The crickets around her sound like the songs of souls shouting hallelujah. Miraculously, she moves from a cloven, we-they world of good and bad to a place where sinners and saved stand together.

O'Connor's story offers a "Revelation," a blinding insight into how we split our worlds, how we separate the familiar into ultimate polar categories and then "fall into hate" like "falling in love."

We call Mrs. Turpin's way of splitting reality between the good and the bad—"There are two kinds of people in the world, the good and the bad, and we good are entitled to say which are which"—a mild form of paranoia. (*Paranoia* is Greek for a second mind standing alongside.) The fundamental paranoid view is that the world, and all those who people it, are essentially untrustworthy. The overriding concern is the question of control. Who is in control of whom? The aim is to get a grip on that which controls the world, or to lament that we are losing it. The visible evidence of this view, with its fears, its control obsession, is the creation of impermeable, defensive and vigilant boundaries.

When One Man's Shadow Falls across Another

In August of 1999, Buford O. Furrow Jr. walked into a Jewish community center in Granada Hills, California, and opened fire on children, wounding two adults and three children. Hours later he shot and killed a Filipino American mail carrier he had chosen as an exemplary target. Furrow, a man with a history of job problems, and a failed marriage to the ex-wife of a founder of a racist group called "The Order" who had threatened to kill her and himself, turned his homicidal impulses onto a chosen target, the Jews.

Furrow's shadow self-exploded in violence. But his pathology, antisocial as it was, was highly socialized by the particular groups that nurtured him and fostered by the larger culture that surrounds him. On both levels, he received models of shadow hate, shadow prejudice, shadow violence. We can learn more from his story of how shadow formation and shadow eruption works, by looking at it through the language lens of what, in psychological language, we call *projective identification*.

In projective identification one casts a dark shadow, so dark that it falls across another, and one cannot see the other in the darkness, only the shadow. In this way, one's negative identity is projected onto another person/group/racial category and, having attributed the inner darkness to another, one claims a purified, empowered, authenticated, and righteous self with new life purpose, behavioral mandates, reasons for being. Viewed from this perspective, Furrow's actions reveal how his disintegrating personality structures were temporarily held together and purposefully focused by his hate. Simultaneously, the projective identification process creates a mental pathway for channeling impulses and emotions of hate and homicidal rage on a target group. The homicidal fury within—which previously had been directed toward himself and his ex-spouse—is now displaced onto the Jews. By identifying with what he considered the "racially superior" Aryan Nations, he has compensated for an inferior self-image. His intense self-hatred is now projected onto his victims. In searching for a way to kill Jews—ironically he even considered attacking the Museum of Tolerance—Furrow is attempting to kill off the hated, disowned, despicable parts of himself. All that is hated within is now seen outside the self, present in a whole race of "inferior people," who may be destroyed with impunity.

When the shadow erupts in projective identification—"I am superman from a superrace; you are vermin from an evil source; I do the world a service by eliminating you"—it has found a comprehensive internal solution to self-hate, a powerful mechanism for the discharge of murderous rage, the perfect instrument for transforming a decompensating, disintegrating self into a heroic figure with a divine mission.

In denying one's own actual human existence—and one's personal moral agency—the "new Aryan self" also denies the separate existence of the victims. Empathy for the targeted group is now impossible, just as self-knowledge is distorted and self-understanding obliterated. The perpetrator is detached from all guilt or remorse over any abuse of the victim. Unencumbered by conscience, compassion, or recognition of the other's cohumanity, nothing impedes the exploitative use of the other.

"I am an innocent and unjustly persecuted victim," the person concludes, and the shadow of blame and hate stretches long, soon blanketing the group held responsible with an impenetrable cloud. With total commitment and deep sincerity, the projecting person experiences the self as victim, but not as victimizer, even though imposing violent control over those attacked. The projective process, although oppressive, rises out of great weakness, and leaves the person feeling powerless, and in a helpless rage. The person weakens even farther by giving away what little remaining power he actually possesses, delegating it to the presumed evil other. The ensuing violence is a grasping for the power that has been so totally squandered in a vain, self-defeating show of bravado. Need we note that this casting of one's dark shadow across another in prejudice and hate is not unique to anti-Semitism; it is present in ethnic discrimination, racism, homophobia, and sexism, as well as nationalism and paralyzing fear of rogue nations. The dark underworld in persons and in peoples is used to tar the other and to justify our refusal to talk with each other lest we come to recognize each other as equally human.

Casting a Common Collective Shadow in Prejudice

Large groups come to cast a common shadow. As the shadow becomes visible in the attitudes and behaviors of a distinct group, one individual arises to personify it, embodying the collective evil. Napoleon, Hitler, Mussolini, Lenin, Stalin, Jim Jones, David Koresh offer such personifications. All were mutilated by utopian ideas; all saw themselves as facilitators of reform whose time had come; each believed he acted for the benefit of humanity at large; all sought to exclude or eliminate from the ideal community those elements which they believed antithetical or incompatible with their vision and view.

As the shadow emerges, the group's identity becomes sharply defined, its beliefs become more rigid, its convictions more passionate. Its perspectives become compulsively dogmatic, unwittingly arrogant, unadmittedly dictatorial, and increasingly intolerant of diversity or challenge.

Political, religious, or scientific movements can erupt with shadow phenomena that narcissistically define what is "right" for all persons, places, times; and what is "wrong" for all peoples, institutions, ages. This is the genesis of enemy formation, and we return to explore it in depth in chapter 8. The most visible form of this collective five-o'clock shadow on everyman's and everywoman's face is prejudice. It is a normative hate that is fostered by, though frowned on, yet permitted within, even while prohibited by, social groups or the larger society.

There is no clear scholarly consensus on how to define prejudice sharply except through the exploration of *normative* decisions. Prejudices are thoughts, feelings, actions that diverge from the norms of a group or society in measurable ways. Prejudice is a social judgment, or more often an antisocial judgment, which can be distinguished from other judgments. A prejudice is positive and socially desirable when it supports rational norms and standards of humanity, justice, and equality; it is negative or socially undesirable when it violates rational norms and standards of humanity, justice, and equality (Bergmann and Erb 1997, 99).

Psychologically, prejudices can be critiqued in terms of their (1) overgeneralization, (2) rigidity, (3) distortion of reality. Sociologically, prejudice is a cluster of attitudes, stereotypes, and judgments learned in the course of socialization. These attitudes then form a schema which determines the social perception of members of the group. These attitudes are both elastic and permanent (in a changed situation they continue to function as methods of integrating contradictory experiences). All prejudice contains these three components: thoughts, feelings, and actions.

1. Prejudicial thoughts: Prejudice as a way of thinking is formed by assembling stereotypes of the other, of some group that is the object of standardized and often-repeated perceptions. The classic anti-Semitic image of the Jews, which grew into a stubborn social structure of insidious suspicions, is a historic example.

These anti-Semitic stereotypes include "the power-hungry Jew," who is judged politically radical and ruthless; "the dangerous Jew," who is sinister, unpredictable, false, conniving, destructive, subversive, and conspiratorial; "the unforgiving Jew," who is arrogant, unreconcilable, and unapproachable after conflict; "the greedy Jew," who is avaricious, acquisitive, grasping, and miserly; and "the religiously superior Jew," who claims superiority as one of God's chosen people and asserts an eternal destiny above all others (Bergmann and Erb 1997, 102). These interlocking and mutually reinforcing images link fear, anger, hate, competition, and inferiority into an organic, malignant creature of social hate.

2. Prejudicial emotions: Negative emotions operate on a feeling level

beneath the rational level of mental process, creating an *attitude*, an *"emotional set"* beneath the *mind-set*, that produces distance from those disliked and results in *societal distance* between groups. The emotional set toward either liking or disliking the other dictates how one will feel toward the representatives of another group or toward the whole group. This emotional set creates social distance by fostering (1) the suspicion of disloyalty; (2) the rejection of the neighbor or coworker; (3) the rejection of association or intermarriage; (4) rejection of not just the primary hated ethnic minorities but all ethnic groups not one's own; (5) withdrawal of a sense of shared nationality or citizenship with out-group members; (6) wish for the ethnic group to be contained, to emigrate, to be unseen and/or invisible (Bergmann and Erb 1997, 125–48). Perceptions exist prior to, within, and in consequence of emotions, so the "feeling" nature of these six affective states floods the person or group with passions that lead to withdrawal and distancing.

3. Prejudicial actions: The inclination to act in prejudicial ways causes one to withdraw, reject, move away from the other to create the desired distance or to carry out intentional discrimination, such as (1) taking personal action against the disliked group; (2) demanding legal discriminatory acts that disadvantage the other and advantage the self; (3) using or tolerating antigroup comments, jokes, attitudes, and actions against other persons or groups.

These three dimensions of prejudice—prejudicial thoughts, emotions, and consequent negative actions—create the complex negative web of bias that alienates us from those we do not know. These structures of prejudice draw their metaphors, similes, and images from the same stereotypes and social myths that are involved in group identity formation. Stereotypes are normally taught to us in our youth and adolescence; we are socialized by the values and rules of family and conventional society so that we learn to hate in the same way we learn to love mother, country, church, and culture. Childhood instructions, jokes from peers, images in school, media, and peer group teach us precisely whom to fear, whom to ignore, who will receive anger, whom to hate.

The Pictures in Our Heads

Columnist Walter Lippmann used the term *stereotype* to refer to the "pictures in our heads," the generalizations we carry to define members of or groups of people. These stereotypes become endowed with transcendent and with diabolical significance; they become archetypes within the shadow that emerge to take us hostage and render our best intentions captive to inhuman judgments. Consider, for example, the following stereotypical cues:

> Group X members: "dirty, lazy, more violent, substance abusers, drug pushers"
> Group Y members: "powerful, shrewd, money hungry, rich, unscrupulous, control media"
> Group Z members: "illogical, emotional, manipulative"

You can identify the group referred to immediately, if you share the cultural literacy of white mainstream America, as women, Jews, blacks, in reverse order.

No one is color-blind, radically unaware, ethnically, economically, politically, or religiously neutral. Stereotypes are universal and inescapable. Dangerous minds deny possessing or using stereotypes; healthy minds recognize them, own them as a part of the mental schema, and question their appropriateness in each situation.

Negative stereotypes, in contrast to tentative generalizations about other groups, have several discernible characteristics. (1) They view every member of a group as identical in terms of negative characteristics. (2) They are not modified by new data, contradictory evidence, or experience. (3) Their enduring power rises from emotional, survival, or security mechanisms rather than insight or understanding. Negative stereotypes do not help us make sense of the world; they localize good and bad, map safe and unsafe, identify friend and enemy, justify and excuse loyalty and hostility, and can be used to explain the surprising exceptions as "different," or a "special case," while continuing to hold the stereotyped image.

Stereotypes, Racism, and Hate Speech

When prejudice is combined with power, racism is the inevitable product. It is as though there were a formulaic process in persons and society: *prejudice plus stereotypes times power equals racism.* Racism involves "the exercise of power against a racial group defined as inferior by individuals and institutions with the intentional or unintentional support of the entire culture" (Jones 1972, 117). Power is the essential ingredient, for it institutionalizes prejudice, marshals the weight of social systems to teach it, specify it, reinforce it. Jones identified three levels of power—individual, institutional, and cultural—at work in producing three kinds of racism.

An example will illustrate the three racism levels: an African American college student is touring campus with her eight-year-old niece and five-year-old nephew. A carload of white male students drives past as she waits at a pedestrian crossing. One student shouts, "Bet you don't know who the fathers are!" The next day she seeks to enroll in a special seminar in her major, but finds it closed due to class size. The Caucasian student behind her is admitted; she is refused. The professor tells her it is an extremely difficult course and she is advised not to take it, although she is a 4.0 student. She applies for a scholarship, and although her GPA is very high, she is denied because of scores on widely used tests normed and standardized on white populations. Currently she is taking a course titled "History of Civilization," which is focused exclusively on the history of Europe, with outside reading permitted on other world regions that played a minor role in history (Harrell 1999, 7–8). Racism is denigrating to the individual, discriminating in the institution, and is continually distorting the culture as it violates the person on all three levels—the individual, the institutional, and the cultural—most often simultaneously.

A vast and historical corpus of racist vocabulary exists in every culture, like a structure of social symbols that defines who is valued, who is not; who is acceptable, who is not; who it esteems as superior, who as not. The person who utters hate speech is quoting from the existing corpus of racist propaganda. He repeats the reasoning of his community, she re-cites the rhetoric of her group, and each appears to be the author of the injurious speech but in reality is only a product of the racist process, not the inciter but the repeated citer, not cause but effect. As Judith Butler argues, although the individual who repeats the habits and harangues of hate tradition is assigned responsibility for creating the hate speech, the whole community should be charged. History rather than the alleged author should be indicted. Do we not scapegoat the messenger so that our common history and its legacy of hatred can be masked? she asks (Butler 1995, 150). This in no way eliminates individual responsibility. Each of us is accountable for the language we choose to use, and in addition we share in the society where we are all together responsible to re-create our language so that it is no longer racist, sexist, ageist, and to reconstruct our thought in forms that support equality, mutuality, and integrity.

Butler raises the possibility of prosecution of persons who repeatedly use hate speech, asking:

> Where and when would that prosecution begin and when would it end? Would this not be something like an effort to prosecute a

history that, by its very temporality, cannot be called to trial? This is not to say that subjects ought not be prosecuted for their injurious speech; I think that there are probably occasions when they should. But what is precisely being prosecuted when the injurious word comes to trial and is it finally or fully prosecutable? (Butler 1995, 156)

Injurious speech has two goals: (1) to provoke the assaulted person to question his or her identity and to perceive the self as inferior and of lesser or no worth; (2) to confirm the speaker's own identity, to define the self as well as to define the other. With every racial remark, we reinstall the racist social structure, occupy the racist role, reaffirm our symbolic identity as a part of a group we consider superior. We appeal to that racist structure—its myths, roles, political power, absolute authority—to confirm our identity and grant us the presumed authority to define others. If those surrounding comply by silently approving or tolerating the attack, and if the victim admits to being the addressee of the words, then each participates in the establishment and functioning of this racist structure and contributes to its power with every racist sentence (Salecl 1998, 120–21).

This prejudicial process in society is used to confirm the racist's identity, to grant authority, to affirm me and my kind as good, superior, loyal, acceptable. Each racist action is a declaration that "I am a true representative of the values of Western civilization," or "I speak in behalf of the white race." When a white racist attacks blacks, for example, it is not an individual act of autonomy, the attacker is the racist system's mouthpiece and speaks for "the white majority" to condemn the other, who is despised. The racist acts as an avowed instrument of the trusted supreme authority to inflict pain on the prescribed victim, who reacts in intimidated pain, thereby fulfilling the drama and justifying the act. Racists require their own perverse community to vindicate their fears, support their dread of the enemy, and share a joint set of beliefs. Naming the object of prejudice as a common enemy serves to unite the community, provides a coherent meaning for their lives, and offers an explanation for all their ills. The fingered enemy, now become the community's victim, is its symptom; the victim chosen reveals the community's inner disorder. "The type of victim" in vogue "at any given moment goes hand in hand with the ideological definition one gives to one's society" (Salecl 1998, 123). A community is better known by the victims it chooses than by the enemies it creates.

Even those who defend free speech condemn hate speech, since it incites violence toward groups of people and demeans and devalues a community. The challenge in critiquing all negative speech is to discern its true motive and function. If the speaker is seeking to destroy another group's privileges or rights, then we have a moral right to despise the speech; but if it is seeking to confront a heinous evil or express legitimate concerns through hostile emotion, then it deserves a careful hearing. As Planalp observes, "In general, it may be easier to recognize the immoral side of emotions that we presume are moral than to recognize the moral side of emotions we assume are immoral" (Planalp 1999, 174).

Empathy: Walking in Another's Shoes

The transforming moment, when empathy cracks the solid wall of prejudice, occurs in the unexpected encounter with another that reveals our common humanity:

C. P. Ellis has lived his entire life in Durham, North Carolina. When he was in the eighth grade his father died, and he quit school to support the family, half his wages going for rent. Life was hard, and he grew bitter. He looked for someone to blame. "The natural person for me to hate would be black people, because my father before me was a member of the Klan. It was the only organization that would take care of white people" (Terkel 1992, 272).

Initiation into the Ku Klux Klan was a momentous life event. Led into a softly lit room, he knelt before an illuminated cross and vowed before four hundred knights to uphold the purity of the white race, protect white womanhood, and fight communism. Ellis rose quickly to be a prominent organizer, then Exalted Cyclops of the Durham chapter. He sat in city council meetings, was welcomed to city leaders' homes, became embroiled in public controversy leading the fight against black activists. One black woman in particular, Ann Atwater, got under his skin, and frequent furious shouting matches erupted between them. A series of events, which began with his experience of being the object of prejudice between classes—Ellis was shunned on the street by a city council member he had aided, which was followed by his being delegated by the Klan to represent them on a joint committee dispersing a $78,000 government grant to help solve racial problems in local schools, led him to finally accept, when asked, to serve as cochair of this interracial committee with, of all people, Ann Atwater. Criticism by old friends increased; support from Duke University where he worked helped, but the pressure on him and his family was mounting.

One day, during a break in their work, C. P. and Ann began what seemed a casual conversation about overloads. Then Ann told of her daughter coming home crying because her schoolteacher had made fun of what her mother was doing in racial reconciliation advocacy. Ellis was thunderstruck by the memory of the same thing happening to his son, who had also come home crying because of ridicule by a teacher. As Ellis explains what happened next, he swallows hard, squeezes back tears:

> I begin to see, here we are, two people from the far ends of the fence, havin' identical problems, except her bein' black and me bein' white. From that moment on, I tell ya, that gal and I worked good together. (Terkel 1992, 275–76)

A dozen years later, Ellis, now business manager of a local labor union with two-thirds black membership, is actively working for a better life for all poor people. When empathy breaks through, with or without tears, a person's shadow is touched by a ray of light, then exposed to the sun.

The most important quality required to improve relations among ethnic groups, as C. P. Ellis's story reveals, is *empathy:* the ability to place oneself in the position occupied by others, not necessarily to agree, but clearly to understand the point of view. The ability to enter the conceptual and emotional world of another is grounded in our at-home-ness in our own inner world. You cannot walk with another over terrain that is totally unfamiliar to you. Knowing your own inner landscape is somehow necessary to trekking with another in the wild places of the other's soul. Claiming increasing portions of the shadow side that lies behind your public side enlarges your ability to understand another's shadow confusion. When we are at peace with the stream of memories flowing from our past, especially those that eddy out of the shadow, we will be able to hear others' memories with respect and not clog or block their flow. Carl Rogers used this metaphor of entering another's stream of consciousness to picture empathy:

> Entering the private perceptual world of the other and becoming thoroughly at home in it involves being sensitive to the changing felt meanings which flow in this other person. . . . It means temporarily living in his/her life, moving about in it delicately without making judgments, sensing meanings of which he/she is scarcely aware. . . . It includes communicating your sensings of his/her world as you look with fresh and unfrightened eyes at elements of which the individual is fearful. It means frequently checking with him/her as to the accuracy of your sensings, and being guided by the responses you receive. . . . To be with another in this way means that for the time being you

lay aside the views and values you hold for yourself in order to enter another world without prejudice. (Rogers 1975, 4)

Empathy recognizes that there is not one world, but many worlds. We differ, our worlds of assumptions differ, and it is through the differences, not the similarities, that we come to appreciate our real humanity. We each live and operate in particular personal and cultural worlds with unique assumptions and convictions, so we do see and think and feel differently. Empathy looks to see how the other has constructed an individual set of assumptions from the wild and varied possibilities available. Empathy seeks a way to "get into the other's world" that will allow an understanding "in their terms" and offer a moment of "seeing as they see" and "feeling what they feel," so that even hatred and contempt become understandable. Empathy enters the other's world as a guest. It does not forget the manners of the guest/host relationship. In the museum of another's memories, one must be even more gentle and respectful than when visiting one's own. Reverence for the sacredness of your own memories and secrets is self-compassion. Compassion for another is a similar reverence for the sanctity of another's soul. Just as our own memories and secrets are precious to us, so we have the duty to defend others' right to treasure and to protect theirs.

Empathy is the key to breakthrough from blind bias to vision both from one's own eyes and reciprocally from the eyes of the other. It is virtually impossible to sustain prejudice while seeing from the other's eyes, or to retain it when returning to see again from one's own. Once one allows the other's perceptions to enter the mind, the dignity of the other as a person, even though distorted or destructive, cannot be denied. Here again we encounter the moment of emotional breakthrough that propels one from *rationalized hate* to truly *moral hate*—to the perception of the right of others to their own world even though we may neither condone nor approve of it. Yet, we can allow ourselves to experience it and feel, in part, the compassion that springs up in the birth of a *just hate*, which sees the distinction between the worth of the other even while judging the worthlessness of the direction or action the other espouses.

Empathy has been often equated with walking a mile in another's moccasins, or standing in another's shoes. The metaphor is so excellent it has been extended unforgettably by Blackman.

Empathy is the ability to step into another person's shoes and to step back just as easily into one's own shoes again. It is not projection, which implies that the wearer's shoes pinch him and that he wishes someone else in them; it is not identification, which involves stepping into another person's shoes and then being unable or unwilling to get out of them; it is not sympathy, in which a person stands in his own shoes while observing another person's behavior. Empathy is standing in the other's shoes while reacting to him in terms of what he tells you about his shoes—if they pinch, one commiserates with him; if they are comfortable, one enjoys his comfort with him. (Blackman 1958, 550)

Chapter Six

The Demon of the Absolute:
The Need to Be Right

[The] Angel of light . . . [is] the demon of the absolute.
—Paul Elmer More

Bigot, *n*. One who is obstinately and zealously attached to an opinion that you do not entertain.

—Ambrose Bierce

Believing ourselves to be possessors of absolute truth degrades us:
we regard every person whose way of thinking is different from
ours as a monster and a threat. And by so doing turn our own selves
into monsters and threats to our fellows.

—Octavio Paz

Proposition for Chapter 6

Absolute judgments, absolute justifications, absolute rationales are needed to give permission
for hateful thoughts and feelings or speech and acts. So the person feeling "malicious hate" or
wishing for the right to express "retributive hate" soon realizes that an absolute rationale—legal,
cultural, moral, philosophical, or theological—is needed to justify such retaliation or revenge.
Prejudice, the shadowy hate of those who differ, explored in chapter 5, creates a platform of
rational arguments to explain its emotional bias. Before taking an absolute step against the
offender, I need to create a basis for believing in the absolute rightness of my settling an old
score. The " absolute" comes to our rescue with absolute principles, invincible reason, ultimate
concerns, and final truth. Either/or thinking soon crystallizes into all-or-nothing conclusions to
give an unquestionable foundation of "absolutes" for our plans for revenge.

In a nineteenth-century short story, "The Art of Hate," John G. Neihardt described a "hate at first sight," a first encounter that "was an insult—a sudden stinging like a slap on the cheek." He dissects the relationship between two men on the frontier: Zepher Recontre, a French half-breed with Blackfoot tribal heritage, and his employer Jules Latour, the swaggering head of the American fur company post. Recontre, the man of mixed French/American Indian parentage, says:

> When I first saw that man, I felt as though he had struck me between the eyes with his white fist. I hated him as I had never hated before, and as I hope never to hate again. It hurts to hate; it eats into a man like some incurable blood disease. . . . We hated each other. I knew how much I hated, . . . but his hate was a great hate—stronger than love can be. And I also knew that this hate would grow until one of us was killed. And it did. (Neihardt 1907, 97)

Neihardt's tale is of a downward spiral of mutual contempt in which "hate can bind two persons as closely as love." The two were inseparable, each doing favors of great sacrifice for the other, each surviving great hardship through the strength profound hate can inspire when each outdoes the other with murderous kindness. They stick close to each other in perilous adventures and dangerous work, each awaiting the moment of triumph when the other makes a fatal error and the witness can exalt in *Schadenfreude*—the delight in viewing the other's misfortune, suffering, and death.

At last, when their boat lies frozen in a winter ice mass, they slowly starve, bodies wasting while their emaciated souls await the weaker man's collapse. Latour, the master, dies cursing the half-breed even as the rescue party is climbing on board and breaking into the ice-sheathed cabin. They enter to find Recontre triumphantly surviving and, never suspecting the duel of absolute malevolence that he has just won, they bless his faithfulness as a servant. He alone knows the meaning of his joy as they set him free from the frozen boat. "Hate had become mania." (Neihardt 1907, 93–109)

Hate, as it did here, quickly becomes the art of the duel and stubbornly risks everything in total commitment to the other's destruction. Hate, in its most passionate expression, leaps to judgments that permit no exception, persists in total self-investment, and pursues ultimate strategies. Retributive hate requires the absolute. The total commitment to a negative goal hides beneath obsequious service, or lurks in the invisible dark side of an ambivalent relationship, or masquerades beneath high-minded philosophy. Absolute judgments can be perfectly concealed by prophetic words spoken from the high moral ground of indignation. Ultimate strategies can be created to vindicate wounded pride or avenge the pettiest slight. Hate and its favored accomplice—the absolute—rarely appear separately. They find an intimate alliance, a passionate affinity, in their commitment to "final solutions."

The elusive abstraction of the absolute is fully visible in the ritual of the duel. In the classic duel situation, the intent is to kill. Each dueler contracts to attempt to destroy the other, to rectify an injury to honor or resolve a hated slur to his social superiority. In the element of chance, they believe, the divine hand will appear.

> The duel situation arises when two men experience a conflict existing between them as absolute, and therefore as capable of resolution only in the destruction of the one by the other. There is no reconciliation, no mediation, no adequate expiation, the hand that deals the blow must not be any of the opponents; but this *is* the "judgment of God." In each there is an aftermath of the belief that men can bring about a judgment of God. (Buber 1971, 73–74)

It is this metaphor that turns dualisms into duel to the death. The myths of heroic warfare, of conquest of territory, of the gunfight in the Old West or the outback, of corporate takeover in the economic equivalent of war, all continue the metaphor of duel as life/death resolution.

"All-or-nothing thinking" lurks in the back of our minds, waiting to offer an absolutely right explanation when one is needed. The ability to see things with perfect clarity in either/or lots—what Melanie Klein called splitting—is necessary in infancy for psychic survival, helpful in childhood to differentiate good and bad, but by school age, at seven, we begin to move beyond the limits of either/or concrete thought to see things as another sees them. Piaget has shown how the child's developing cognitive schemas change at age seven, allowing the child to perceive things from the opposite point of view, to step outside her frame of reference and look at the self from the other side. Hereafter, all-or-nothing splitting is no longer of much use, except in the service of fear or hate. Being capable of seeing the other side does not mean that such vision becomes a regular way of thinking. All evidence suggests that infants think in absolutes and keep love and hate separate; the ability to see the other as both good and bad is not yet present, and a return to infancy can happen as quickly as a flash of temper or an age-two tantrum. We retain this ability to regress in times of stress to the absolutism Klein called *all-good* or *all-bad*. When as adults we fail to see that another can be both good and bad at the same time, we are stuck in infantile schema, unable to move to the next emotional and cognitive level of recognizing that as I am not all good, even in my most self-righteous moments, or all bad, even in my most depressive blues, neither is the adversary.

The Demon of the Absolute

The adversarial "all good vs. all bad" tension is not only as old as infancy, it is as old as prehistory. As metaphor, consider Cain and Abel. Cain hears God say to him: "Do good, be loved; do bad, you are evil." Cain, in the same bind as his parents, like them chooses evil, and violence "is a demon crouching at the door" (Gen. 4:7). In the Hebrew Scripture, adversarial thought is the satanizing of the other person. We have lost this meaning of "satan" by absolutizing it, capitalizing it into a proper noun. In Hebrew, "satan"—the adversary—is the root word for alienation between humans. To create an enemy, to perceive a hated adversary as evil, is satanic behavior. *Diabolos*, the Greek word for devil, means "to throw between." Evil, in essence, is the *wedge* that cuts between, the *wall* that we create to separate, the adversarial means of breaking connectedness. Rollo May offers this twist:

> The Greek word is *diabolos;* "diabolic" is the term in contemporary English. Now it is fascinating to note that this diabolic is the antonym of "symbolic." The latter comes from *sym-bollein*, which means to "throw together," to unite. There lie in these words tremendous implications with respect to an ontology of good and evil. The symbolic is that which draws together, ties, integrates the individual within himself and with his group; the diabolic, in contrast, is that which disintegrates and tears apart. Both of these are present in the *daimonic*. (May 1969, 137)

In the great stories of Jesus' being tested by the diabolic, the symbolic attractions offered were, in the final analysis, all temptations to rupture connectedness to God and solidarity with humanity. Alienation is the essential dynamic of human evil. Estrangement from the other is definitive of all destructiveness. Coconspirators may bond in common hatred, but the relationship, defined by the shared foe, is grounded in mutually committed estrangement. In service of the same absolute intention, the demonic excavates the abyss, erects the wall, sows land mines along the border to "throw a barrier" between self and other—or, as we perceive it, between sacred self and evil other. Literary critic Paul Elmer More wrote:

> The demons that haunt human society include the Moloc of violence, the Beelzebub of treachery, the Belial of lying flatteries, the Mammon of gold, the Mephistopheles of scepticism, the hobgoblin of fear, and other of the Stygian Council escaped through the open gates of hell—these disturbers of the peace have always been stalking the world, plying their trade of malice. . . . But there is one demon who retains so much of celestial glamour, who so wears the robe of authority, that he still moves about unnoticed or passes for an angel of light. And the mischief of his art is that the finer minds are often those most subject to his wishes. I mean the Demon of the Absolute. (More 1928, 1)

"This Demon of the Absolute," More argued, "is nothing else but reason run amok." Disregarding fact, it sets up its own absolutes as the truth and asks us to act thereupon. Reason is a guide, an inner mentor that prompts us to act consistently, consequentially, humbly, and wisely, and avoid the either/or.

> There are no absolutes in nature; they are phantoms created by reason itself in its own likeness, delusions which, when once evoked, usurp the field of reality and bring endless confusion in their train. Their end is chaos. (More 1928, 2)

The absolute can take over in all aspects of our lives. In politics, either/or thinking may be elevated to nationalistic good versus an evil empire; in religion, the contrast is between an infallible church and undisciplined individualism; or in spirituality, the choice is between faith in an omnipotent, predestining God with absolute sovereignty or no God at all. Absolute thought-forms lead to either/or values, and these values in turn justify ultimate decisions about who shall live and who shall die. The Demon of the Absolute inspires judgmentalism, empowers prejudice, and justifies discriminatory systems, racist laws, and ethnocentric practices.

Hate speech is constructed from absolute propositions; hate crimes carry them to their inevitable and logical/illogical conclusions.

"The Demon of the Absolute" rules in polarized minds and paranoid community. As all persons are categorized as either/or, good or evil, all thinking proceeds in clear, decisive dualisms that become absolute in definition and, in time, in action. When human reason bows to the demon of the absolute, rationalizations can justify violence, excuse exploitation of others, or sacralize domination; oppression, or even genocide, can be created to serve our needs. The phantom of exalted reason becomes the monster of absolutism.

> The demon says to reason, "What is wrong with you? Here you are all ready to be god and too shy to put on the robes. Is there not an Almighty, a Big Boss, in your head? Make that Almighty into the emperor of the Universe. Then serve him well. And do not let anyone challenge his authority." (Wentz 1993, 70)

When reason has claimed an absolute authority, we can act with confidence that our mandate is infallible, claim knowledge of truth that is incontrovertible, and make decisions that need no review or reparations. In ancient Rome, fathers had absolute power over sons, daughters, wives, and slaves, including the right to condemn them to death (Gordon 1990, 147). It is hardly surprising that sons often hated their fathers; wives and daughters, mere chattel, feared him; and slaves betrayed him.

But no matter how absolute the authority one may pretend for the self, no one is invulnerable to challenge or criticism, even when self-criticism has been silenced. Then comes the master stroke of invulnerability. By discovering a God—a god in whose own image I exist (or is it vice versa?)—one resolves this dilemma. My absolute, elevated to supremacy, is now inaccessible to critique, worshiped and served with unquestioning obedience, available to be imposed on others. In defending oneself against all challenges, our use of the divine can range from saying, "But I have prayed about this" to the ubiquitous use of "God Bless America." When in doubt, we appeal to the absolute, preferably an absolute of our own design, and infallibility comes to the rescue.

Taking exception to the construction or use of absolutes as the way to ensure authority, Abraham Heschel notes that such idolatry replaces God with our vision of what is good:

> There are no ultimate laws, no eternal ideas. The Lord alone is ultimate and eternal. The laws are His creation, and the moral ideas are

no entities apart from Him; they are his concern. Indeed the personalization of the moral idea is the indispensable assumption of prophetic theology. Mercy, grace, repentance, forgiveness, all would be impossible if the moral principle were held to be superior to God. (Heschel 1962, 217)

As Heschel goes on to show, the absolutist looks to some grand scheme or idea of truth above and beyond all else. In contrast, the prophetic tradition looks to a person. The absolutist wants truth exclusive of all other truths; the prophetic calls exclusive absolutes into question. The absolutist insists truth is one; the prophetic recognizes truth may have many faces, may reside in competing claims or in the balance of one correcting and/or completing another.

Elie Wiesel, in *Night*, struggles with continuing belief in a God who is absolute, and asks:

Why should I bless the Eternal? Because he had thousands of children burned in His pits? Because He has six crematories working night and day, on Sundays and feast days? Because in His great might He had created Auschwitz, Birkenau, Buna, and so many factories of death? How could I say to Him, "Blessed art thou, Eternal, Master of the Universe, who chose us from among the races to be tortured day and night, to see our fathers, our mothers, our brothers end in the crematory? Praised be Thy Holy Name, Thou who hast chosen us to be butchered on Thine altar?" (Wiesel 1960, 78)

The accusation of misrepresentation—in the face of the evidence that the Almighty, the Absolute, is anything but all-powerful and ultimate—set Elie, the young man, over against God: "I had ceased to be anything but ashes, yet I felt myself to be stronger than the Almighty." The Absolute no longer exists for him; if there is a god, who, why, what is this god? Yet in the midst of such profound questioning and doubt, Wiesel also finds an alternative—an opposing answer whispers within him in response to a hanging.

Three men are executed by the SS. The youngest is a boy with a refined and beautiful face, loved by all in the concentration camp. The three stand on chairs beneath the gallows, the nooses drop over their necks, the commandant gestures, the chairs are tipped. The two adults die quickly; the child is too light to draw the noose tight. For more than half an hour the child struggles, eyes full of terror, tongue red. The inmates are marched past to witness the cruel death.

"Behind me," Wiesel reports, "a voice asked 'Where is God now?' And I heard a voice *within* me answer him. 'Where is He? Here He is—He is hanging here on this gallows'" (Wiesel 1960, 76).

Does Wiesel mean that the existence of any almighty, absolute deity ended as the child died? Or that such an omnipotent god must die—the idea of such a god makes no sense in the horror of the child's hanging? Or perhaps that God is there with the lad, there in the terrible suffering, one with him and with the onlookers? Or that this is the only face of God we now know, humanity suffering the most heinous evil? Or all of the above? Clearly he means that the old hopes of an almighty arm of justice intervening in brutish inhumanity are forever dead, but is there a God beyond this god? He spends his life contradicting, confronting, arguing with this God in loyal controversy. After Auschwitz, whether Jewish victim or non-Jewish bystander, we must join him in the debate.

Postmodernism: An End to Absolutes?

Postmodernism, the dominant contemporary philosophical perspective, has challenged modernity's old secure claims to final, adequate and unquestionable answers on the universe and life within it. It critiques the confident modern claims of overwhelming consensus that permit us to speak of possessing absolutes and proclaiming universals. In 1984, Jean-François Lyotard, in *The Post-Modern Condition*, initiated the dismantling of what he called "grand ideas" or "grand narratives" of universal truths that had received virtually unquestioned assent. He called for the discarding of all "metanarratives," those totalizing explanations of existence that lay claim to universal agreement. Instead of continuing our pretentious claims to world consensus, Lyotard advocated "dissensus," which respected the right of each group to define its identity by its own localized "language games," not by one metanarrative that some reputed "consensus" insists must be true for all humans. For Lyotard, there are no longer viable universal and absolute networks of truth that define us all, but "language games" that define what is truly *just* in their own unique ways. He did attempt to salvage one universal, justice, as an overarching value, but failed to recognize that each group also has its own idea of justice. In his search for a nonuniversal justice, he finally ended with the call to play our language games nonconflictually—"Let us play . . . and let us play in peace" (Lyotard 1984, 131).

Postmodernism has undermined all assumptions of one group's right to define truth for another, to dictate justice to another. Each and all *oth-*

ers must be heard and their ways of defining truth and justice called into dialogue. We must search for justice together in the postmodern world; justice has become an arduous journey, not an easily found destination. No one has the perspective or the unique position to speak universally, as Enlightenment rationalism allowed us to do in the age of modernity. Those who claim the prerogative to define the human condition absolutely and unilaterally do so with no wider consensus of authority than their own followers. For example, the right to define Japanese personality and character from outside the closed borders of Japan, as Ruth Benedict did just after World War II in *Chrysanthemum and the Sword,* is no longer granted to any scholar. Each culture speaks for itself with its uniqueness intact. "Language games" that speak for the whole human race are intellectually indefensible, although they are still popularly employed and politically exploited. No field of thought is exempt, none has the right to claim universal authority—not even science.

> Postmodernism sees science as one myth among many, and the enlightenment heritage that has elevated science to supremacy, as totalitarian and culturally imperialistic. Instead of the modern idealization of the words "rational, principle" and "dominance", postmodernism gives place to emotion, intuition, personal experience, the particular rather than the general, the mystical as well as the real, the mysterious as well as the empirical. Its goal is not to formulate an alternative set of assumptions but to register the impossibility of establishing any such foundation or underpinning for epistemology. (Hiebert 1999, 53)

Postmodern thought is interested in the actual, not the absolute, the particular rather than the general, the unique rather than the universal, the unrepeatable instance rather than the recurring pattern that can be scientifically replicated. This rejection of old ways of mapping universals and making generalizations has influenced all fields of thought with the possible exception of politics, where the day of utilizing "language games" that speak for the world has not passed.

Former president Richard Nixon, writing in the 1980s about defining international identities, particularly West vis à vis East, argued for absolute metaphors:

> It may seem melodramatic to treat the twin poles of human experience represented by the United States and the Soviet Union as the

equivalent of Good and Evil, Light and Darkness, God and the Devil; yet if we allow ourselves to think of them in that way, even hypothetically, it can help clarify our perspectives on the world struggle. (Nixon 1980, 5)

The problem is that when one divides the world in such either/or categories as in these words by Nixon, or Reagan's "evil empire" address, or George W. Bush's "axis of evil" language, the poles are pressed to their farthest reach. Following the terrorist attack on the World Trade Center towers, most political spokespersons, including President George W. Bush, spoke with such certainty regarding absolute good vs. evil that their language was more reductionist than even Nixon or Reagan. An absolute stance is not just a political position but, in actuality, a theological confession—a political theology of humankind. Statements about the Absolute, whether philosophic or political in nature, affirm a "grand narrative" that points to the goal of history. In messianic absolutism, which projects an ultimate value or center of values for the march of history, absolute statements are, inevitably, theologies.

Every great spiritual tradition has had wise persons who were not worshipers of the Absolute, but followers of the mysterious God who courts, covenants, and creates enduring relationships. They learned and taught that we encounter personal, vital, eternal truth when we give up the search for, or the claim to have found, absolutes that remove all question or doubt.

The contrasting visions of God in, for example, the Hebrew tradition vary from the God who is the Absolute Other, to the God who is the Intimate Lover who comes to Abraham offering a covenant of mutual loyalty and promising, "I will make of you a great nation, . . . and in you all the families of the earth shall be blessed" (Gen. 12:2–3 RSV mg.). This is a God beyond all those gods familiar to Abraham's family tradition—those of deified ethnicity, deified territorial safety and sanctity, deified prosperity and fertility, deified triumph and military dominance, deified masculinity and gender supremacy, deified systems of law, reason, mythology; deified revenge, just retribution, or any other form of special pleading. This God who offers Abraham a covenantal relationship is a God beyond all formerly known gods. This vision of God—covenanting faithfulness, pledging loyalty, promising to be unfailingly present as cotraveler—carries Abraham, leaving home and family in Ur to begin a pilgrimage of discovery, through the confusion of human affairs. The word *Absolute*, when attached to this god, refers to unwavering faithfulness—God is absolutely faithful, absolutely constant in unflinching reliability, in unwavering grace. It drains the word absolute of the perfect sense of mathematical infinity, "pure act" finality, static regularity, the first of all causes. All these may possess some truth beyond our comprehension, but the Absolute we come to know as God is absolute relatedness: presence, constancy, faithfulness, relational availability. Russian theologian Berdyaev declares this Hebrew understanding of the God who comes to meet us:

> You cannot pray to the Absolute. No dramatic meeting with it is possible. We call that the Absolute which has no relation to another and has no need of an other. The Absolute is not a being, is not personality, which always presupposes a going out from itself and a meeting with an other. The God of revelation, the God of the Bible, is not the Absolute. In Him there is dramatic life and movement, there is a relation to an other, to humanity, to the world. (Berdyaev 1944, 84))

Berdyaev protests the philosophical captivity of our ideas of God that have changed the dynamic God of the Bible into a philosopher's concept of "pure act." "When we have attempted to know God Himself as Absolute, the God Who reveals and not conceals Himself, then a monarchical understanding of God has been accepted, which is a source of theological seduction and slavery. The Christian revelation of the Son of God Who sacrificed Himself, suffered and was crucified, saves us from that. God is not an absolute monarch. God is a God Who suffers with the world and with humankind. He is crucified Love" (Berdyaev 1944, 85).

Mature faith affirms that there is no god but God; this God has challenged all absolute judgments, all ultimate human actions, all self-divinizing idolatry of our theological systems modeled on human hierarchies and power gone wild. The God who is "Absolute" Other must also be "absolutely" related to all that is, or this God is not the God of Jesus Christ, the Suffering Servant who is also the One who fills all in all. This God is full of grace and truth—not cold truth alone, not tolerant grace in supremacy, but Truth in relationships, Holiness in Solidarity. God is Love, Life, Light: the giver and grace of Love, the origin and lure of all Life, and the goodness and justice of eternal Light.

A pure, ideal absolute abstraction is an idol—a god who offers ultimate certainty, a very attractive god indeed, but a false face for the demon of the absolute. The true God is a moving, transforming reality; in God's Being, there is also becoming; in God's gracious giving there is also loving receiving; in God's transcendent majesty there is also immanent identification and presence with us in our suffering and pain. But every image we use to describe God too easily, too definitively, becomes a humanly created image that violates the Second Commandment. No sooner do we formulate it in a satisfying way than we reify it into an idol and prefer it to the Mystery that stands behind it. As Wentz says with irony, "One can barely speak of this God without the soft touch of something landing on the shoulder—the demon of the absolute. A quick peek, a snap to check, he isn't there. Can I catch him unawares?" (Wentz 1993, 71). Theologian anthropologist Hiebert notes how these images of an absolute God which we create reflect our cultural world and are soon imposed on other cultures and distort their worlds.

> Idealist theologies preserve the certainty of objective truth and absolutes. They reject the relativism that leads us to nihilism, but the price of this certainty is high. To claim that what is in the human mind is objective reality is to deny the ultimate reality of God and his deeds in history. It is to locate truth in the self and to deify the human mind. And, as many Third World theologians point out, it can lead to Western theological colonialism and a failure to take them seriously. (Hiebert 1999, 59)

Once an absolute deity is conceived, an absolute religion created, and absolute positions on the moral high ground claimed, it is not difficult to make absolute decisions, take absolute actions, and justify violent solutions to what are, in actuality, relative situations. It is the worship of the absolutes that leads us to fanaticism and violence.

> There is never any hope for a world that serves absolutes. Such service can only lead to violence. There is no victory, only hatred and revenge. The only genuine hope is in our response to human suffering. You can whip me into submission, but there will be no advancement of the human story in your success. I will either become vengeful and serve the righteousness of my absolute claim against you, or I will accept the suffering knowing that neither your god nor mine is really absolute. In the latter case, there is hope. In the former, there is none. God is the discovery in the midst of suffering that there are no absolutes. (Wentz 1993, 73)

The secure possession of the absolute, the loss of all ambiguity, the excision of the conscience, the loss of or the coopting of God, all are necessary for the rise of despotic leadership in country, corporation, or church. In our time perhaps no one has exemplified the embodiment of the absolute, indeed all four of the qualities just named, more fully than Hitler. (Although, since Hitler, history has offered us multiple candidates.)

> The secret of Hitler's effectiveness lies, in fact, in his complete and fundamental absence of restraint. Such a belief in oneself is ordinarily only possible to one who feels himself, in the fullest sense of the term, commissioned and empowered by the absolute. Those who do not believe in any absolute cannot believe in this sense of the self, but the absence of restraint is accompanied by the natural ability and perfected readiness to avoid that reflection on oneself that would make one's own emptiness apparent. (Buber 1957, 111)

"Remember, it was Hitler who said, 'Conscience is like circumcision, a mutilation of the human being.' He appears to have restored the mutilated member through becoming the man without conscience," Buber says, with Jewish tongue in cheek (1957, 153).

Hatred as Absolutism Become Fanaticism

Absolutism, either when inspired by urgent love of cause or empowered by intense hate of its opponents, becomes fanaticism. The relationship of hate and fanaticism is like two sides of a coin—fanaticism is "heads," hate is "tails," and the coin itself is absolutism.

"Fanaticism is the major component of hate, and vice versa. More precisely, not all fanatics are filled with hate, but those who are filled with hate are fanatics. Their conduct leads inexorably to the destruction of the Being in being" (Wiesel 1999, 372). "How are we to explain fanaticism's attraction for so many intellectuals, to this day?" Wiesel asks. "And what can be done to immunize religion against its pull? For, once it absorbs absolutist trends, religion becomes aggressive. The fanatic inspires and breathes fear. It is the only tie that binds him to his fellow-man and God. Whether his dictatorship is intellectual or theocratic, he pretends to possess a unique and eternal truth. Insist on a discussion, and he takes offense. He accepts questions only if he alone has the right to answer them. It comes to this: the fanatic accepts only answers—his own—while his tolerant adversary prefers questions" (370).

Fanaticism, argues German pastoral psychologist Josef Rudin, is a universal problem, present in every ethnic group and in every period of known history. Racial, geographical, climatic, gender, or age differences carry little or no weight here. Fanaticism is a psychic, social, political phenomenon that can exaggerate almost any or all areas of life and culture, investing it with absolute importance or authority. Rudin focuses on three characteristics of fanaticism that must be examined to understand its power to motivate persons, groups, and movements: intensity of drive, distortion of motives, disorder of the whole personality (Rudin 1969, 16ff.).

1. Fanaticism is an *intense drive.* The degree of energy with which one lives, feels, thinks, wills, works, and confronts the objective world can actually be quantified. The kinds of drive that can be measured include: (1) Instinctual arousal. Intense fanatic excitement (explosive, eruptive, violent, enraged). (2) Emotional temperament. Intense fanatic passion (vehemence, impetuosity, impulsiveness, emotional tenacity). (3) Intellectual obsession. Intense fanatic rage of will (intelligence, determination, abstract idealism, overfocusing, monomania, unscrupulousness). We can picture these as levels that form a layer-specific model of intensity. In fanaticism, these three—the instinctual, the emotional, and the intellectual—may combine or one may predominate. Rudin suggests that Hitler and Kafka illustrate the first; Savonarola and John of Leiden (Jan Beuekelson), the Münster theocrat, illustrate the second; Lenin, Stalin, Calvin, the third.

The sources of these intense emotions are many and varied, what we might call the "vital psychic backgrounds of fanatic intensity." Such intense arousal, emotion, or obsession may well up as a spontaneous expression of situational vitality (rock concert, disco dancing, Mardi Gras); or, more enduringly, occur from compensation for a deficiency in the self (attempts to nullify a defect, balance a false equilibrium, silence a repressed doubt); or they may be evidence of an intellectual obsession such as a consuming search for the absolute (invoking divine authority, claiming the supreme and ultimate truth, identifying self as God). The personality is overpowered by psychic energies that create a tornado of passion, obsession, even violence. Delusions of omnipotence, indefatigability, or absolute certainty may result. "Fanaticism is the brother of doubt," Jung emphasizes, and the more alarming the doubt, the greater the need for absolute truth (Rudin 1969, 19–20).

2. Fanaticism is *distortion of motives,* a problem of an all-consuming value. A dominating absolute value is chosen as one's life project, and all else is measured by this value attitude. The value, having become an imago of the self, grows to claim central dominance as the organizing

principle of a person's life in a lopsided, overvalued investment of energy. One fanatic may be dominated by an absolute authority from above (a professional warrior, SS man, political party stallion, company functionary, cultic devotee, true believer, intellectual faddist); another is dominated by a goal of pursuing absolute perfection (in *personal style*, such as impeccable manners, flawless aristocratic behavior, unassailable class status; *public lifestyle*, such as defining legal/cultural regulations; *creative art style*, such as perfection of technique, supreme mastery of an art form; *ethical style*, such as promulgating codes, laws, or goals of a particular cause of justice); a third kind of value fanaticism occurs with the social or religious prophet who seeks the embodiment of a higher vision of truth. Great personalities such as Tolstoy, Gandhi, King, Mother Teresa, Mandela come to mind.

3. Fanaticism can become or result from a *disorder of the whole personality*, from pathology. Fanaticism pushes the envelope, challenges all borders, is often an area of borderline functioning—on the border between rational and irrational, healthy and unhealthy, sane and not sane, normal and abnormal in the personality. The pathological fanatic is often a prepsychotic personality, almost out of control or about to break down. This is complex, and any description must be varied beyond any simplistic or reductionistic categories. Yet patterns of mental disorder are visible. These are most pronounced in (1) fanaticism as hysteria (excessive and uncontrolled emotionality); (2) fanaticism as disordered thinking (rigidity, delusion); (3) fanaticism as compulsion (powerful inner force that is accepted as a *mission* and fulfilled as a *task* resulting in a *fixation* producing *aggression*).

Rudin concludes that the multilayered character of fanaticism, the multiplicity of its forms, the malignancy of its psychic power to overpower the personality reveal how unique and varied yet how similar and simpleminded fanatic processes truly are. All of these characteristics are familiar. The sports fan who can recite the scores of players from decades ago, the critic who cannot experience art for the flooding of analysis and deconstruction, the perfectionist who is unable to make contact with the actual out of love for the ineffable are all in our daily life.

Prophylaxis for fanaticism must include teaching a clear hierarchy of values, fostering solid-core identity formation, reinforcing an open questioning attitude, and inspiring a commitment to worthy, enduring, balanced, and convincing life goals (Rudin 1969, 134–89).

Absolutism is the ultimate end of Christian orthodox fanaticism, just as the Inquisition is the final end of Catholic infallibility, perfectionism is the far end of revivalism, and nationalism the blind end of patriotism. Several of these are illustrated by the following letter from Cotton Mather, which shows how fanaticism can invoke the will of God in pursuit of sectarian prejudice.

In the year of Our Lord 1682

To ye aged and beloved, Mr. John Higginson:

There be now at sea a ship called *Welcome*, which has on board 100 or more of the heretics and malignants called Quakers, with W. Penn, who is the chief scamp, at the head of them. The General Court has accordingly given sacred orders to Master Malachi Huscott, of the brig *Porpoise*, to waylay the said *Welcome* slyly as near the Cape of Cod as may be, and to make captive the said Penn and his ungodly crew, so that the Lord may be glorified and not mocked on the soil of this new country with the heathen worship of these people. Much spoil can be made of selling the whole lot to Barbadoes, where slaves fetch good prices in rum and sugar, and we shall not only do the Lord great good by punishing the wicked, but we shall make great good for His Minister and people.

Yours in the bowels of Christ,

COTTON MATHER
(Phillips 1941)

The "bowels of Christ" is a reference to the biblical words for compassion—in the Hebrew the root of the word is "womb," in the Greek "bowels," as a location of deep concern from the center of one's being. The Reverend Mather's gut feeling about the Quakers was projected in biblical language upon the diety, and returned with a godlike authority as a basis for absolute exclusion and the purchase of West Indies rum. The hate of the Quakers, the absolutism of the Puritans, the willingness to sell a brother into slavery as a service to God, the fanaticism of the settlers creating a new and pure England emerge in these few lines. This letter of 1682 is little different in attitude from those found any week in any American newspaper, and if we review our history, we know what sort of absolute actions we are capable of making with so little consideration of the full human cost.

The Hiroshima event reveals that it takes very little, in the midst of a war, to prepare a nation like America to inflict a heinous atrocity on an enemy society in order to send a message or "make a point" to the world:

> Only months later the United States Government was to set up a court for the trial and punishment of Japanese civilian and military leaders who violated the laws of war in a manner much less significant than the violations associated with the atomic attacks. Our moral arrangements permitted us to engage in indiscriminate terror against the civilian population of Japan, while holding Japanese leaders accountable for adherence to the letter of the law. (Lifton and Falk 1982, 197)

As I walked in the Peace Park at Hiroshima last summer, I asked myself: "What kind of mood does a fundamentally decent people have to be in, what kind of moral rationale must it make, to prepare it to incinerate as many as a quarter of a million human beings for the sake of making a point?" A fundamentally decent and responsible people are able to adjust their moral values to think and do the unthinkable, as long as all political parties agree that it is necessary, justified, and therefore right. The call to support absolute positions, approve absolute actions, pursue absolute goals always comes in time of national threat. Military action—the absolute clad in armor—has won the approval of ethicists and theologians since Augustine in the fourth century blessed the cause of Rome by use of criteria that discriminated between just and unjust wars. The rationale for designating a war as "just" has been reformulated again and again. "'Just war' is . . . *just* . . . *war*," theologian John Howard Yoder often said in debate. He has not been refuted. The unresolved dilemma is how Christian theologians, of the same faith family, on both sides of a conflict, can use similar principled arguments to declare their war just. If it is possible for Christian ethicists of high integrity to simultaneously declare a war just, but from opposing sides, then there is something fatally wrong with the criteria or the process. In the last century, German Christians destroyed French and Dutch Christians, and vice versa. English and American Christians decimated Italian and German Christians. Over the centuries, European Christians in tiny next-door states have slaughtered their brothers and sisters in Christ by the millions. The Christian Scriptures are clear that solidarity to fellow Christians in any other land is more important than loyalty to any secular nation state. Croatian theologian Volf, who writes from the heart of the Balkan struggle, challenges attempts to find absolutes that can justify resorting to final violence:

There are Christians who have a hard time resisting the temptation to seek religious legitimation for their (understandable) need to take up the sword. If they give in to this temptation, they should forego all attempts to exonerate their version of Christian faith from complicity in fomenting violence. Of course, they can specify that religious symbols should be used to legitimate and inspire only *just* wars. But show me one warring party that does not think its war is just! Simple logic tells us that at least half of them *must* be wrong. It could be, however, that simple logic does not apply to the chaotic world of wars. Then all would be right, which is to say that all would be wrong, which is to say that terror would reign—in the name of the gods who can no longer be distinguished from the devils. (Volf 1996a, 306)

Often rational justifications are constructed in hindsight to sanctify the evil done or the means employed. We must also lay aside all facile attempts to rationalize the horror of war, even at the highest level of philosophical accounting for evil in the construction of theodicies or the attempted creation of theory to identify some meaning, some useful significance or reasonable outcome, from atrocities. Rieff, in rejecting the construction of absolute justifications for devastating actions, presents a lament that is unrefutable:

What supernatural hubris could lead [anyone} to imagine that anything can be done to "redeem" the deaths of Verdun and Auschwitz, the Gulag Archipelago and the Algerian war of independence, Hiroshima, the Cambodian killing fields, and the mission stations of Rwanda? To imagine that there is anything human beings could do, up to and including reducing the risk of nuclear war or mitigating the worst abuses of tyrants and torturers, to somehow "make right" or make less vain such horrors and sufferings, is either the most astonishing act of self-aggrandizing hubris or the blindest naivete. Nothing can make these things bearable to anyone with a conscience, and it is vainglorious and self-serving to pretend otherwise. (Rieff 2001, 4–5)

Discovering the Absolute

In *The Meaning of Revelation*, H. Richard Niebuhr writes of three basic convictions: (1) "Self-defense is the most prevalent source of error in all thinking and perhaps especially in theology and ethics"; (2) "The great source of evil in life is the absolutizing of the relative, which in Christianity takes the form of substituting religion, revelation, church or Christian morality for God"; and (3) "Christianity is 'permanent revolution' or *metanoia* which does not come to an end in this world, this life, or this time" (Niebuhr 1941, ix–x).

Neibuhr's theological analysis of human error exposes the constant process of using our absolute constructs to protect our selves, our entitlements, our values, our unwillingness to challenge them or be challenged to examine them. *Defensiveness* closes our eyes to the surrounding realities, such as an overpopulated, hungry world in conflict, with "haves" trying to maintain entitlement in the face of challenges from "have-nots" without privilege. It assists us in creating a reasoned, although not always reasonable, justification for maintaining the status quo. *Absolutizing* the relative excuses us from questioning these rationales, and permits us to worship a religion that points toward God rather than to worship and serve the God who is above and beyond all religion. It trusts naive appeals to absolute revelation without humility before its central goal and trajectory. It acts from rules rather than seeking just ends. Concretizing Christianity, or any other religion, into sacralized, static finality cuts it off from the God who is constantly at work "making all things new," transforming things toward ends we do not grasp, and ultimately bringing resurrection from death. Whether we do this absolutizing consciously or unconsciously, the result is the same. G. K. Chesterton once wrote that "There are two kinds of people in the world: the conscious dogmatists and the unconscious dogmatists. I have always found myself that the unconscious dogmatists were by far the most dogmatic" (1928). As Niebuhr commented on our need to use theological ideas of divine revelation with tentativeness and humility:

> The patterns and models we employ to understand the historical world may have had a heavenly origin, but as we know and use them they are, like ourselves, creatures of history and time; though we direct our thought to eternal and transcendent beings, it is not eternal and transcendent; though we regard the universal, the image of the universal in our minds is not a universal image. (Niebuhr 1941, 7)

Hatred as Evil Imagination

Imagination—the creating of an image of another and substituting the partial image for the actual other—is the essence of hatred. Hatred, viewed theologically, is a human capacity to *imagine evil* toward the other, so evil imagination is the earliest biblical and theological language for conceptualizing the moral nature of hatred. Evil imagination is our primary way of conceiving, visualizing, desiring, and ultimately plotting and acting in destructive ways toward another. Hate is the willful construction of evil images of the neighbor and delight over the hateful destruction of both image and reality.

H. Richard Niebuhr, writing on "evil imagination," provides an intriguing entry point for an ethical analysis of hate and hostility. (Niebuhr did not explicitly address the functions of hatred, but his thought has been insightfully argued to this end by Ryan LaMothe, to whom I am indebted for much that follows [LaMothe 1996, 185–98].) For Niebuhr, evil imagination has three tragic tendencies which distort our attitudes toward the neighbor:

1. Evil imagination is "the totalitarian tendency," which, like the Babel myth, "inclines us to believe that our outlook yields not only the truth but all the truth there is" (Niebuhr 1941, 118). This tendency absolutizes the relative; substitutes religion, revelation, church, or a moral system for God; claims that the thought or experiences of a particular historical group is the *only* true, dependable, universal source of truth. This is original sin, the tendency toward idolatry.

2. Evil imagination is the proclivity toward making self-preservation the first law of life. The elevation of self or group preservation justifies a group's taking ultimate actions that sacrifice others for its own safety or survival.

3. Evil imagination is the tendency toward self or group glorification. The person or the group "thinks of itself as the center," enthrones images, symbols, and doctrines of God as the highest or only true manifestations (Niebuhr 1941, 74).

For Niebuhr, two interrelated assumptions are at the heart of this tendency: (1) all human knowledge in general and revelation in particular are neither eternal nor unchanging—the human images and symbols of God may change and die, but God does not. Evil imagination confuses one's symbols and images of God with Godself. (2) All history is partial and relative—one among many—and follows the course of all other histories: change and death. In evil imagination one's personal, social, or religious history is elevated as absolute and all else is relative. In contrast, Niebuhr called us to embrace the reality of God while confessing the ambiguity of human history and knowledge.

In the Hebrew Scriptures, evil imagination, as the earliest definition of human destructiveness, occurs in the Noah epic, the story of the flood. God's judgment against the human race comes because "every imagination of the thoughts of his [man's] heart was only evil continually" (Gen. 6:5 RSV; see also 8:21).* Evil imagination, or hate, is the inclination toward idolatry in Deut. 29:19, 31:21, the inner core of human motivation that distorts human relatedness, wholeness, integrity (1 Chron. 28:9), and one of the original seven deadly sins—pride, untruth, murder, evil imagination (hate), eager impulsive evildoing, perjury, sowing dissension (Prov. 6:18). In the Christian Scriptures, it is cited in Mary's song, the Magnificat, that God has "scattered the proud in the imagination of their hearts" (Luke 1:51 RSV). Paul uses the term to define the depths of human evil (Rom. 1:21), which, he affirms, can be transformed (2 Cor. 10:5–6).

Evil imagination has its roots in two fundamental conditions of human existence: the experience of *absolute dependence* (we are each completely contingent) and *absolute powerlessness* (we are powerless to create a particular existence or to avoid death). We are thrown into and taken out of existence by mysterious and unchangeable powers beyond ourselves. Thus we must confess, "I live but do not have the power to live" and "I may die at any moment but am powerless to die" (Niebuhr 1963, 114). This reality carries with it a deep fear and anxiety. We "fear the loss of selfhood, not simply of life; it is a fear of the exclusions from the community of selves. It is a fear of death not as a biological but personal event" (Niebuhr 1989, 75).

Violence and its justifications, *hostility* and its rationalizations, *hatred* and its concealments are all expressions of evil imagination as an effort to secure one's identity and continuity against coming destruction, loss, and forgottenness. Hostility, violence, fear, and anxiety, linked together by their common ground, emerge in response to absolute dependence, powerlessness, and the awareness of coming destruction. As LaMothe observes: "Whenever we see persons or groups glorify themselves, any time we hear a person or group espouse the belief that they possess *the* universal truth, whenever a person or group makes self-preservation the first law of life, hostility and anxiety are present" (LaMothe 1996, 191).

---

*The Hebrew word is *yatzer,* "to shape or to fashion." Devisings, strategies, plans, match our idea of imagining and conspiring to do evil (Gen. 6:5; 8:21).

Faith and Evil Imagination

The person, for Niebuhr, is inherently social, and the self lives, moves, and has its being within the matrix of faith. This is revealed in the questions we ask in all our relationships. "We are forever being asked and asking: Do you believe me? Do you trust me? Are you trustworthy and believable? Are you faithful to me and our common cause?" (Niebuhr 1989, 22). We come to *belief* by *trusting* the other's *fidelity*. The three primary dialectics of faith—*belief–disbelief; trust–mistrust;* and *fidelity–infidelity*—he argued, demonstrate the social character of all faith.

> The self not only acknowledges the other as another knower but in believing and disbelieving him or her, it trusts or distrusts . . . another self that has the double freedom of being able to bind itself by promises and yet break them also. . . . Trust is a response to and an acknowledgment of fidelity. The two are so interrelated in the reciprocal action of selves that one cannot speak of faith simply as the trust which appears but must speak of it also as fidelity to which trust is a response. (Niebuhr 1989, 47–48)

We ask these questions of fidelity by exercise of "reason" and accept the answers through imagination. Reason and imagination join to create the faith needed to build relationships with others and to find one's social location in the world.

Evil imagination is a particular kind of faith—either absolutized faith or inverted faith. When absolutized, the belief-trust-faithfulness to one's community's images and symbols of God are regarded as absolute, universal, eternal, and glorified over all other faith histories. When inverted, the dark side of faith is manifested in disbelief, disloyalty, hostility, distrust, and infidelity that is directed toward those who do not hold the same absolutized images, symbols, and religious histories or against those who threaten one's own hegemony to this faith, its eternal security or finality.

This hatred, hostility, disbelief, and disloyalty is more often than not unconscious, and paradoxically coexists with positive belief in deep ambivalence. One may consciously exult in an absolutized God and unconsciously fear, hate, and distrust this all-powerful Being in love–hate, worship–fear, devotion–dread. So faith is mixed with fear, subverted from darker depths. Consciously the person is faithful to the images and symbols of God held within his or her community, while unconsciously responding to the shadow cast by these absolutized beliefs. The imagined brightness of self-glorified image ("My God and I are right") may cast a contrasting shadow of horrifying and sinister darkness. The face of hate and the face of the holy may each be the obverse of the other.

One may explore this ambivalence by asking: "Do I suppress awareness of my own ultimate powerlessness and absolute dependence by absolutizing and glorifying my images and symbols of God? Am I sometimes tempted to defend these with stubborn insistence on their total accuracy and their finality? If I think for a moment that I possess the ultimate truth of the Eternal, then *I* need not fear my finitude, frailty, contingency? Do fears of my own impermanence tempt me to cling to certain symbols, images, and propositions? Has the thought troubled me that if one of my images of God dies, I too will die; if my symbols for God are not maintained, I will not be sustained?"

These are troubling questions evoking insecurity and provoking hostility. We are thrown into a life of intolerable insecurity, and this is reason for anxiety and protest. But our anger, we fear, dares not be directed at an all-powerful God. So a substitute is selected. In virtually every group, a scapegoat is necessary to the inner harmony and balance of the group; it may be an out-group that is despised or a variant within, like gays, Jews, blacks, browns, chosen to contain our and our group's hostility and hatred.

> The faith of evil imagination must seek a substitute, a denigrated "other" in order to (a) maintain an elevated view of itself, (b) secure a sense of identity and continuity against the vicissitudes of life (e.g., powerlessness and absolute dependence), and (c) contain the group's unconscious hatred for and distrust of an absolute, all-powerful and dangerous God. As Hitler once remarked, if there had been no Jews it would have been necessary to invent them. (LaMothe 1996, 194)

The denigrated other is not trusted or believed and deserves no fidelity, no loyalty. The enemy, now named, is freely hated. A substitute has been chosen by processes beneath consciousness. Those who cannot accept ambiguity, finitude, and the reality of "knowing only in part" need an enemy who is absolutely wrong so that they can claim to be absolutely right. If liberals are exposed as total relativists, then conservatives can lay claim to truth; if conservatives can be seen to be corrupt, then liberals are in the right; if gays epitomize moral depravity, then the sexual violations of heterosexuals can be excused; if the atrocities of the Islamic world are compared with the virtues of Christendom, and not vice versa, then we can reassure ourselves of possessing absolute values.

In 1726 satirist Jonathan Swift offered *Gulliver's Travels*, the ironic analysis of hate as evil imagination, with the account of Lemuel Gulliver's visit to the miniaturized kingdom of Lilliput. Swift, who was said to hate "man" but to love individual men, produced one of the most caustic social commentaries in the English language. After Gulliver's capture as "the man-mountain" and his socialization into the kingdom, he encounters their protracted war with the neighboring kingdom of Blefuscu. As Swift tells the tale:

> Two mighty powers have been engaged in the most obstinate war for six and thirty moons past. It began when . . . his present majesty's grandfather, while he was a boy, going to eat an egg, and breaking it according to the ancient practice [on the big end] happened to cut one of his fingers. Whereupon the Emperor, his father, published an edict, commanding all his subjects, upon great penalties, to break the smaller end of their eggs. The people so highly resented this law that, our histories tell us, six rebellions were raised, one emperor lost his life, and another his crown. These commotions were fomented by the emperors of Blefuscu, since the exiles always flee to that country for refuge. It is computed that eleven thousand persons have, at several times, suffered death, rather than to submit to break their eggs at the smaller end. (Swift [1726] 1952, 22)

As Swift portrays the controversy, hundreds of volumes have been written on both sides, but neither side reads the other's. Religious doctrine now sacralizes both positions; each refutes the other. Both have elevated their preferences to ultimate authority, each uses them to absolutize their sacred doctrines and practices. These beliefs offer a unique identity, an assured continuity as persons and as a people, an illusory defense against intolerable anxiety over coming loss or destruction. Their absolutism provides a simulacrum of power to dispel and deny feelings of powerlessness and dependence. Their habituated hatred and protracted hostilities guarantee endemic violence will provide satisfaction of their needs for denying death and finitude for generations to come (LaMothe 1996, 196).

This story is replicated in all conflicts that seek absolute rather than joint solutions. Cumulative violations lead people to cut each other off if they cannot cut each other down. As Volf observes, "Too much injustice was done for us to be friends; too much blood was shed for us to live together" are the words that echo all too often in regions wrecked with conflict. A clear line will separate "them" from "us." They will remain "they" and we will remain "we," and we will never include "them" when we speak of "us." Such "clean" identities, living at safe distances from one another, may be all that is possible or even desirable in some cases, at certain junctures of people's mutual history. But a parting of the ways is clearly not yet peace. Much more than just the absence of hostility sustained by the absence of contact, *peace is communion between former enemies* (Volf 1996a, 126).

"We have just enough religion to make us hate," Swift once wrote, "but not enough to make us love one another." The danger of claiming ownership of the absolute is that it authorizes absolute judgments followed by absolute actions, as religion so frequently does, when in reality the heart of all religion is found in neighbor love and of all true religion in enemy love.

Chapter Seven

The Ultimate Triumph of Hate: The Horror of the Holocaust

In the beginning there was the holocaust. We must therefore start over again.

—Elie Wiesel

Sure, there are people who have hated each other for centuries. But that one kills people so systematically, with the help of physicians, only because they belong to another race, that is new in the world.
—Brother of Joseph Mengele, chief S.S. Auschwitz doctor

We have been struck with a harsh truth: in Auschwitz, all the Jews were victims, all the killers were Christians.

—Elie Wiesel

Proposition for Chapter 7

Humans are capable of creating principled rationales for any form of hate—a reason for vengeful hate, a mandate for retaliatory hate, a justification for moral hate—with tightly argued ethical arguments. Whole societies may join in carrying out hate programs of gigantic proportions, with gross inhumanity. This inexplicable capacity for collective evil done on the basis of rationales that persuade so-called advanced societies to join in the commission of heinous inhumanity forces us to conclude that any society can induce its citizens to become perpetrators of horror and creators of hell. In the last century, one of the most developed and articulate Western societies—intellectually, scientifically, aesthetically, spiritually—did! By understanding how hate can foment and motivate violence, we can act to reduce it and say with passion, "Never again."

Jedwabne, Poland. In the town center, a commemorative stone marker bears the inscription:

> Place of martyrdom
> of the Jewish people.
> Hitler's Gestapo and gendarmerie
> burned 1,600 people alive,
> July 10, 1941.

The true story is much different. On July 10, just weeks after the Germans took control of the region, the Polish Christian neighbors of the Polish Jews of Jedwabne poured from their homes in and surrounding this small town in east Poland. From nearby villages and the neighboring countryside, they came by foot and by cart bearing knives, axes, clubs studded with nails. With Nazi support, but not Nazi participation, they massacred sixteen hundred Jewish men, women, and children, even babies. Half the town's population died that day.

Neighbors slaughtered neighbors. Families and clans who had lived, traded, played, built this village together for over five hundred years suddenly divided, and Christians became a community of executioners. The victims were Jews they knew well, friends, business associates, fellow citizens. That morning they forced them to pick up the heavy statue of Lenin and carry it to the Jewish cemetery. There they were compelled to dig a giant grave, push the statue in, then all would be murdered and thrown on top of the toppled Soviet leader.

The atrocities multiplied—beards were set on fire, people stripped nude and mocked before their throats were cut. At evening, all who survived were driven into a barn, the doors locked, the whole soaked with petrol then torched. Sixteen hundred people massacred—neighbors who had lived just down the street.

There is a soul-wrenching horror about this terrifying behavior by the peasants of Jedwabne who exploded in the baleful unity of gleeful hatred to murder their Jewish neighbors en masse.

Jan T. Gross has documented this heinous atrocity in the courageous book *Neighbors* (2001). One reviewer summarized its message by saying: "My tale is simple and horrible, it seems to say; listen to it and remember it and pass it along. Hatred like this runs deep in human nature and is ever ready to erupt again. Be warned" (Frank 2001, 4).

To learn what human hate is capable of designing, we need only look at the systematic, state-sponsored incarceration, persecution, and murder of nearly six million Jews by Nazi Germany and its collaborators in captured countries. The "Final Solution" exterminated two-thirds of Europe's Jews, and one-third of the world's Jewish population, including one and one half million Jewish children under the age of fifteen. Only 11 percent of European Jewish children alive in 1939 survived. More than half of those murdered were Polish, where the genocide was 90 percent complete. The Nazis also executed millions of non-Jews: Gypsies (Roma and Sinti), the handicapped, Jehovah's Witnesses, homosexuals, Soviet prisoners of war, and political and religious dissidents (Rittner and Roth 1997, 1).

The holocaust (burnt sacrifice), or to use the more appropriate Hebrew word, Shoah, meaning "catastrophe," is unique among all human horrors in that the methodically precise extermination of a people was a central mission of a nation-state. Historically, philosophically, religiously the event is incomprehensible. "Both thinkable and unavoidable, the Holocaust persists as unthinkable because it was avoidable. It did not have to happen. That recognition leaves humankind, morality, religion, and even God on trial" (Rittner and Roth 1997, 3). We shall never explain it and we shall never cease to wonder how and why the specific genre of hate called anti-Semitism prepared the culture, shaped the public attitudes, empowered the leaders, silenced Christian consciences, filled the death trains, and opened the doors to gas chambers.

Jean-Paul Sartre, in 1946, in "Portrait of the Anti-Semite," described those who hold opinions that attribute misfortunes to and propose discrimination against and expulsion or extermination of the Jews. His portrait, in summary, provides a troubling case study:

A man can be a good father, a good husband, a zealous citizen, a tolerant, cultured, and philanthropic person, and at the same time an anti-Semite. Anti-Semitism is not an idea, it is a passion, a profound sentiment, a bodily repulsion that extends even to hysteria. The predisposition to anti-Semitism attributes a wide range of evils, faults, betrayals, and injustices with no logical or factual basis, purely on the basis of emotional reasoning.

No external factor induces anti-Semitism—it is an attitude totally and freely self-chosen, a passion of hate and anger not provoked by any actual event or act; it precedes any fact that is said to arouse it; it interprets facts in its own way to render them totally offensive.

Since the anti-Semite has *chosen* hatred, we are forced to conclude that hatred is the emotional state that he loves. Choosing hatred is choosing impermeability, the durability of stone, the avoidance of change, the fear of openness and truth. The anti-Semite has chosen hate because he believes hate is a religion that places him on a superior level, above reason, logic, consistency, or belief in words. Yet he is not superior, indeed, he is average, mediocre, even anti-intellectual.

The anti-Semite sees the Jews as entirely bad, unclean, filthy, sullying all they touch, *free to do evil*, not good, indeed, with a *will to evil*. He believes that evil comes to the world through the Jew, that all the evil in the universe is located in him, so he must be ejected. Unmasking, denouncing, raging against evil is the anti-Semite's "job"; his curiosity is sexual, sadistic, bent on death and destruction. This is a sacred struggle requiring sacred destruction.

He is a man who is afraid of himself, of his own conscience, of his freedom and instincts; a murderer who represses his penchant for murder. Anti-Semitism is fear of human fate, thus he seeks to be a pitiless stone, a furious torrent, a devastating lightning: in short, everything but a man (Sartre 1946).

Sartre's portrait is precise enough to identify the individual characteristics, yet broad enough to include Christian and atheist, fervent believer and convinced agnostic. Here lies the most puzzling of riddles. Could a person committed to Christian ethics create a rationale that distorts its central principles and embraces polar opposites? Why has Christianity been the seedbed of the worst elements of anti-Semitism? How does a religion of grace, forgiveness, and enemy love become the mandate for hate?

Christianity and Anti-Semitism

What is it in Christianity that lends itself to or inclines it toward anti-Semitism? Out of those cultures that are most shaped by Christian thought and practice has come the most virulent hatred of a particular people and the most heinous crimes against them. What is its base, its reason for being, its essential cause?

The holocaust reveals something fundamental about the presence of evil in the human condition and about the beliefs that shaped all participants' worldviews and moral values. Particularly, it calls into question the essential framework of Christianity, the religious matrix of all the perpetrators. What is it within Christian thought that permitted—if not contributed to—the indescribable evil of the "final solution"? As surely as the victims are a problem for the Jews, the killers are a problem for the Christians (Wiesel 1978b, 14).

In spite of the obvious facts—Jesus was a Jew, the first Christian believers were Jews, the Jewish Scriptures were the only Christian Bible for the first two centuries—across two millennia individual Christians and groups of Christians have expressed vitriolic hostility toward their parent religion. The twisted charge that the Jews were guilty of killing the Son of God emerged very early, perhaps in retaliation for the humiliation Christians felt at being excluded from Judaism. But why did this resentment grow into hatred, prejudice, anti-Semitism, persecution, pogroms, genocide, and the holocaust? And how can thinkers in any discipline of the social sciences, the arts, philosophy and theology, the economic and political sciences do any constructive work without recognizing this most heinous event, which cuts a critical fault line across all fields? We must view with suspicion and dismay all philosophy, psychology, or theology written after the holocaust that ignores the holocaust. It stands alone in world history and in the history of religions. Anyone who thinks critically since 1945 about humans in all their multifaceted relationships must include the Shoah factor in every proposition about good and evil.

It is much too simplistic to attribute anti-Semitism to any one theological theory, but in six theological concepts we may discover the support for anti-Semitic attitudes.

1. The *sacred executioner* theory—that a substitutionary theology requires a particular people willing to carry out the role of "Christ killers."
2. A *theology of victimization* that alleges the Jews are eternal victims, cursed to be such because of their rejection of the Messiah.
3. *Family rivalry* between two streams in Jewish thought, and sibling hatred that set the younger, Christians, over against the older, Judaism, as competitors for the blessing and birthright as Abraham's children.
4. *Hatred for the lawgiver.* Since the Law was delivered by Moses and Judaism, there is antipathy for those who brought us the law and thus were messengers of prohibitions.
5. *Anti-Semitism* is a distinct and separate counterreligion, a religion of race, blood, and violence that borrows and utilizes Christian images in constructing its own ultimate values.
6. The *"Augustinian principle,"* which supports fatalism, despair, and a passive acquiescence to evil by advocating submission to a divine providence that controls all by a master design.

These six concepts, taken individually or in some combination, offer partial answers to the questions—Why anti-Semitism? How is it possible? How can the teaching of Jesus—of all such teachings of the Jewish tradition—be turned back in hostility against their community of origin? How can the words of the one who spoke the Sermon on the Mount be used to engender the darkest of human hates? What is so fundamentally twisted in the Christian tradition that it has given birth to such rabid racism? This fundamental contradiction, deserving our most critical thought, is central to all theological reflection on hatred. What answer do we offer to the question of Christian culpability for this unthinkable crime against humanity?

The Sacred Executioner Theory

Hyam Maccoby (1986), following Jules Isaac (1971, 233), has argued that the diabolization of the Jews is a fundamental in Christianity that stands uniquely apart from all other world religions. This antipathy did not arise from the Jewish rejection of Jesus, but from the Christian myth of Jews as murderers, or deicides, of Jesus.

Murder alone—even of a great leader such as Socrates—could not produce this depth of loathing. Only the mythologizing of the death of Jesus into a *cosmic sacrifice* (not necessarily a malicious myth, but a disastrous one) and the demonization of Judas, the diabolical betrayer, as the ultimate representative of the Jewish people as a whole, could create this metaphysical fear. The classic myths of sacrifice—even deicide—invariably contain an executioner who is ostracized, Maccoby argues, and the Jews have performed the role of *sacred executioner* for the Christian society. In such myths, the guilt of the people—who wanted the execution—is shifted onto the executioner. The greater the hate, the more the members of the tribe feel absolved for the murder they themselves arranged.

The remedy for this deep hatred of Jews by Christians, he concludes, lies not in excising the passages in the New Testament that are "rejectionist," nor in exhortations to offer respect to Judaism as an independent religion, but in radical criticism of the central Christian myth of redemptive violence through substitutional salvation as a means of shifting guilt and responsibility through hatred (Maccoby in Braham 1986, 1–7).

Maccoby's argument focuses on the central position of violence in Christianity. The murder of the divine redeemer figure who brings universal salvation places blame on the Jews as representatives of cosmic evil, giving them an evil universality as enemies of the universal solution to the human problem. He points to Paul as the primary creator of the form of the Christian myth:

> It was Paul who created the Christian myth by deifying Jesus for the first time, and by regarding his death as a cosmic sacrifice in which the powers of evil sought to overwhelm the power of good, but, against their will, only succeeded in bringing about a salvific event. . . . [T]he Jews are the unwitting agents of salvation, whose malice in bringing about the death of Jesus is turned to good because this is the very thing needed for the salvation of sinful mankind . . . so incidentally creating cosmic villains, the Jews, too, while retaining the historical salvation-scheme of Judaism. (Maccoby 1986, 9)

Paul's work was a political stroke of genius. It diverted Christianity from being in conflict with Rome. By depoliticizing the historical Jesus, divesting him of all political attributes as a Jew of his period, Paul turns him into a visitor from outer space with a purely spiritual mission. Rome, no longer the enemy, is merely a political entity. But on the spiritual plane, the Jews become the enemy. The Gospels, Maccoby maintains, bring this to full imaginative life, the history of the church elaborates and further demonizes the Jews, excludes them from ordinary social relations, assigns them the morally "dirty" work of the society. Although hated and despised, they become necessary to perform the assigned tasks and to lift the guilt of Christians for their delegated deicide.

Christian responses to Maccoby's challenge argue that the "straight-line method" of historical accounting is not possible in this instance, and that the early Christian controversies with their Jewish spiritual parents must be understood with more sensitivity to positive attachment, appreciation, and indebtedness as well as the separation, disagreement, and conflict between the two groups.

In fact, Paul and all other New Testament authors were and remained Jews, and whatever hostility they expressed toward Jews and Judaism was exclusively religious in character, never ethnic, racist, or nationalist. This distinction, made by Samuel Sandmel, demonstrates that "the nineteenth- and twentieth-century word *anti-Semitism* is a completely inappropriate term when transferred to the first and second Christian centuries." Specifically, early Christian hostility toward Judaic thought and Judaism as a religion were theological and religious in character, not racist or nationalist as was the anti-Semitism of the nineteenth and twentieth centuries (Sandmel 1978, xxi). The polemics in the Gospels and in Paul are not anti-Jewish, he points out accurately, but rather are against rabbinic positions in Judaism, and critique Jewish practices from within the Jewish frame of reference.

Thus a chronological, straight-line argument seeking to establish historical links is not possible. From the first century to the end of the first millennium Jews, although seen as nonbelievers, were respected as fellow religionists "tolerated on humanitarian grounds, and indeed preserved on theological grounds" (Trachtenberg 1943, 164). It was not the Jews but the pagans, who professed no belief, who were considered intolerable and excluded from Christian community.

The Middle Ages created a new conception of the Jew. Demonic stereotypes were formed that, centuries later, Nazi anti-Semitic rhetoric used to bolster its propaganda machine. Thirteenth-century passion plays created myths of redemption in which the Jewish people and their representative, Judas, were assigned both guilt and responsibility for the death of God.

Eugene Fisher also disagrees with Maccoby, specifically in his description and interpretation of "the Christian myth." Deicide, he notes, is not a Christian doctrine. God is not killed on the cross; Jesus as the human-divine union of God become man is executed, but the one God transcends and continues beyond all. The set of beliefs that Maccoby posits were held only by various heresies—Docetics, Gnostics, and Cosmic Dualists—and by certain popular groups such as the passion play celebrants (Fisher in Braham 1986, 23).

However, even if viewed as a commentary on Christianity at its worst, its most perverse, Maccoby's critique is a probing attempt to explain the contradictions of Constantinian Christianity, its compromise with the state to ensure its safety and security, and its strange and utterly inconsistent strain of malignant violence and viciousness toward the Jew. If Christians are to refuse such theories as Maccoby's, then we have a responsibility to come forward with our own repentant recognition of the evil strands within our theology and practice that fostered the unthinkable. Our silence and our denial must be faced:

> To try to use secularization, the Enlightenment, or racism as reasons why Christianity played no role in the development of the holocaust and modern anti-Semitism is, to my mind, impossible. We must face the awful truth that there is a most deadly relationship which cannot be ignored. Intellectual honesty demands no less. (Everett 1986, 33)

A Theology of Victimization

A second theory of explanation—a theology of victimization of the Jewish people—can be set forth more succinctly. This strand of Christian thought taught that the Jews' alleged role in the death of Jesus and their rejection of the claim that he was the Messiah of Israel were acts of such rejection of God that God has rejected them for all time, cursed them as a people:

> The Church of Christ has never lost sight of the thought that the "chosen people" who nailed the redeemer of the world to the cross must bear the curse of its action through the long history of suffering. (Bonhoeffer 1970, 222)

Bonhoeffer's terse summary of the Christian tradition of blaming the Jews, in early writings he later renounced, pinpoints the attitude. Among Christian advocates, the anti-Semitic rationale had many corollary arguments. They are victims of a divine curse. Their land, their temple, their autonomy as a people were forfeited. They are dispersed as eternal victims, in permanent exile, deserving of any suffering. They are enemies of God; in service of the Devil; never to regain their homeland; without power, sovereignty, redemption, place within God's favor, or the Christian world's respect.

After Constantine, Christian laws made Jews outcasts, victims of oppression, subjects of forced baptism, persecuted with threat of and reality of death. No crime was too heinous, no prejudice too horrific, to lay blame at the doorstep of this people in exile from their own land, from their God, from their alleged Savior. The rhetoric of the church included any number of charges: All their suffering was the result of divine wrath and just punishment. All God's promises now belong to the Christian church, all curses to Israel. The New Israel has a God of grace, of love, of exclusive redemption; the Old Israel has only a God of law, vengeance of imperfect primeval darkness. Therefore the new religion of love is entitled to pour out hate on its predecessor.

This ideology of the victimization of a people permeated the context of the holocaust, supported the justifications used by its perpetrator, comforted observers in their passivity, silenced protesters from expressing outrage. This theological tradition, malignant with hate, has occupied an influential place in the body of Christ, as Everett writes:

The theology of victimization of the Jewish people has been employed by Christians to justify their belief that Jews should be victims for nearly two thousand years. But this theology has really been a cancer in the soul of Christianity. It has made a mockery of Christian love. It permitted Christians to ignore the evil consequences of its theological tradition. It compromised the integrity of the Church as a moral agent. It deformed the Christian character. It ultimately involved the Christian community in the attempted genocide of the Jewish people. (Everett 1986, 39)

It is the worst of blasphemies to believe—as Christians have done for two millennia—that in order to love Jesus we must make his people, the children of Abraham, victims deserving of hate, and in Jesus' name hate them. And even more blasphemous is the idea of avenging the death of the crucified One who died speaking words repudiating all vengeance. Honest reflection by Christians cannot minimize or overlook the vengeful attitudes implicit in many theological positions, from principled arguments to popular prejudices, that explain the meaning of the cross in anti-Semitic intimations and innuendoes:

The passionate hatred some Christians display toward the Jews illustrates how deep is the vengeance instinct and how great the desire to find scapegoats among minority peoples. One of the greatest injustices of all time has been the revenge of Christians against the Jews for presumably having killed Jesus. Those identifying themselves as Christians have been the most anti-Jewish in the history of the world. Hitler, for instance, used the passion play of Oberamergau to whip up anti-Jewish feelings in Nazi Germany. (Redekop 1990, 50)

In the name of the same Jesus who suffered capital punishment unjustly, millions have suffered the same capital punishment. The obvious sacrilege of this contradiction is minimized when mentioned, and often largely ignored in the doing of theology or the interpreting of Christian history.

Family Rivalry, Sibling Hatred, Covenant Competition

A third explanation is rooted in the long tradition of brother displacing brother, Cain murdering Abel, family members in rivalry like Jacob and

Esau, Joseph and his brothers. It concludes that family rivalry and sibling hatred offer an explanation for the origin of a hostility that did not die. "As we all know," Rudin observes, "family rivalries are usually among the most intense and the most bitter" (Rudin 1969, 49).

Jesus was a Jew; the audiences that heard his preaching were Jews; the twelve apostles were Jews; early Christians were Jews. Yet the sibling rivalry between Christianity and its older brother, Judaism, which erupted by the end of the second century, had reached a virulent stage by the late fourth century in the teaching of John Chrysostom. In 387, Chrysostom preached from the pulpit of Antioch to a congregation of Gentiles become Christian.

> I hate the Jews. . . . I hate the synagogue. . . . It is the duty of all Christians to hate the Jews. . . . None of the Jews, not one of them is a worshipper of God. . . . Since they have disowned the father, crucified the Son and rejected the Spirit's help, who would dare to assert that the synagogue is not a home of demons. God is not worshipped there. It is simply a house of idolatry . . . worth no more than a theatre . . . it is a place of prostitution. It is a den of thieves and a hiding place of wild animals . . . not simply animals but of impure beasts. . . . God has abandoned them. What hope of salvation have they left? . . . The Jews live for their bellies, they crave for the goods of this world. In shamelessness and greed they surpass even pigs and goats. . . . [Y]ou should turn away from them as from a pest and a plague of the human race. (Chrysostom 1857, 843)

By the thirteenth century, Christians unanimously called Judaism a religion of "error" and ruled that "error has no rights." The "teaching of contempt" continued to escalate in the bitter rivalry that appears in the writings of the Reformation—Martin Luther is an unfortunate example— and spread throughout Europe in popular prejudices, social discrimination, and the repeated violence of pogroms, and reached its apogee in the holocaust.

The holocaust is the ultimate denial of God's covenant relationship with Israel, the "chosen people." The special character of that unique bond evokes the most primal sibling rivalry between Christians and their sister faith, Judaism. Like Jacob coveting Esau's possession of the birthright, Christians have sought to supplant their predecessors, claim their heritage, usurp their position in the covenants of Noah, Abraham, and Sinai, by occupying Jeremiah's promised new covenant (Jer. 31:31–34).

As Christianity became the metastory of Western civilizations it often denied the central formative role of Judaism, and appropriated it in the creation of its own traditions. But this plagiarism was stymied by the continued stubborn survival of Judaism in its ethnic and religious descendants: (1) The Jew represents the promise of an eternal covenant, or birthright, between God and Israel. The presence of the Jew reminds all other believers that the covenant still stands, that covenant partners are celebrating Sabbath and Passover as a sign and symbol. They are—and always will be—reminders of God's special chosen people. (2) The belief that God is sovereign, that providence is not a fiction, and that the Eternal has entered human affairs hangs on the preservation of the Jew and the persistence of the Jewish community. (3) So if we destroy the Jew and eradicate the community, then either (a) we have stolen the birthright and established the new kingdom of God (or the Third Reich, which is a counterdeity), or (b) we have demonstrated that there is no God, no providence, no special chosen people, no continuing covenant birthright. We are God; we create the kingdom; we decide who shall live and who shall die.

Ironically, Jewish and Christian faith share a common heritage, scriptural text, common God, and when rightly understood, a largely common belief in justification by faith. The hatred by Christian of Jew is rendered more intense by the similarities between the two. Freud called the hatred of neighbor, colleague, or sibling "the narcissism of minor differences." Human beings express their most virulent hatred toward those who are only slightly different, not vastly opposed, to themselves. These minor differences pose a greater psychological threat to one's core sense of self than do great contrasts, and the most heinous acts of aggression are done against those most near. The slight difference—which becomes the element of threat to one's core identity—can provide an essential hatred that can be further fanned with paranoid fears, projected evil, political conspiracy theories, and clean/unclean taboos to create the tidal wave of categorical hatred capable of engendering genocide.

The Jews of Germany identified more closely with being German, with the culture of German identity, than did non-Jewish Germans, whose hatred then denied the identity of those Jews who had become the leading citizens in the arts, education, philosophy, and political thought. Corroborating evidence of such hatred of the neighbor whose slight difference is visible, we might note in the fratricidal conflicts of Bosnia, Serbia, Albania, and other Eastern European countries; of Irish Catholics and Protestants; of the Hutus and Tutsis in Rwanda; of the intertribal hostilities of Sri Lanka, Cambodia, and Afghanistan—all similarly reveal this discharging of hatred with a narcissistic rage over minor differences.

Hatred and the Law

The fourth argument is that the hatred of the Jews is metaphysical, an antinomian *hatred of the imposition of the law*. The Talmud itself considers this question, and asks, "Why is the mountain on which the Torah was given to our master Moses called Sinai? Because that is where the word *sinah* [hatred] comes from." Hatred of the Jews was born with the Torah, and the Torah predates Christianity. There was anti-Semitism among the Romans, who were pagans; they were not Christians, yet they hated the Jews. It cannot be said, therefore, that Christianity alone spawned the hatred of the Jews that we see throughout history. There would have been anti-Semitism even without Christianity, although Christianity certainly contributed to its spread throughout the world (Wiesel 1990, 38).

This hatred is fed by feelings of inferiority, guilt, imperfection, and inadequacy that are awakened by the Torah. The demands of the law stir up the dark resistances of the unconscious, the rebellious depths of the soul. In his analysis of anti-Semitism, which he calls Jew-hatred, George Steiner writes: "Nothing is more cruel than the blackmail of perfection. We come to hate, to fear most those who demand of us a self-transcendence, a surpassing of our natural and common limits of being" (Steiner 1988, 164).

In Wiesel's *Beggar in Jerusalem*, Kalman the Kabbalist says: "The Jews are God's memory and the heart of mankind. We do not always know this, but the others do, and that is why they treat us with suspicion and cruelty. Memory frightens them. Through us they are linked to the beginning and the end. By eliminating us they hope to gain immortality" (Wiesel 1970a, 137).

Rather than continue to examine ourselves in the light of the law—an ideal of morality—and fall short, we quickly reverse the process to compare ourselves with the ultimate evil. The polar swing of hatred relieves self-critique by substituting self-righteous judgment of those who shame us or those we find delight in shaming.

The dehumanization of Jews into scapegoats is the reverse side of the coin whose face is the deification of the Nazi leader. The representative of the "good" is turned into a virtual god, while those labeled "evil" are vermin worthy of extermination. One pole of a magnetic field cannot exist without its reverse; the "good polarity" of idealization creates the negative polarity of denigration (Dicks 1972, 247). And naming the negative pole allows the namer to claim the moral high ground. The evil of the others, once judged, certifies our righteousness; if they are evil, we must be good—one implies the other. If we can locate all evil in one place, our own address is the home of purity, and so:

The evil of the Nazis justifies our carpet bombing of Dresden.

The Soviet downing of KAL 007 over Sakhalin Island in 1983 revealed their evil and allowed us, outraged, to feel virtuous vis-à-vis "the evil empire."

Stalin's heinous atrocities proved the Soviets to be "monsters," as Reagan frequently named them, while we are "possessors of more godly values."

The suicidal/homicidal terrorism that brought down the New York World Trade Towers justifies our war targeting a people rather than a police action against perpetrators.

The apartheid policies of South Africa during much of the twentieth century provided the opportunity for many other nations, by fingering another's flagrant racism, to overlook their own.

The Holocaust as Religion

The holocaust was a religious event, produced by religious values, some have argued in an attempt to find something at least fragmentarily understandable in evil beyond understanding.

The holocaust religion, they say, was founded on race and blood as ultimate values. It placed idealistic, event-transcendent values above the worth of human beings and the dignity of living peoples. It espoused religious values with total commitment to absolute ends. It carried these values to a consistently applied conclusion. Persons had no significance if they were outside the transcendent categories of this faith system. For Hitler, religion was not an issue of belief, but a matter of being. If one was "Aryan," one was elect, redeemed, within the circle of salvation; if one was Jewish, one's essence was unredeemable, one's existence denied, one's extinction necessary in racial extermination (Brockway 1982, 56).

The humanitarian and humanistic values central to the teaching of Jesus are based on faith that constantly challenges human structures, systems, and categories. These latter are inherently foreign to religion, as both Barth and Bonhoeffer have argued. The faith that motivated Jesus made persons more important than abstractions, people more precious than religious boundaries. He modeled the love of God which is present only in those who love as God loves, love all persons without preference to age, belief, color, gender, or nation. Living by such values of faith in a diverse, overpopulated, resource-deficient, shrinking world is virtually impossible, but the alternative is unthinkable. Yet most of the world's religions provide criteria to justify who is privileged and why, who will prosper, and who wills it. As Brockway argues, however,

> What the holocaust should have taught us is that religion, no matter what its form, leads to hatred, destruction of people (who are individuals with their own hopes and dreams and daily lives), and governmental forms that institutionalize that hatred and destruction. (Brockway 1982, 60)

The holocaust requires of us not just a hermeneutics of retrieval, which interprets the past to find in tradition the revelation that illuminates the now; it requires of us a hermeneutics of suspicion, which calls into question any easy and easily sentimental notions of God as a God of love. It requires us to retrieve the negative theologies of Job, Lamentations, Amos, and Isaiah as well as the negative elements in the classical theologies of Irenaeus, Augustine, Aquinas, Luther, Calvin, Hans Denk, Barth, Bonhoeffer. With Bonhoeffer we may come to believe that "only a suffering God can help us now," with Soelle we may "view with suspicion all theology that is pre-pain." With David Tracy, we must hear in the voices of the sufferers (the unspeakable suffering of the six million) the voice of the suffering of God:

> For all those who hear that voice—the voice of our suffering betrayed God (betrayed by us) and the voice of God's suffering betrayed people (betrayed by us)—that voice can become the bond that unites us all in calling out together, with them and with our God, "Never again!" (Tracy 1982, 106)

The Augustinian Principle: Fatalism and Despair about Evil

Friedrich Heer argued that anti-Semitism is the product of a long-standing attitude which he calls the "Augustinian principle." This vision sees the world as essential sin, resulting in fatalism and despair about its possibilities:

> There is a straight line from the church's failure to notice Hitler's attempt at a "Final Solution" of the Jewish Problem to her failure to

notice today's and tomorrow's endeavors to bring about a "Final Solution" of the human problem. The murder of millions of Jews during the Hitler era anticipated the murder of millions and perhaps hundreds of millions of human beings who would die if the great war returned—a war that could only end in mass murder and genocide. (Heer 1971, 29)

The core Christian belief in essential evil, he says, desensitized the institutional church to the encroaching decay of civility, the approaching decadence of anti-Semitism, the erupting necrophilia of the holocaust. "Evil we have with us always," the churches moralized, and thereby rationalized the atrocity into tolerable eccentricity. The identical blindness afflicts us in our justifications of nuclear preparedness, our equivocations that create just war theories, our anticreationism, which permits and promotes the despoiling of the environment in global suicide.

This centuries-old process of psychological self/world negation is now potentially cataclysmic global suicide. Heer's response is to call for a relinquishment of the Augustinian principle and a return to Christ's own piety, which was rooted in the earliest strands of Jewish thought—the worth of persons and reverence for creation. His goal is for followers of Jesus to seek to believe what Jesus believed, not believe in the Jesus of tradition, who has come to be whatever the tradition wants and needs in a leader or divine exemplar.

The Myth of the Devil-Jew

German anti-Semitism was grounded in the myth of the Devil-Jew. This pervasive myth offers a seventh explanation of anti-Semitism. The omnipresence of this myth in German literature, across the centuries, and most explicitly during the nineteenth and twentieth centuries, reveals a durable prejudicial stream of hatred that influenced the attitudes of people both within and without the churches. The myth explicitly, during World War II, sought to make the Jews bear responsibility for the wars of 1870, 1914, and 1939.

Julius Streicher, the inspirator of racist theory, offered three maxims in his weekly *Sturmer*: (1) The Jews are the cause of war. (2) To fight a Jew is to fight the Devil. (3) The Jews are our calamity. Paradoxically, the three basic accusations the wider world directed at Hitler match these unequivocally: He caused World War II; he was the devil incarnate; he was the calamity of Europe. In actuality, Hitler was claiming a negative, destructive, identity, but seeking to proclaim it a positive and constructive destiny. To accomplish this, he chose innocent victims, demonized them as the enemy, and made them the recipients of all his projections. The Nazis, by joining him in this process of projecting their own evil— the dark shadow of themselves—onto the Jews, sought to empty themselves of all disorder, set all things in order (Fornari 1975, 75).

How could the culture that produced Luther and Kant have been so swept away by this demonization and elimination of a people? How could the nation that gave birth to Beethoven and Barth have bought wholesale into Hitler? How could the land that gave us Goethe and Nietzsche have created Nazism?

In answer, the work of Robert Jay Lifton is particularly illuminating. Post–World War I Germany, he argues, suffered a historical "sickness unto death"—a category from Kierkegaard, a total breakdown of cultural symbols and sources of meaning. The nation sank into a depression that can best be characterized as a "collective sense of immersion in death, bodily and spiritually," Lifton says, concluding that a national malaise "could not have been greater than that experienced in Germany after the First World War" (Lifton 1986, 468). The nineteenth century had witnessed a national quest for German immortality, for the cultural transcendence of internal differences in new self-definition as a people of artistic and intellectual destiny to lead the world, and an inclusive project of seeing ultimate meaning in their nation and culture's superior place in the history of mankind.

All this had been dashed by the disillusionment of the First World War, resulting in a profound experience of "failed regeneration." "With the defeat, adult Germans were to become the most devastated survivors: of the killing and dying on an unprecedented scale, and of the equally traumatic death of national and social visions, of meaning itself" (Lifton 1986, 469). What they longed for was "the vision of a total cure, the promise of shared vitality and renewed confidence in collective immortality. . . . Hitler provided that vision not only of a national rebirth, but also of recuperation and regeneration of German community life. He promised a glorious future of vitality and national immortality" (Lifton 1986, 471).

Hitler, as agent of transcendence, as guarantor of the endless life of the people—the fatherland, *das Volk*—offered the message of a savior demanding ultimate loyalty and willing sacrifice. He could call forth "an ecstatic state of feeling outside oneself and swept up by a larger force that could connect or reconnect one with ultimate spiritual principles" (Lifton 1986, 474).

Ironically, our recognition of this inversion holds up a mirror that reveals our own shadow. Hitler the devil is the projected image of the bad parts of every person, his system of evil, of every human system. Our tendency to eject the cause of World War II and project it totally on Hitler inevitably raises the question of our own projection of our bad parts and our selective perception in seeing the ultimate evil of which humanity is capable as supremely resident *only* in him.

The Mystery of Doubling

All studies agree that Nazi commanders of concentration camps were not sociopaths, but administrators interested in doing an efficient job who became desensitized to heinous suffering (Dicks 1972; Gilbert 1950). How did they do this as "normal" human public servants? By what mental process could they come to view neighbor and colleague Jews as their mortal enemies? By what psychological maneuver could they justify their systematic mass killing? Those who carried out the holocaust were humans, not devils, trusted physicians, not obsessed exterminators. These gifted doctors went home at night to greet their wives and play with their children. We are not able to understand the double lives of these men who carried out unspeakable hate crimes by day and lived normal, routine loving relationships by night.

Psychiatrist Robert Jay Lifton has called this phenomenon "doubling," and explained it by means of five characteristics: (1) In doubling, two selves function autonomously, yet are connected. The doctor with two selves needed the Auschwitz self in order to function psychologically in an environment completely contrary to his previous moral standards; and he needed his prior self to sustain an identity as a humane physician and a loving father and husband. (2) The Auschwitz self would work efficiently in the concentration camp role, connect effectively with the entire prison environment, making contact as a fully functioning physician in an all-inclusive way. (3) But the Auschwitz self, as a means of psychological survival in this death-dealing and death-dominated context, coped with this terrifying dilemma by creating a "killing self" that carried out orders in order for him and his family to survive. (4) Doubling offered relief from guilt to the first self by assigning the blame to the second self that performed the dirty work. (5) Doubling thus provided two levels of experience, a *conscious level* of coping with and serving in two worlds of incompatible experience and an *unconscious level* of internal disconnection from responsibility that could allow a conscientious physician to embrace evil without the restraints of conscience. The doubling ran deep into the personality—its depth into the psychological makeup of the doctors is stunning, its power to eliminate conscience in the "normal" self and turn it into conscientiousness in the Auschwitz self was a kind of transfer of conscience between selves. The conscience of the human self was usurped by the conscience of the prison self, which had its own criteria for what is good—duty, loyalty to the group, improving camp conditions, dedication to the Nazi project. "Conscience gave way to conscientiousness; and saving lives became associated with killing" (Lifton 1986, 401).

The elimination of moral conscience and its transfer to obedient system conscience are illustrated by the case history of Dr. Edward Wirths, chief of medical staff at Auschwitz (1933–44). As a private physician, Wirths was sympathetic with Jewish patients, clandestinely treating them during early Nazi persecutions. When ordered to Auschwitz, to stop the persistent typhus epidemics, he established rigid standards of cleanliness, ironically by introducing zyclon-B gas to disinfect barracks. Later it would be used to kill millions as a means of "purifying the culture." Wirths took stands against camp brutality and random acts of abusiveness, and, deeply disturbed by thousands of dead bodies and revolted by all he encountered, he wrote his brother, Helmut: "I have seen such terrible things, things unimaginable, I can never go home again and look in the eyes of my children" (Lifton 1986, 400).

Wirths opposed the military selection-for-execution process, contemplated leaving Auschwitz, but finally acquiesced to his father's command, "There is no place in the whole world where you can do as much good as in Auschwitz. Endure." At the outset, hoping to do good, Wirths initiated a new physician-controlled selection process, which determined who would work, who would die, to save those fit for work from the gas chambers. Believing he could improve the evil project by modifying its process, Wirths adjusted his conscience to rationalize participation.

"Once more conscience gave way to conscientiousness; and saving lives became associated with killing," says Lifton. When a colleague selected two thousand Jewish subjects for the gas chamber, Wirths conspired with sympathetic doctors to arrange for them to remain alive, then a few days later he selected two thousand people from a subcamp to complete the quota. Thus he could resist with one self in front of good friends and comply in private to legitimize his need to follow orders. In his apologia he would later claim he was doing God's work. "I had 'a sign from above [that] I should and must fight on' in preserving Jews." He concluded in exonerating himself, "It probably can be credited to me that Jews are alive in Europe at all today" (Lifton 1986, 401). He wrote to his wife on January 13, 1945, when being criticized by Gestapo chief Maximilian Grabner, "I can say that I have always done my duty and have never done anything contrary to what was expected of me."

When Wirths surrendered, the British intelligence officer processing him clasped his hand and then said, "Now I've shaken hands with the man who . . . bears responsibility for the death of four million human beings." Wirths's Auschwitz self was finally forced to confront his real self; there was no mercy between the doubled selves. That night one self pronounced sentence on the other; Wirths hung himself. Cut down, he died several days later (Lifton 1986, 384).

The doubling allowed one part of the self to disavow another part, then when forced to confront each other, allowed the prior part to execute the criminal self. One awareness had been disconnected from another awareness, one reality and its meanings dissociated from another reality and its meaning. This division of awareness and meaning allowed the doctor to select with painstaking attention which person would die, but the meaning was denied. It was not interpreted as killing, not seen as murder. Lifton named this inner process "psychic numbing."

Psychic numbing is a "general category of diminished capacity of inclination to feel." It includes derealization (divesting oneself from the actuality of what one is a part of, not experiencing it as real) and disavowal (the rejection of what one actually perceives and its meaning) in "an interruption in psychic action—in the continuous creation and recreation of images and forms that constitutes the symbolization or 'formative process' characteristic of mental life" (Lifton 1986, 442).

In contrast to what it saw as "weak" Freudian psychoanalysis, based on the principle of empathy, German psychiatry espoused "the absence of empathy" in treating patients, and this further contributed to the blunting of awareness, individual psychic numbing, and group numbing.

The Nazis crafted language to alter reality. Selecting prisoners for extermination became "ramp duty" or "medical ramp duty" or "prisoners presenting themselves to the doctor." *Killing* was never used. (In tens of thousands of Nazi documents it occurs only once, in reference to an edict not about humans but dogs.) Instead of "killing," *transfer, evacuation, resettlement,* or "the final solution of the Jewish question" were commonly used.

Lifton interviewed twenty-nine surviving Nazi doctors over a two-year period (1978–1980), and in response to questions of moral reflection he reports "none of them—not a single former Nazi doctor I spoke to—

arrived at a clear ethical evaluation of what he had done and what he had been part of" (Lifton 1986, 8). Josef Mengele, chief medical officer of Auschwitz, illustrates the radical doubling at its worst. A fellow doctor said of his behavior:

> He was capable of being so kind to the children, to have them become fond of him, to bring them sugar, to think of small details in their daily lives, and to do things we would genuinely admire. . . . And then, next to that . . . the crematoria smoke, and these children, tomorrow or in a half-hour, he is going to send them there. Well, that is where the anomaly lay. (Lifton 1986, 337)

Mengele, more than any other of the physicians, showed traits of classical antisocial personality disorder. In contrast to those who show an adaptation to the atrocity situation, he reveals more of a lifelong pattern, with extraordinary numbing, an absence of emotional ties in personal life, total lack of feelings for victims, no signs of any enjoyment, the inability to make any sustained eye contact, tendency to sadism, pretensions of omnipotence, instant "shifts from being attentive and jovial, and then within a fraction of a second, cynical and brutal" (Lifton 1986, 376).

For example, Mengele debated the diagnosis of two eight-year-old Gypsy boys who were part of his research on twins. The two were favorites of all the doctors, including Mengele. The dispute was over distinctive joint symptoms, which Mengele linked to tuberculosis; the others argued other causes. Mengele excused himself from the discussion, then returned in an hour reporting, "You are right, there was nothing." Then, after a long silence, he said, "Yes, I dissected them." While they held their case conference, he shot the two favorite boys in the neck, and examined them organ by organ while still warm (Lifton 1986, 351).

An Irresolvable Dilemma: Christian Conspiracy, Complicity, Culpability

The dilemma remains—stupefying, scandalizing, constantly haunting any thinking and feeling person. How can good people ferment hate into horror? How can hate triumph so utterly? How are humans capable of such evil? And above all, how can a world shaped by Christianity offer up its parent faith, Judaism, on the sacrificial altar—the meaning of the word "holocaust"? Recall what Judaism and Christianity share in common:

- Both see the human as created in the image of God.
- Both affirm the preciousness of the person.
- Both proclaim a God who cares for all humankind.
- Both are religions of redemption.
- Both are covenantal religions accountable to God.
- Both are predicated on divine initiative in redemptive acts.
- Both call forth committed human responses in ethical living.
- Both require participants to live out their salvation in love of neighbor and enemy.
- Both believe justice, mercy, and humility are the evidence of religious sincerity.

By what stretch of imagination could one envision either of these groups offering any part of any rationale, contributing to any cultural biases, closing its eyes to any act of complicity? Yet the holocaust is a total assault on all of the above statements. It is, Irving Greenberg argues, "a counter-testimony which undercuts the persuasiveness of both religions and contradicts the hope which they offer. . . . God's nonintervention during the Holocaust suggests the absence of a covenantal partner or a breakdown of covenantal responsibility. The fact that Christian Anti-Semitism is implicated in furnishing ground for the hatred which was exploited to set up the Jews for victimization; the apathy or hostility of Christians during the Holocaust; the participation by people who considered themselves Christians or, at least, God-believers, in the mass murder process all strike further at religion's claims" (Greenberg 1982, 71).

If either Judaism or Christianity were to testify to its traditional beliefs as though the holocaust did not happen, its credibility would be destroyed. Judaism cannot do this, but Christianity can and has largely returned to business as usual. The resulting religion is an empty sound, like the gong of a cymbal, a Pollyanna illusion possible only as believers block out the realities of history. As Greenberg challenges:

> It is clear that Christianity will not be able to overcome its legacy of guilt for the Holocaust without a major purging of its sources of Jew hatred. This will take head-on confrontation with the Gospels' and church fathers' tradition of supersessionism [Christianity usurping the story and text of Judaism as their rightful property] and anti-Semitism. (Greenberg 1982, 85)

Every aspect of one's cultural, religious, or theological tradition that overtly or covertly degrades others or nurtures hatred must be rigorously challenged. If this requires that we challenge even the commandments of God if they are used to support human genocide or the exercise of violence, or detract from our capacity to resist it, even these words of God must be challenged as a witness for the God who is fully revealed in the Suffering Servant, in the One on the cross. Acquiescence to degradation of human life, to violence and destruction, is witness against God.

"The 'final solution' utilized the industrial processes and the managerial techniques which enabled European civilization to dominate the world" (Feingold 1981, 5). The massive technology of transportation and production made the continuing mass murder possible with detached efficiency. Greenberg is insightful here:

> In past persecutions such as the crusades, the explosion of *religious hatred* which led to killings soon burned itself out once it was blooded. Eichmann and the other administrators of the final solution prided themselves on not *hating* Jews. The S.S. even set up courts officially for the purpose of punishing corruption or excessive abuse on the part of the S.S. camps administrators. While in fact an enormous amount of abuse went unpunished, the underlying idea was that this was an idealistic process, administered with integrity, and not an outburst of *hate*. The sense that this was a job enabled the bureaucrats to do their work with zeal and efficiency and with self-image intact. "To have stuck this out and . . . to have kept our integrity," said Himmler, is a "page of glory" in S.S. annals. (Greenberg 1982, 68)

Naming the evil done, ending the denial of hatred, owning responsibility, learning from the truth revealed are the real signs of integrity. Richard Freiherr von Weizsäcker, then president of the Federal Republic of Germany, in a speech to the Bundestag, May 8, 1985, gave an unflinching and excuse-free enumeration of the crimes of the Nazis and the association of millions of German people in the years 1933–1945. He concluded a litany of atrocities by owning the complicity and knowledge of Germans high and low.

> To implement his unfathomable hatred of these our fellow men, . . . Hitler had never kept it from the public, but rather made the entire nation the tool of this hatred. . . . [E]very German could witness what Jewish fellow citizens had to suffer, from cold indifference through veiled intolerance to open hatred. Who would remain innocent after

the burning of the synagogues, the looting, the stigmatizing with the Jewish star, the withdrawal of rights, the unceasing violations of human worth? Whoever opened his eyes and ears, whoever wanted to inform himself, could not escape knowing that deportation trains were rolling. (Shriver 1995, 109–10)

Whoever closes his eyes to the past becomes blind to the present. Whoever does not wish to remember inhumanity becomes susceptible to the dangers of new infection. Neither Catholic nor Reformed theology challenged conforming personalities to refuse to carry out orders for the sweeping extermination of a people. In a time when the absolute worthlessness of Jewish life is shown by the 1944 administrative decision to burn children alive to save one-half of a cent's worth of gas, why were Christians silent? Since such events, any glib speech about God and divine concern is unforgivable. Since such a world existed, theological reflection must be done with delicacy or restraint. Since such complicity, the Christian heritage and traditions of the perpetrators cannot be lightly dismissed. Remember that Heinrich Himmler insisted that all S.S. men believe in God, arguing that "otherwise they would be no different from the atheistic Marxists" (Greenberg 1982, 76). And the church did nothing about this. Wiesel asks:

> How is one to explain that neither Hitler nor Himmler was ever excommunicated by the church? That Pius XII never thought it necessary, not to say indispensable, to condemn Auschwitz and Treblinka? That among the S.S. a large portion were believers who remained faithful to their Christian ties to the end? That there were killers who went to confession between massacres? And that they all came from Christian families and had received a Christian education? (Wiesel 1978b, 13)

How is one to explain it? How indeed, except by full confession that the hate which Christianity denied, yet transmitted generation to generation, ultimately resulted in the destruction of a people. In killing Jews, the holocaust destroyed more than Jews. When the Western Christian tradition goes amok and denies and destroys the Jewish people, it denies and destroys the Christ. In response to a student's question in an Oregon classroom, Elie Wiesel said:

"I am convinced that had Jesus Christ lived during the holocaust, he would not have done anything about it because he would have been a victim. And who knows? I wonder whether deep down the killers did not try to kill Jesus by killing the Jews" (Abrahamson, 1985).

Poet Uri-Zvi Grinberg, in a piece titled "They have killed their God?" describes the appearance of Jesus in a small place somewhere in Eastern Europe. He goes about the village looking for his brothers and sisters— for his people. Finding none, he finally asks a passerby:

> "Where are the Jews?"—"Killed" says the passerby—"All of them?"—"All of them"—"And their homes?"—"Demolished"— "Their synagogues?"—"Burned"—"Their sages?"—"Dead"— "Their students?"—"Dead too"—"And their children? What about their children? Dead too?"—"All of them. They are all dead." And Jesus begins to weep over the slaughter of his people. He weeps so hard that people turn around to look at him, and suddenly one peasant exclaims, "Hey! Look at that! Here is another Jew. How did he stay alive?" And the peasants throw themselves on Jesus and kill him too, *killing their God*, thinking they are killing just another Jew. (Wiesel 1978b, 183)

If we are to enter this story with any possible fellow feeling, we must realize that our most earnest attempts to experience empathy with the immeasurable suffering and horror of the holocaust victims or survivors requires not words, but silence. Compassion results in our being struck dumb. Simon Wiesenthal, in his book *The Sunflower*, opened his soul and let us feel the awful decision of forgiving or not forgiving evil. He was asked to do what seems the right thing to do—forgive a dying man—but in the circumstance he could not. While imprisoned in a Nazi concentration camp, Simon was summoned one day from his work detail to the bedside of a dying officer of the S.S. Haunted by the heinous crimes in which he had participated, the officer wanted to confess to—and obtain absolution from—a Jew, any Jew. Faced with the choice between compassion and integrity, between mercy and justice, Wiesenthal said nothing. He silently turned away. That night he searched his soul before his cellmates, and they assured him he had done the right thing. But years after the war had ended, he continued to review his action. Had he indeed done the right thing? In his book, fifty-three thinkers reply, people from many professions, religions, cultures, and tragic experiences. Some argue for a generosity of spirit that forgives unconditionally, others for a more costly grace, and still others see the impossibility of Wiesenthal's situation. Who is he to speak in behalf of all those who suffered and died at this man's hands? By what moral right is he their voice? Could only the victims speak the word of forgiveness? He has silenced their voices forever. As I read this troubling book, I wonder, "If the dying man is repentant, and repentance is prerequisite to forgiveness, why has he not asked the orderlies to carry him the few miles to join the victims in the concentration camp and die in solidarity with those whose forgiveness he seeks?"

The many responses move one deeply, but one of them is particularly appropriate as we end this chapter. It is the soul-searching answer given by Martin Marty, who says: "I hear the question framed like this: 'What would/should a Jew have done?' and 'What does a Christian say?' And in that way of stating it I can only respond with silence. Non-Jews and perhaps especially Christians should not give advice about the holocaust experience to its heirs for the next two thousand years. And then we shall have nothing to say" (Wiesenthal 1997, 210).

If any empathy is possible, it is silent; if any true compassion, it will be mute.

Chapter Eight

The Fear of the Other:
The Faces of the Enemy

I have learned that God is not the enemy of my enemies. God is not even the enemy of God's own enemies.

—Martin Niemoeller

No false prophet can ever conceive of God as being the God also of the enemy.

—J. A. Sanders

If evil shall lead to evil, where shall the chain of evils end?
—Sophocles

Proposition for Chapter 8

Hate needs an enemy. When we meet the enemy, and respond with enmity, we mirror the enemy and in time we become the enemy. Our worst fears of what is *out there,* when we begin to hate are replicated *in here.* The enemy we fear and hate is now within our own souls. The rationales of principled hate that we create to justify our hatred of those who threaten or oppose us block our moving beyond retributive hate, blind us to the possibilities of moral hate. As long as the other is hated as an enemy, there is little likelihood of our experiencing truly just hate.

Ayoung man approaches you on a late evening walk along a deserted street. From a distance, judging from his gait, he appears familiar. A neighbor boy, you assume.

As he passes under the streetlight a half block ahead, you sharpen your gaze. His color differs from yours. He is totally unfamiliar. You straighten your back, seeking to appear taller; square your shoulders to look more fit. Fear flits through your thoughts. The light glints on an earring, a tattoo is visible on his arm. He is carrying something long and round in his hand. You see his eyes, fixed on you, sizing you up. His face, seen more clearly now, is the face of a potential enemy. He is smiling. In threat? A ploy? A precursor to assault? Fear accelerates your heartbeat. A film of sweat shines on your upper lip. You glance both ways seeking support. There is none, you are on your own. Tomorrow's headlines will report . . .

"Good evening, professor," he says warmly. "How fortunate to find you here." He extends the club—a rolled sheaf of paper. "This is the research project I owe you. My extension is until tomorrow, and you asked me to drop it in your mailbox at home. Thank you for giving me the extra week."

As you accept the paper, his name on the cover allows you to greet him personally. The warmth of your response is intensified by the adrenaline pumping through your bloodstream. "Please come along for a cup of coffee and you can tell me a bit about your work," you say. And the two of you—friends—walk down the street, your hand falling on his shoulder.

The transformation from distant neighbor to threatening foe, to presumed enemy, to trusted friend took only seconds—seventy seconds of your life. Positive perceptions of a neutral neighbor to be respected can undergo a rapid transformation to negative judgments about a treacherous enemy to be feared. The familiar sequence is: (1) seeing the other; (2) encountering differences; (3) accessing stereotypes; (4) fearing the stranger; (5) collecting cues of possible threat; (6) anticipating danger; (7) feeling spiraling fear. Anxiety reinforces itself with overlays of dismay, disease, disgust, and anticipatory hate. Fear is compounded by vulnerability, threat is suddenly contaminated by rage at *the enemy*.

Creating the Enemy

Enemy creation, as in this example of an individual encounter with fear, is an immediate, reflexive process that springs one back to childhood fears and reflexive responses. In threat, we regress to earlier chapters of our developmental process—often all the way back to the first: primal trust vs. mistrust. One can recapitulate this primal process in a matter of seconds on a walk in the dark. The earliest task of psychosocial learning is coming to trust our attachment to significant others. The birth of trust is the first sign of positive growth, and the second is the ability to question that trust—that is, to both trust and mistrust. Achieving a balance between trust and mistrust, as Erik Erickson has taught us, creates hope, what he called the first of the virtues, because hope trusts and risks while recognizing its fears. When the balance is not achieved, despair, not hope, results, which is soon followed by its emotional expression, hate.

Enemy hate, whether momentary fear or momentous rage, is connected to this familiar primal agenda—trust, mistrust, and the feeling of hopelessness that we call self-doubt. "I hate being helpless, I hate feeling hopeless, I despise any circumstance or person that triggers these feelings." Self-doubt, that dubious aggregate of anxiety, mistrust, vulnerability, despair, disgust, and self-devaluation, is intolerable. And we can alleviate the intense discomfort of such feelings by turning them outward to any available actor or target—the enemy, the neighbor. The neighbor returns the blessing in what is, in reality, an actual exchange of wastes:

> The enemy system (a shared delusional system) involves a process of two or more enemies dumping their (unconsciousness) wastes in each other's backyards. All we despise in ourselves we attribute to them. And vice versa. Since this process of unconscious projection of the shadow is universal, enemies "need" each other to dispose of their accumulated, disowned, psychological toxins. We form a hate bond, an "adversarial symbiosis," an integrated system that guarantees that neither of us will be faced with our own shadow. (Keen 1986, 21)

If both parties reciprocate with similar enmity, the mutual exchange of personality toxins allows them to dispose their emotional crud on each other's territory. Blind to the projection process, we are equally oblivious to the detritus accumulating in our own backyards. This emotional toxic dump of residual hatred pollutes our attitudes as we get caught up in a continuous exchange of hostilities.

An enemy can be an enemy all alone, but it takes two to get a dance of enmity going. One person unilaterally disliking another is common enough—hate often runs one way—but enmity rapidly becomes bilateral. Mutual unease quickly matures into interacting cycles of fear and avoidance. The move/countermove, plot/counterplot meet similar needs for each. Both sides develop expectations and make predictions, each makes the little detours of evasion. In time, both sets of perceptions take on a remarkable similarity in a dance of prophecy and fulfillment. The two steps are symmetrical: we hate as we are hated, we hate our enemies as we hate ourselves. Our love or hate for our enemy *out there* mirrors love or hate for the dark side *in here*.

"We have met the enemy and he is us," is the celebrated wisdom of

Walt Kelly's little cartoon philosopher, Pogo. But he didn't go far enough. The rest of the truth is, "We have met the enemy and that is *how* we became us." In fear, in conflict, or in hate, as one opposes the enemy, move for move, we mirror each other, we create images of each other, and we become the other. "You always become the thing you fight most," Carl Jung wrote after World War II. "It is a fact that cannot be denied: The wickedness of others becomes our own wickedness because it kindles something evil in our own hearts" (Jung 1954). "Whoever fights monsters should see to it that in the process he does not become a monster," Nietzsche warned. "When you look long into the abyss, the abyss also looks into you" (Nietzsche 1924, 89). The face of the enemy, when stared at long in hate, becomes our own.

The Faces of the Enemy

In *Faces of the Enemy*, Sam Keen (1986, 16–88), using propaganda posters, cartoons, and sketches, named and illustrated thirteen archetypes of the enemy. These apparitions of the hostile imagination reside in the collective unconscious of each modern culture and in each of us. Keen called it a "phenomenology of the hostile imagination," which creates "enemy apparitions."

1. The Enemy as Stranger. By creating the division of us vs. them, insiders vs. outsiders, the tribe vs. the enemy, we create a hostile imagination that assumes what is strange is evil. The unknown is malevolent and must be destroyed.

2. The Enemy as Aggressor. By splitting reality into defensive dualisms—we are innocent, they are guilty; we tell the truth, they lie; we inform, they issue propaganda; we only defend ourselves, they are aggressors—we create a paranoid, self-fulfilling as well as self-protecting prophecy.

3. The Enemy as Faceless. By erasing distinction, we create stereotypes, dehumanize the opponent, objectify those we desire to eliminate—we do not kill a person, but an idea.

4. The Enemy as Enemy of God. By demonizing the other, we no longer face fellow humans. They are devils, demons, dark powers. Warfare is applied theology, a battle between good and evil; it is a just war in which the sacred blood of our heroes is sacrificed to hallow the ground under the feet of the chosen people of God.

5. The Enemy as Barbarian. By portraying the foe as culturally rude, crude, and uncivilized, he may be viewed as an irrational, morally primitive

member of a savage horde. The enemy is brutal, bestial, domineering, immoral, and destructive.

6. The Enemy as Greedy. By defining the enemy as insatiable, with no limits to aggression, no boundaries to stop his advance into others' territory, he may be expected to pursue conquest in order to satisfy an enormous appetite for empire.

7. The Enemy as Criminal. By seeing the enemy as anarchists, terrorists, outlaws, we split our reality cleanly: we are law-abiding, they are outlaws; we honor our treaties, they break them freely when it is their advantage; we abide by the rule of international law, they violate international accords; we stand for justice, they brutalize and tyrannize; we give foreign aid, they export revolution.

8. The Enemy as Torturer. By describing the torturous and atrocious character of the enemy, we build a reputation of sadism, of heinous crime, of unrestrained slaughter and indiscriminate carnage.

9. The Enemy as Rapist. By painting the enemy as a villain with unadulterated lust defiling innocent womanhood, destroying motherhood, molesting, violating, abusing without compunction, we justify any action necessary to stopping the despoiling of women.

10. The Enemy as Beast, Reptile, Insect, Germ. By reducing the enemy to vermin requiring extermination, we are free to escalate our warfare.

11. The Enemy as Death. By visualizing the enemy as a death's-head, we move him beyond being an agent of death to become the Grim Reaper himself.

12. The Enemy as Worthy Opponent. By creating the myth of heroic warfare, this one tradition seeks to dignify rather than diminish the enemy. Combat becomes a ritual of purification, a means by which we progress or evolve toward greatness, a deadly game between worthy opponents.

13. The Enemy as Abstraction. By transforming the enemy into bits of data, the technological approach allows the modern warrior to be coolly detached in calculations of efficiency. The automated battlefield offers the final insult: the other is only a statistic.

As the enemy evolves, it/he/she can become multifaced, serving many of these functions simultaneously as interlocking justification for our own actions. So the enemy wears a different face in response to our differing fears, our multiple reasons for hate. What is true for individual enemies is magnified for the enemy of a group or nation. The enemy group takes on the collective face of its leader, or the representative activist, infamous terrorist, or solitary offender. Each group comes to see the part as the whole, the one as the many, the hated individual as the nation or people. As fear takes control of national consciousness, a paranoid process emerges in the collective mind, and we find ourselves persuaded by feelings that a few months before might have been shaken off easily.

The Paranoid Solution to Inner Conflicts

Paranoia is the curious, ubiquitous mechanism by which we humans disown what is unacceptable in the self and attribute it wrongly to someone else, either in suspicion or in idealization. Idealization, the feeling akin to worship that characterizes "falling in love," is a form of projection that Freud called "the psychosis of normal people." In romantic love we enter a mythological world that suddenly seems transformed by the magical influence of the beloved into a place of sweetness and light inhabited by the kindest, noblest, most caring of all persons. We can also, as Storr has noted, "fall in hate":

> "Falling in love" is generally recognized as being a common state of mind, and, in spite of Freud's diagnostic label, is not considered abnormal. Its opposite, "falling in hate," is not so widely acknowledged. Yet I believe it to be about as common, and a great deal more dangerous. Both states of mind belong to a very early state of emotional development in which "good" and "bad" are widely separated absolutes. (Storr 1972, 87)

"Falling in hate," the rush of negative feelings seizing control of the mind, is a response to an "absolute." All good is split away from the bad, and the bad may now be hated without reservation. Discovering the absolute brings an end to ambiguity and ambivalence. All is now clear; the truth is at last visible, tangible, undeniable. We have seen the enemy's face, and it is all we have always loathed. What relief from self-doubt to find a scapegoat, someone to blame, somebody to bear the weight of our rage, the burden of our bad conscience. Alice Miller writes of a young woman who joined the *Bund Deutscher Maedel*, the female branch of Hitler youth, although she had no previous contact with Jews. She had been raised by strict, controlling parents and felt thwarted in preparing for her desired career: "Much later she told me with what enthusiasm she had read about 'The Crimes of the Jews' in *Mein Kampf* and what a sense of relief it had given her to find out that it was permissible to hate someone so unequivocally" (Miller 1981, 188).

She was actually being exploited by her parents and was also envious of her siblings' careers, but as a well-behaved girl, Miller notes, she was not permitted to have these feelings. With great relief she had come upon a substitute target, a place to displace her rage, which was sanctioned by an authority, celebrated by a group, and therefore self-permissible. She embraced it with passionate commitment.

Paranoia, and the paranoid perspective, is a stage in viewing reality that every human psyche must pass through. We are all born paranoid, and "good enough" parenting has served to help us grow beyond the paranoid position. "Every normal person," Freud writes, "is only normal on the average. His [her] ego approximates to that of the psychotic in some part or other and to a greater or lesser extent" (Freud 1937, 23:235).

In paranoia, a person loses the sense of centeredness and lives before a world of critics or conspirators. The fundamental paranoid view is that the world, and all those in it, are essentially untrustworthy. The overriding concern is control. Who is in control of whom? The aim is to get a grip on that which controls the world, or to lament that we are losing it. The visible evidence of paranoia, its fears and its control obsession, is the creation of impermeable, defensive, and vigilant boundaries. A brief introduction to paranoid process will show the primary role that paranoia fulfills in the processes of *simple, malicious, revengeful,* and *retributive* hate. Its fingerprints become obvious in *principled* hate when the rationales presented reveal the suspicion, fear, and blaming that are at its core.

To establish a baseline for comparison, we need a common understanding of healthy personhood. The person who is emotionally and relationally mature (1) shares the center stage in *mutuality* with another; (2) *attends* to the other's concerns; (3) values self and other with *equality* of worth and significance; (4) maintains *individual* responsibility for the self; (5) experiences a sense of *safety* in the interchanges; (6) extends *trust* to the other as well intentioned; (7) shows *humility* in comparison of self with the other; (8) respects *authority;* 9) is capable of *intimacy* and sexual communion; and (10) lives in a world of shared consensual *reality.* While no one exhibits all these characteristics at all times, in most circumstances it is possible to maintain a balance among them.

In paranoid thought, each of these ten factors becomes, as you will see, increasingly disordered as the thinker moves from mildly to moderately to markedly troubled thinking and feeling.

1. *Mutuality.* A person moves from enjoying shared reciprocal existence to a sense of *centrality,* the feeling of being at the center—"It's usually about me"—of significant other people's interest (mild disorder). As the

sense of centrality grows, the person begins to suspect that others are talking about her (moderate dysfunction) and subsequently becomes convinced that others' words, acts, and thoughts are "unquestionably about *me*" (marked disorder). Expectations become suspicions, which grow into frozen contempt and fear, and hatred follows.

2. *Attending to others' concerns.* From having a warm interest in others the person shifts to an anxious sensitivity to people's responses and the tendency to feel easily slighted or wronged (mild); which extends into feelings of mistreatment, abuse, or persecution (moderate), reified into delusions of persecution (marked disorder). Resentment is the inevitable result.

3. *Equal self-valuation.* Instead of equally valuing self and others, the person's feelings of equality are heightened into superiority, pride, unjustified conceit, and exaggerated self-sufficiency (mild); shift into feelings of being overlooked, ignored, and cheated of deserved recognition or credit (moderate); and form into delusions of grandeur. When others do not recognize this entitlement, they become the enemy.

4. *Healthy individuation.* An exaggerated sense of autonomy takes over, accompanied by a growing concern over losing control (mild); which changes into fears that others are seeking to seize control, exploit, or take advantage (moderate); and then moves into delusions of being controlled or programmed via inserted thoughts, blaming others for one's hateful feelings (marked). The impulse to hate is out of control.

5. *A sense of personal safety.* Instead of feeling safe in interchanges, the person constantly protects the self with habitual guardedness, questioning of others' "real motives" (mild); which deepens into suspiciousness, cynicism, surveillance (moderate); and then settles into fixed delusions about plots, evil intentions, or secret motives (marked). Now the enemy is clear, the threat unequivocal, the need to hate essential.

6. *Trust.* Confidence in others erodes as conspiracy theories gain credence. At first the hunch is that events, circumstances, external factors "conspire" to cause failures (mild); then it intensifies toward blaming others who interfere, thwart, or defeat hopes or plans (moderate); and at last comes "illumination" through a vision of systematized opposition, an incontrovertible insight into a master plot that stymies our best efforts (marked). The enemy is now a part of a larger conspiracy that is acting in hate toward us, therefore justifying our hatred in return.

7. *Humility in relationship* is altered as the person becomes convinced of the righteousness of his or her stance, the divine right to define justice, and begins crusading for causes (mild). This belief grows into vengeful

actions toward specific groups who deserve punishment (moderate); then sanctifies an urge to annihilate the foe and purify society of an evil menace, or an impulse to exclude or kill the enemy (marked). Righteous indignation and moral outrage are followed by holy war.

8. *Authority relationships.* The capacity to work harmoniously with authority figures is lost as resentment develops at working "under" others (mild); which grows into fear of being dominated, controlled, forced to submit (moderate); and compounds into fear of authorities, a resistance to submission in working relationships, an aversion to participation in any organized function (marked). Adversarial reactions to authority build in hostile or hate-shaped ruminations.

9. *Intimacy and sexual union.* The person fears intimacy, maintains distance, is plagued by feelings of sexual inadequacy or vulnerability (mild); which grows into frenetic hypersexual activity or phobic withdrawal from sexual contact (moderate); this freezes into sexual crisis over impulses, attraction, or actions in sexual obsessions (marked). The impulse to hate is fueled by repressed arousal and attraction.

10. *Reality.* Finally, the person leaves the world of shared consensual *reality* and begins taking inner direction from absolute conscience or authority (mild). This mystery develops into illusions of absolute insight, goodness, rightness (moderate); then freezes into auditory hallucinations/voices with commands from absolute authority (marked). The inner turmoil is projected onto others—in the blaming, resenting, suspecting, mistrusting that unite in hate.

These ten tendencies, as they become incrementally disordered, contribute to hate formation. An analysis of any given hate speech, exploration of the motives and explanations for hate acts, inevitably reveals most of these movements from mild to marked distortion. (The hater takes a central special position of superiority to the hated; fears a loss of autonomy; defends his security against a suspected conspiracy; judges it from a righteous position, claiming the authority to speak, act, command; submerges all feelings of inadequacy; and acts in obedience to an inner imperative that justifies ultimate acts against the enemy.)

Collective Fear and Hate

What happens as a person moves from balance to imbalance, from a sense of safety and security with others to defensive fear and paranoid actions, also happens in a paranoid marriage or deeply troubled family, and to whole societies that are swept by corporate fear and hate. Any of us over fifty know what it is like to see the collective shadow of fear and hate fall across their land, or remember what it feels like when consensual paranoia sweeps across a society and we again become, willingly or unwillingly, members of a war-justifying people: An enemy is identified, the group pulls together cohesively in a negative and fearful appraisal. Then we jointly claim the moral high ground in order to certify purity and goodness of our own group and attribute evil and hostility to the enemy. Good and evil get split farther and farther apart. The unacceptable parts of the group's collective soul, which we call the shadow, are projected onto the enemy and seen as independently present in the foe, so that the cruelty, sadism, hostility, and greed that one fears and hates become increasingly visible in the other.

Enemy formation reduces our anxiety. Shame and guilt are decreased as malevolence is transferred to the enemy and denied in the self. Filtering of information eliminates any data that might contradict the fundamental assumptions about the malevolence of the enemy. Real and imaginary dangers become indistinguishable. Now we are ready to fight righteously against the manifest evil. Violence becomes not only justified, but virtuous. We have become our shadow. And we do not see, in the darkness, how it has altered our own face. This regression to paranoia (the natural process of the infant psyche) stimulates fear of our own powerlessness (childhood helplessness) and terror at the enemy's omnipotence (the all-powerful parent), whose malevolence (the bad parent), whose ultimate destructiveness (the neglectful, abandoning giant who could have saved us but would not) leaves us no choice but violence.

As a group or nation allows fear of enemy to turn into hate of enemy, its thinking changes from an open to a closed system. When things go wrong, the enemy is suspected; when tragedy strikes, the enemy is blamed. The center of responsible agency migrates from within the group to be located without in the actions or behavior of the foe. The control of how *we* see, think, decide, or act is now located in how *they* decide and act. As *they* become corrupt and evil in our eyes, *we* find that our motives become more pure and justified. As the system balances itself by transferring *our* dark side to *them*, we become willing to act with impunity in order to maintain not just safety and survival but also prosperity and unlimited access to resources. In a closed system way of thinking, defending our freedom includes protecting our way of life, which entails the freedom to dominate the world market, to consume produce and protean from developing nations for our fast-food industries, and to have unrestricted access to the oil necessary to fuel SUVs and recreational vehicles.

"The paranoid style," Richard Hofstadter has called this collective politics of fear, using the clinical term to describe a political and social mental disorder. It appears in the "use of paranoid modes of expression by more or less normal people . . . as a way of seeing the world in the paranoid style in which the feeling of persecution is central and it is indeed systematized in grandiose theories of conspiracy" (Hofstadter 1966, 4). The vital difference between clinical and social paranoia, "though both tend to be overheated, over-suspicious, over-aggressive, grandiose and apocalyptic in expression," is that the clinical paranoid sees all this evil directed specifically at him or her; the social-political paranoid sees it against a nation:

> The central image of the paranoid vision is a vast and sinister conspiracy, a gigantic and yet subtle machinery of influence set in motion to undermine and destroy a way of life (in fact, there are conspiratorial acts in history, and there is nothing paranoid in taking note of them). The paranoid style, however, sees a "gigantic" conspiracy as *the motive force* in historical events. History is a conspiracy, set in motion by demonic force of almost transcendent power, and what is felt to be needed to defeat it . . . is an all-out crusade. (Hofstadter 1966, 29)

The apocalyptic language of paranoia—dealing with the inevitable death of whole worlds, political orders, systems of values—warns of impending doom, as time is running out. The enemy is clearly identified, sharply defined as a perfect model of malice, sinister, ubiquitous, powerful, cruel, sensual, a free superpower that is an agent of the devil. It is catastrophe feared that elicits paranoid thought, rhetoric, and strategies. The world of power is seen as sinister, malicious, and distortedly omnipotent. Somehow, the paranoid has failed to develop the sense of how things do or ultimately do not happen, which we call basic trust. As Hofstadter concludes: "We are all sufferers from history, but the paranoid is a double sufferer, since he is afflicted not only by the real world, with the rest of us, but by his fantasies as well" (Hofstadter 1966, 40).

Obviously, we have actual enemies—objective foes, not just the mythical figures we create from our communal unconscious or the subjective interlocking enemies reciprocally generated by our fear of each other. But no act of enmity happens outside of the ongoing history of both parties. The creation of the enemy is a cultural mechanism that needs careful scrutiny before we enlist in hating some person or group identified as the foe. Following World War I, columnist-philosopher Walter Lippmann cited a historical story as a parable of enemy creation:

> There is an island in the ocean where, in 1914, a few Englishmen, Frenchmen, and Germans lived. No cable reaches that island, and the British mail steamer comes but once in sixty days. In September it had not yet come, and the islanders were still talking about the latest newspaper, which told about the approaching trial of Madame Caillaux for the shooting of Gaston Calumette. It was, therefore, with more than usual eagerness that the whole colony assembled at the quay on a day in mid-September to hear from the captain what the verdict had been. They learned that for over six weeks now those of them who were English and those of them who were French had been fighting in behalf of the sanctity of treaties against those of them who were Germans. For six strange weeks they had acted as if they were friends, when in fact they were enemies. (Lippmann 1922, 3)

From the moment the news was heard, friends and neighbors looked at one another with new eyes, communication ceased, friendship was severed. The face of the enemy looked back from familiar yet suddenly strange features.

Four years later, on a Thursday morning, the armistice was signed, and at the news people celebrated the end of the war in unutterable relief that the war was over. Yet in the five days that followed until the actual armistice could be fully established, the battle between enemies continued and several thousand young men died on the battlefield fighting a war that was already over. They had not learned that they were no longer enemies. Creating and uncreating enemies in obedience to national policy is a process of adjusting one's loyalties to conform to political reality while denying human realities. Nations that have blended cultures through immigration from many lands and peoples can still create enemies of brother, neighbor, friend by demanding that people feel hostility and direct hate toward former fatherlands, against the mother nation of their birth. We create enemies in two basic ways, no matter the culture: by (1) responding to enemy images and (2) reacting to enemy challenges.

1. *The response to enemy images.* In the normal process of acculturation, the human mind feeds on images—absorbing, digesting, re-creating them as a means of understanding and decision making. The flow of images transmits a stream of cultural views, some of which connect and others that alienate. Enmification is a part of a paranoid system that substitutes

pathological symbols for reality; those named as enemies become images that dehumanize the other side and authorize actions of exclusion (Rieber 1991, 18).

Two examples: As the American frontier moved west, settlers encountered Native Americans who had a thousand-year claim to the land. By redefining the owner as enemy, by characterizing the indigenous person as malevolent, ignorant, inhuman, and savage, the settlers obscured the moral dilemma. The eradication of those now designated as "savages" could proceed unimpeded by the moral reflection reserved for conflicts with European nations.

J. Edgar Hoover was able to flout state boundaries and give federal power to the FBI by creating a "Ten Most Wanted" list of "public enemies," even while his own organization became an enemy of the rights of states and frequently of citizens with whom it disagreed. For three decades, enmification by the Federal Bureau of Investigation facilitated the surveillance and harassment of moral leaders who challenged the unjust status quo of the nation, such as Martin Luther King Jr. and Daniel and Philip Berrigan.

2. Reaction to enemy challenges. When an enemy threatens some value of the group, the enemy can be quickly drawn into a symmetrical position of mirror-image hostility so that we behave as we charge our enemy with behaving. Ronald Reagan's bombing raid on Libya, an act of undeclared war against civilian targets, failed to assassinate his enemy Muammar al-Qaddafi. This act of retaliation for suspected terrorism was a stroke of terrorism that killed two of Qaddafi's children. The American logic expressed was "We are entitled to do to him what we accuse him of doing to us."

When a person or group allows fear to develop into a full paranoid reaction, enmification floods all thoughts and decisions. The individual becomes totally preoccupied with the enemy, and all of life becomes related to the conflict, until the struggle becomes the essential reason for living. The group, in similar fashion, draws together in intense cohesion, mobilizes its energies and resources, and commits itself to action under the inspiration of the common enemy. Rhetoric is radicalized into total antipathy against the foe. In the thirteenth century, for example, Pope Gregory IX preached a crusade, a call to holy war, against the Mongols following the European defeat led by Batu Khan in 1241, saying:

> The Mongol princes, who have dog's heads, eat the bodies of the
> dead leaving only the bones to the vultures. The old and ugly women

are divided into daily portions to feed the common folk, while the pretty young women, having been ravished, have their breasts torn open and are then reserved as tidbits for the grandees. (Leach 1977)

We now know, Edmund Leach comments wryly, that "the dog-headed Mongol cannibals against whom Pope Gregory IX preached his crusade were representatives of a far more sophisticated civilization than anything that existed in Europe at that time." His rhetoric launched a crusade whose continuing legacy contributes to Muslim-Christian relations, to East-West political decisions of the twenty-first century. Radical polarization is not a relic of the years 300 or 1241, it is the tactic of a Nixon, a Johnson, a Reagan, a Bush, as well as a Qaddafi, a Hussein, a Bin Laden. It is the familiar tactic of summoning people to join in absolute thinking and ultimate acts. In radicalizing any conflict, social activist Saul Alinsky contends that "Before people can act an issue must be polarized. People will act when they are convinced that their cause is 100 per cent on the side of the angels and that the opposition are 100 per cent on the side of the devil. . . . Then when the time comes for negotiation it is really only a 10 per cent difference" (Alinsky 1971, 78).

Demonizing one's adversary has great costs, however. When a leader weighs the merits and demerits of a situation, finds it 52 percent positive vs. 48 percent negative, and yet chooses to demonize the conflict to 100 percent good vs. 100 percent evil, the polarization blinds us. When looking at the 52 percent devil, we cannot see the 48 percent ally. Demonizing blocks the possibility of discovering how we might be allied with the adversary if we moved beyond an either/or mentality to a both/and or a creative neither/nor approach.

Enemy Fear and Filth

Northrop Frye, the master of literary criticism, writes about the strange association linking fear and filth:

> People with unusually silly prejudices against social groups different from their own have a strong attachment to the word "dirty." . . . Dirt has some psychological connection with excretion, and is linked to whatever we want to separate ourselves from. (Frye 1990, 263)

The language of enmity is the vocabulary of the unclean. The enemy in essence represents death and putrefaction; described as dirt, filth, refuse, garbage, and excrement; in character is called pest, vermin, plague, or disease; in source, the enemy issues from the "dregs" of society, "the bowels of the underworld," the intellectual gutters; it is an alien-generated disease or disorder; it is demonic, diabolic, or of the devil.

Although etymologically unrelated, there is an illuminating coincidence in two adjoining words in the English dictionary, enemy and enema, argues James Aho. Psychologically they are linked in both the individual's and the Western society's unconscious reserves of hatred (Aho 1994, 108–9). The public enemy provides the public enema—the campaign to expel the offender, purge the social body of its refuse (what it refuses), its waste (we must waste the enemy). In its expulsion of hatred, the social body experiences relief from tension.

The anality of hatred, Aho observes, is a central motif in the Nazi purge of Jews.

> It is perhaps no mystery, then, why those accustomed to speaking of the Jews in explicit scatological terms would see fit to sanitize the Fatherland (*Judenreinmachen*, literally, "make clean of the Jews") by means of a perverse anal arsenal: Systematic denials of sanitary devices for defecation, regimented once-daily latrine use for all inmates including the predictable sufferers of dysentery, the requirement that one use his eating bowl for evacuation at other times, latrine duty without hand tools, torture by facial immersion in filled receptacles, and so forth. (Aho 1994, 111)

Lest we think of this as happening only there and then, anality was a central attitude of American military personnel in Vietnam. The almost universally used slang word "gook," a variant of "guck," was a disparaging term for an Asian, whether from North or South Vietnam. And the action taken against them was "to wipe out" or more commonly, "to waste." Applying Edmund Husserl's phenomenology as a methodology for exploring the conscious world of the contemporary Western citizen, Aho asked two questions: (1) What are the experiential features of the enemy—what are these enemy apparitions that give them the essence, the *eidos* of *enemy-hood?* He answers, "The enemy is dirty, garbage, refuse, enema." (2) How is the enemy possible? How are human beings rendered into evil things? He answers, "In an actual attribution of the viewer's own mental traits onto these others. The hater's own putrefaction is attributed to the enemy. The process is twofold: one's own excremental qualities are displaced onto the foe, and then, having created a monster, one takes for granted the other's filth while denying any culpability in creating the 'enemy.'" (We look to positive mutual empathy as the only basis for creating harmony; in reality, empathy may also be a negative reciprocal device that creates enmity.) In negative empathy, the hater projects his own evil on the foe as an extension of himself; he perceives actual evil in the other and then magnifies its size, intensifies its passion, exaggerates its malevolence, endowing it with evil grown beyond all recognition (Aho 1994, 115–21). Monstrous evil does exist outside of our projections, of course, but rarely does the reality match the fantasy; eventually we find that our foe is made of the same stuff as we. Still, some—Stalin, Hitler, Amin, Pol Pot—have served as objects of hate in time of conflict, and when the particular war or period of oppression was past, the judgment of history heard, the wider world was justified in its hatred. In historical retrospect, the Nazis were virtually the perfect enemy, Adolf Hitler the quintessential enemy. He shaped his century. Long after his defeat and death, we are still paying for the luxury of having such an evil enemy. He not only matched, but surpassed the caricatures we created in the normal construction of a wartime enemy image. The characterizations we drew from our own fears woven into the fragmentary information available about the evil in the Third Reich turned out to be true beyond our most paranoid suspicions. Not only Hitler's evil, but the corruption of his inner coterie of coconspirators and the complicity of countrymen and country-women appeared to justify our worst actions, such as the carpet bombing of civilians in Dresden and Hamburg.

America did not enter the war against Germany because of the genocidal atrocities, for the awful realities of the "Final Solution" were not well known until after Germany fell. The oppression of German Jews and the rising anti-Semitism of the Nazis were widely known in the 1930s, yet few efforts to assist Jews or to allow them to immigrate were made. There is no evidence that Nazi racism played any part in the American decision. The reason we went to war was to halt Nazi military expansionism (Rieber 1991, 23).

Until its forced unification under Prussian domination in 1870, Germany was no more than a collection of independent principalities, each with its own foreign policy and incapable of concerted effort on the world scene. Bismarck, and his successors, pursued foreign policies of belligerent posturing which escalated into the catastrophe of the First World War. Defeat and the ensuing humiliation of the negotiation table were soon followed by the Great Depression. The German state and its authority were bankrupt.

The 1930s brought a strange transformation. Under the skillful guidance of Hitler and Goebbels, Nazi ideologues persuaded the depression-plagued citizenry of the Weimar Republic to embrace a new image of themselves that replaced their national sense of shame with a sense of honor. The Nazi vision was to build a pure Aryan *Volk* (people) grounded in a unique cultural and racial definition of elite blond supermen, an invincible warrior force, reminiscent of Wagner's Valhalla and the myths of heroic demigods. In hindsight, the Nazi belief system is astoundingly incomprehensible, based on nonexistent racial distinctions of spurious scientific theory and appalling moral lapses. Yet, in a grim economic depression, shameful post–WWI psychic numbness, and desperate social disintegration, they offered to a beaten and humiliated people a strategy for survival and a harbinger of the fulfillment of national hopes.

What was distinctive in Nazi ideology was the creation of a "biocracy," as Robert Jay Lifton (1986) has called it, which prescribed biological perfection of the people as the way to social transformation, national glory, and the Third Reich. An Aryan race did not exist—it was a fallacy of mythologies constructed from early theories of philology and anthropology soon to be totally discredited by the applications of scientific methodology in these disciplines. Yet through these doctrines of eugenics, Nazism created a new national enemy—the inferior races of Jews, Poles, and Slavs.

The inferior races—the enemy—especially the Jews, were now defined as a disease. The cure was the extermination of these polluting gene pools—the genetic, cultural, political pollution was to be medically and biologically removed. "Anyone who wants to cure this era, which is inwardly sick and rotten, must first of all summon up the courage to make clear the causes of this disease" (Hitler 1942, 304). So wrote Hitler in *Mein Kampf*, and Nazism succeeded in transforming the image of a peaceful, industrious, artistic, and religious community into that of a dangerous, implacable, physically repugnant, sexually ravenous, obese, or excessively frail horde of diseased parasites endangering humanity. This was not simply the creation of "public enemies," it was pathological enmification, which denigrated a people to a bestial category appropriate to genocidal elimination.

> The sin against the blood and the degradation of the race are the hereditary sin [original sin] of the world and the end of a humanity surrendering to them. (339)

These are Adolf Hitler's concluding sentences in "My years of suffering in Vienna" in *Mein Kampf.* That it is deluded, and more than a little paranoid, is self-evident, but its massive persuasive power for the German nation set loose a tidal wave of Nazi vengeance and passion for vindicating "the fatherland" against a foe created from their own collective shadow.

Hate: A National Resource

Clyde E. Weaver, a Church of the Brethren peacemaker, was answering a Soviet official's questions on why he had, earlier that day, gone to a hospital in Moscow to give blood as an expression of his solidarity with humankind. "I am neither Russian nor American but human," he explained. "I live by the rule of love, not hate." The Russian, a Kremlin representative, puzzling over the paranoid division of the two countries— it was the '70s, the height of the cold war—finally concluded, "The difference between you and me is simple. I was taught to fear you, but you were taught to hate us." He was accurate in his judgment, Weaver told me. "The Soviet Union was invaded often, and virtually everyone knew what it was to have lost a family member in warfare. My country had never been invaded. We did not know fear. We were taught to see them as the enemy. We were taught hate."

This is, of course, a perfect characterization of paranoid thought, on both sides: To hate another people, to fear another people, because they are a threat. We have just ended a half century of international paranoia— a *folie à deux*—between two nations. "The single most striking feature of American public life in the . . . four decades (1950–1990) has been the consistent fervor with which the Russians have been identified as the enemy. . . . Perhaps never before in history has one society so hated and feared another for so long—during a period of prolonged peace" (Rieber 1991, 5). Thought patterns were assumed normal once they became the norm— the norm of paranoia delicately argued, carefully nuanced, artfully concealed in accurate descriptions of the other's malevolence, justified as self-defense that was sadly necessitated by the unfortunate situation. Over half of the population of both the United States and Russia were born into, raised within, nurtured by "the reality of mutuality interlocking hatred and fear." In both nations, citizens were taught to see the other as the enemy and to prepare to destroy them as they were prepared to destroy us. MAD, the doctrine of mutual assured destruction, became the final guarantee of "safety and security" during the last half of the twentieth century. Simply stated, this doctrine held that as long as each nuclear power retained enough weapons to annihilate the population of the other, even after a first strike against its own weapons, then the decision to initiate a nuclear exchange became irrational and presumably impossible. In the logic of arms control, the production of arms became a moral good, the protection of populations by weapons of mass destruction a moral value that was ethically defendable. As long as each side has a sufficient stock of weapons safely hidden from surprise attack and capable of retaliating destructively, then each nuclear power held the civilian population of the other country hostage.

Secretary of Defense Robert McNamara explained the premise of MAD to Soviet prime minister Aleksey Kosygin during the Johnson administration. Kosygin, hearing it promulgated openly, protested—"But that is immoral." As a neighbor of genocides—Hitler against the Jews, the Turks against the Armenians—and a survivor of Stalin's even greater purges of tens of millions of his own people, he knew the terrors of genocide. Yet he and his successors adopted the "mutually assured destruction" theory and joined the United States in planning, preparing, and investing virtually half of the annual budget in tools to commit mutual genocide. Although balance was maintained to assure that it did not happen, both nations were forced to prepare technologically, psychologically, spiritually to ensure capability. Spiritually, the nations committed themselves to being fully prepared in corporate enmity to commit genocide. Ultimately, there was no place left on the planet unaffected by the mutual dance of fear and hate. With the end of the cold war, we emerged from a half century of captivity under a double bind that affected not just the first and second worlds, but also the third world.

Fear and Hate as a Double Bind

A double bind is composed of three contradictory and intersecting parts—a threat, a counterthreat, and a command against all escape. The first two contradict each other, and the third immobilizes the victim by forbidding recognition of the evil being done, or prohibiting escape from the evil situation; it forbids awareness, resistance, or flight. The cold war was a global bind that held all participants frozen. There was no pairing of one who binds and one who is bound, since both East and West fulfilled both roles in the struggle.

The three legs of the cold war bind stated most tersely were: (1) You are threatening to destroy me and I must, if I value justice, prepare to respond in kind to the threat offered. (2) I can only justify my action of planned violent retribution by believing profoundly in my own potential victimization—my right to rectify the wrong I fear would be done. (3) But in planning to retaliate for an injustice, I must take justice into my own hands, which is unjust—I must confront evil, but to do so I must utilize the same evil action that is intolerable in you. In short form, it says: You threaten genocide; I must threaten genocide in return; since you are capable of genocide, I must be capable of it too. I must not see the evil contradiction in this logic, not think about it, not question its sanity.

Unconsciously we rationalized our position by a deeper bind: (1) You and we threaten each other with weapons of mutually assured destruction, but we each must believe that our motives are purely self-defense. (2) We need you to justify a war economy based on arming the world; we need you as enemy to receive our hate and rage to boost our gross national product, but we must believe that we are peaceful and well-intentioned. (3) We dare not see that we are both reacting to and creating each other as enemies; we cannot face that we both fear you and need you. As a further way of expressing this bind, consider these three interlocking attitudinal sets:

> The world is made up of the good and the bad.
> We are good, the foe is evil.
> The enemy must be controlled or eliminated.
> *We are righteous, acting only in self-defense.*

> If we had no evil enemy out there,
> we would have to face the evil in here.
> We need you out there to protect us from us.
> *But we deny that we are a danger to anyone.*

> We hate you but cannot live without you.
> We need you, but we are willing to destroy you.
> We dare not see that this is contradictory,
> we dare not recognize that this is irrational.

The three legs of the double bind—double binds always have three conflicting threats acting in conjunction—are the triad of paranoia, enmification, and denial. Paranoia sets up the either/or situation of threat, while blaming the other for the whole of it; enmification creates the treacherous foe while denying any responsibility for it; and denial blocks our ability to recognize or think critically about our part in the standoff. Once we are accustomed to the double binds, we find that enemies unify us as a group, help us pull our many differences together and define a joint identity. Enemies become interchangeable when convenient to larger goals. Syria, America's "implacable foe," is welcomed as a long-lost brother when the conflict with its Iraqi neighbor, Saddam Hussein, breaks out; Saddam, earlier America's ally and stalwart defender of "civilized values" in contrast to neighboring Iran's fanaticism or Syria's terrorism, is now considered an evil "Hitler." Iran, as America leaps into the Gulf War with Iraq, now curries favor with her recent foe, the "great Satan" America, who is now allied with Russia, formerly Reagan's "evil empire."

Enemies become indispensable. The USSR and the U.S.A., over forty years, served to form each other's core commitments. For a half century, anticommunism bound Americans as a people, and when deprived of their old adversary they needed another foe. Aho makes the impertinent observation: "Without an enemy, there could be no heroic community with which to identify. . . . Although admittedly this is an overdrawn claim, it may be argued that America needed a petty Hitler, and thus set about manufacturing one to meet its specifications. Its name: Saddam. This is not to say that Saddam Hussein, out of his own stupidity, greed, and treachery, did not freely stumble into the strobe projected by the American psyche, thereby becoming archdemon in a reenactment of the American dream of world redemption" (Aho 1994, 15).

The "mysterious need" for an enemy is more than a need to oppose; it can be the need for an organizing center for our creative energies, a need for clear self-definition, clear values, and sharp, definite boundaries. It may be a need for a legitimate foe, a righteous cause, a just crusade, an unambiguous moral order. But the challenge of moving beyond enmification in order to support or initiate social change requires a wisdom that can work for justice while looking at the needs on both sides. As peace activist Fran Peavy writes:

> Working for social change without relying on the concept of enemies raises some practical difficulties. For example, what do we do with all the anger that we're accustomed to unleashing against an enemy? Is it possible to hate actions and policies without hating the people who are implementing them? Does empathizing with those whose actions we oppose create a dissonance that undermines our determination? I don't delude myself into believing that everything will work out for the best if we make friends with our adversaries . . . but our challenge

is to call forth the humanity within each adversary, while preparing for the full range of possible responses. Our challenge is to find a path between cynicism and naivete. (Peavy 1985)

When our goal is achieving justice, not eradicating those who have acted unjustly, then confronting evil offers us a life focus with moral intentionality. We then work at real issues of justice without relying on fear of enemies to pull us together, harmonize our differences into a fearful defensive unity, and justify acting unilaterally when concern for the welfare of both sides is needed. When a person is committed to pursue such concerns as equal economic opportunity or equal human rights, or adequate health care, or full gender equality, rather than the extermination of all those who oppose one or more of them, then the drive to seek justice gives life direction with social passion. Instead of living by enemy orientation, the morally passionate person finds a justice vision that goes beyond opposition, to inner direction.

Such a transformation requires sorting out one's hatreds. The stranger cannot be automatically identified as the enemy. Western societies have a long history of ideas about strangers. In a number of ancient languages, Latin among them, a single word was used to designate strangers and enemies. Over the centuries, though, there have been those who could distinguish between the two, such as the good Samaritan in the story told by Jesus, who experiences the transforming double vision to see the other as stranger and fellow human in need. Once we can make such a distinction, those once targeted as the foe are seen differently. Howard Gruber writes of this transformation in our own day:

> First, we must criticize the language of Satanism and its opposite member, sanctimony. Whenever we feel ourselves becoming self-righteous, we might murmur "My Lai, Hiroshima, Nagasaki," if we are Americans, or other suitable confessions of national complicity in creating the present state of affairs. The point of this exercise is not to indulge in guilt-making, but to remind ourselves that, just as We are human, They are human.
>
> Second, we need to adopt the language of a commonly shared humanity. There are no We and They, there is only one side—humanity.
>
> Third, since there are real dangers, it behooves us to identify them carefully, so that we can take aim against them . . . the greatest Enemies are hedonism, self-interest and passivity. (Gruber 1991, xii)

These three dangers—hedonism, self-interest, and passivity—fuel the hatreds that combine to grow into the greater conflagrations of joint inhumanity—warfare. Military historian Michael Howard argues that "the dialectic between war and peace has been the central organizing principle of societies through the centuries." He cites British jurist Sir Henry Maine's dictum: "War appears to be as old as mankind, but peace is a modern invention." Peace is not and never has been the natural state of humankind. Peace is artificial, intricate, and highly volatile. The likelihood of maintaining it, once established, depends on the creation of a global peaceful order in the world community that might share some of those characteristics that make domestic order possible—communication, economic interdependency, educational exchange, friendship, and civility—goals that can only be reached by joint action and cooperation (Howard 2001).

The roots of war are embedded deeply in our worldviews about conflict, historical records that use war as the framework for recording significant events, cultural assumptions about the nature of competing ethnic groups, and religious convictions that support myths of redemptive violence. All these contribute to the view of the inevitability and efficacy of war. Among the values attached to military institutions that we must question are: (1) the glorification of war (companionship, bravery, worthy cause, honor accrued for the nation) as the sign of true greatness in individual and national identity; (2) the celebration of military leaders (Alexander, Napoleon, Patton), in spite of the destruction they led; (3) the justification of war ("realist" thinking and "just war" theories), when recent history records even greater radical changes accomplished by peaceful means; (4) the inevitability of war (instrumental calculations of utilitarian good) as a final solution to opposed national wills; (5) the sacredness of self-defense (the elevation of self-interest as ultimate and inviolable) in contrast to seeking safety as a human right for all peoples; (6) the national interest (collective greed or self-seeking expansionism is justifiable when institutionalized) as a legitimizing argument for military action.

Such values are attached to our ways of seeing the world. Our deep antipathies toward other nations can and do lie dormant for long periods, and then undergo tectonic plate shifts as national alliances realign, allies alienate, or new coalitions form. When enemy fault lines move, invisible loyalties and their obligations undergo a seismic shaking. The power of managed fear, of political antagonism, of corporate institutional greed to define who is "the enemy" should be humbling to us each time we see paranoia sweep across a nation. We will only root out the penchant for

seeking an unjust safety, an immoral security, an inhumane national hegemony at the expense of other nations and peoples, when we deal with the
enmification processes of rationalized principled hate.

From Reacting to Responding

Coming to terms with national and social hate means coming to face our
reactive hate. In growth toward maturity, each of us must learn not to *react*,
but to *respond* in considered and thoughtful reordering of our personal
experiences of enmity. Reactive defensiveness that externalizes the
responsibility for enmity onto others or reviews and relives the pretexts
for hate binds us to the past. Responsive nondefensiveness opens us to
learn from the enmity and take steps toward personal maturation. Such
steps toward maturity include: (1) Naming our enemies without denial,
owning whatever part of the enmity is ours, then accepting responsibility
to work only on our own half. Dealing with our part in the enemy relationship, whether it is the smaller or larger portion of the problem, is the
first step of integrity and useful intervention. Trespassing into the other's
half of our relationship—placing blame, passing judgments, or taking
responsibility for their emotions and actions or any other attempt to
change another—is of no help to them or us. We must deal with our own
inclination to hate rather than point to the other. (2) Recognizing that the
proper response to the enemy is moving beyond enmity to restore respect
for his right to perceive the world differently; another's enmity is not a
valid reason for withdrawing respect for a nation as a nation or a person
as a person. One can feel repugnance at distorted and destructive elements
in another's intentions and actions, yet stubbornly continue to extend
enemy love. (3) Acting in life-affirming, person-honoring, relation-
renewing ways. Loving the enemy is acting toward the other in the way
we wish for him to act toward us—the simplicity of the Golden Rule of
reciprocity should not mislead us from recognizing how it is grounded in
deep empathy. ("Do to the other as he wants us to do" would be acquiescence and subservience. "Do as we want to do unto him" may be retaliation and revenge. "Do to him as we want him to do to us" is empathic
understanding that uses our own needs as the frame, the other's potential
for good as the picture, and the courage to risk doing good in the face of
another's continuing evil to bring the picture to life. That an enemy
chooses to be our enemy does not determine our choice of response.
Equal concern for the welfare of foe and friend is the nature of agape love,
and such love is the sole response that is finally freeing.

Yevgeny Yevtushenko, the Russian poet, tells of a moment of iridescence on the streets of Moscow. In 1944, Yevtushenko's mother took him from Siberia to Moscow. The city was in shock from Hitler's violence on the one hand and Stalin's on the other. Yevtushenko and his mother joined the thousands who witnessed the procession of twenty thousand German war prisoners through the Moscow streets.

> The pavements swarmed with onlookers, cordoned off by soldiers and police. The crowd was mostly women—Russian women with hands roughened by hard work, lips untouched by lipstick, and with thin hunched shoulders which had borne half of the burden of the war. Every one of them must have had a father or a husband, a brother or a son killed by the Germans. They gazed with hatred in the direction from which the column was to appear.
>
> At last we saw it. The generals marched at the head, massive chins stuck out, lips folded disdainfully, their whole demeanour meant to show superiority over their plebian victors.
>
> "They smell of perfume, the bastards," someone in the crowd said with hatred. The women were clenching their fists. The soldiers and policemen had all they could do to hold them back.
>
> All at once something happened to them. They saw German soldiers, thin, unshaven, wearing dirty, blood-stained bandages, hobbling on crutches or leaning on the shoulders of their comrades; the soldiers walked with their heads down. The street became dead silent—the only sound was the shuffling of boots and the thumping of crutches.
>
> Then I saw an elderly woman in broken-down boots push herself forward and touch a policeman's shoulder, saying, "Let me through." There must have been something about her that made him step aside. She went up to the column, took from inside her coat something wrapped in a coloured handkerchief and unfolded it. It was a crust of black bread. She pushed it awkwardly into the pocket of a soldier, so exhausted that he was tottering on his feet. And now from every side women were running toward the soldiers, pushing into their hands bread, cigarettes, whatever they had. The soldiers were no longer enemies. They were people. (Yevtushenko 1967, 34–35)

This is not a miracle; it is the very human story of recovery, of seeing humanity in other humans. A person can be perceived as worth-ful, in spite of the evil past that stands between us—indeed, as none other than our brother. This is the heart of the teaching of Jesus of Nazareth in the Gospels, and in a great life reversal it becomes the central theme of Paul's life and thought. The centrality of the concept of reconciliation in Paul the apostle stands in stark contrast to his earlier life. The reformation of vigilante to peacemaker is an inexplicable life narrative, except when viewed through the mystery of Jesus. The enigma of Paul's story provides a fitting conclusion to any discussion of enemy creation.

The Enigma of Christianity's First Theologian

One of the greatest enigmas in the history of religions is the contrast between the beginnings of Christianity—an antihate, proreconciliation, nonviolent movement following the teachings of Jesus of Nazareth—and the militant, political, violent, inquisitorial church that emerged after the fourth-century alliance and accommodation with the Roman state. The impenetrable riddle is how the writings of the key theologian of the primitive Christian movement, Saul of Tarsus, later Paul of Jerusalem, could have been foundational to this political synthesis of "Christian" Church and violent state, since Paul, of all Jesus' proponents, uniquely grounds his understanding of Jesus in the radical concept of revolutionary concern for and compassion toward enemies. One-third of the Christian Scriptures were written by Paul or by followers in the Pauline tradition. The pivotal issue of his theological thought is "God and enemy love," which he develops into a unique concept and practice of reconciliation. Paul the thinker-theologian is shaped by his history as Saul the inquisitor-executioner. The story of his radical change of identity from a bitter enemy of the Christian movement to its most vocal advocate and apologist offers a fascinating series of passages that address early Christianity's central concern of reconciling adversaries. Paul's letters are grounded in the concrete experience of receiving enemy love that revolutionized his life, thought, and work.

Paul, before his conversion serving as inquisitor and chief prosecutor of heresy, was the archenemy of the primitive Christian Church. The historical record reads: "Saul . . . was harrying the church; he entered house after house, seizing men and women, and sending them to prison" (Acts 8:3). It reports that Saul served as prosecutor, as chief accuser at the trial of charismatic leader Stephen, and gave legitimacy to his execution (Acts 7:58–8:1). Saul, "breathing murderous threats" against Christ's followers, then set out for Damascus to find and bring to trial those charged as seditionists (Acts 9:1–2). But a transforming moment occurred en route that produced a total shift in his identity, loyalties, community membership, and life project.

Carl Jung observed: "Saul owed his conversion neither to true love, nor to true faith, nor to any other truth. It was solely his hatred of Christians that set him on the road to Damascus, and to that decisive experience which was to decide the whole course of his life. He was brought to this experience by following with conviction the course in which he was most completely mistaken" (Jung 1953).

Four aspects of this radical reordering of a brilliant man's life from oppressor to advocate of the oppressed must be considered in understanding the total corpus of his thought.

First, Saul is the nemesis of the emerging Christian movement and of all those sympathetic to it. Something occurs that reverses his identity and role from pursuer and prosecutor to advocate and ambassador. (In Greek, "ambassador" [*presbeis*] refers to the go-between who negotiates peace between warring sides in a conflict.) This reversal happens when, perceiving himself as Jesus' enemy, he discovers that Jesus is not the enemy of those who consider themselves Jesus' enemies. Instead, Jesus welcomes the enemy as a friend. Jesus is not wrathful, but offers Saul a way to resolution of his inner conflicts. Jesus himself confronts Saul and calls into question Saul's vocation as prosecutor, asking, "Why are you persecuting?" He names Saul's painful tortured conscience in a graphic metaphor—"It is hard for you, this kicking against the goad" (Acts 26:14)—then offers reconciliation.

Second, Jesus welcomes the enemy through his representative. Ananias, a leader of Christians in Damascus, is Saul's first contact with the movement Saul has been exterminating (Acts 9:13–19). In the dramatic interchange between Ananias and Jesus, Ananias receives a command to go to such and such a house, where a man is in need. Ananias, realizing who the man must be, replies, "No, he is an adversary—a *diabolos*—a devil." Jesus persists: "I have chosen this man; he will be not an adversary but an advocate, an ambassador." Ananias goes to accost the feared inquisitor, identifying himself to the hunter as one of the hunted. He touches Paul, saying, "You will see again, now," thus initiating healing of his spiritual, relational, historical, ideological, and physical blindness. Then he says, "Come into the community of the Spirit through baptism," inviting him into the circle of the fugitives, and "So, my brother, come, eat and drink," celebrating inclusion in community. Saul's self-perception is: "I am Jesus' primary, most infamous and devoted enemy."

But Jesus' response is: "You will be my primary, most infamous and devoted ambassador."

Third, enmity toward an actual, concrete community of people, "from the start and at its heart," is enmity toward God; hate of neighbor is hate of God. Reconciliation is turning from enmity to acceptance, with real people; it is a sociological reality, not a psychological renewal. Outer reconciliation with one's enemies, not inner spirituality of good intentions, is the concrete means of our turning toward God. There is no vertical reconciliation achieved first, followed by a horizontal consequence. The two are one.

Fourth, the experience of Saul, the man, becomes a revelation to Paul of the "gospel of reconciliation." The event that transformed him became the transforming word—God has justified, graced, loved his enemies—not because justice is done to them, nor because injustice is overlooked, or excused. God justifies the unjust, welcomes them into a community that loves justice and grace, where we can do justice, love faithfully, live in peace (Rom. 5:8–10; Eph. 2:8–22). "'Reconciliation,' the unique Pauline metaphor for God's saving act in Christ, originated on the Damascus road. For on the Damascus road, Paul experienced God's reconciling him, a hostile enemy, to himself, forgiving his sins and making him a new creature by his grace" (Kim 2002, 214, 237).

The enigma remains. Enemy love is both end and beginning of the Jesus story. It is largely missing in the story of the church, which rarely dares to follow its founder in the central genius of his thought and life. In the compromise to be spiritually loving but socially and politically allied with the forces of retaliative hate, Christians became successors, not followers of Jesus, and neither messianic nor apostolic succession is worth much unless there is the willingness and the urgency to follow in his steps.

In the spiritual renaissance that may be coming to birth, Walter Wink argues, it will not be the message of Paul that will galvanize hearts this time, as it did in the Protestant Reformation or the Wesleyan revival, but the figure of Jesus, whom Paul pointed to but the Reformers and revivalists missed. This is the Jesus whose teaching of nonviolence and love of enemies is the truth most relevant to the twenty-first century. The ultimate religious question will not be Luther's guilty query, "How can I find a gracious God?" Rather, it will be "How can we find God in our enemies?" "There is, in fact, no other way to God for our time but through the enemy, for loving the enemy has become the key both to human survival in the nuclear age and to personal transformation" (Wink 1992, 263).

From Enmity to Empathy

Eugene Debs, American social activist and prophet, was imprisoned during World War I as a conscientious objector. He was placed, as punishment for being a despised "conchie," in a cell with the most feared inmate in the prison—a man who was considered incorrigible, devoid of any spark of goodness, totally isolated from others in his rage. He had spoken to no one since his imprisonment and had responded to other prisoners' initiatives with cold disdain and visible hatred.

Debs quietly observed the rage for a period, then, using his cell mate's language of silence, began a nonverbal process of stealing past defenses (Debs, although white, understood the man's anger at the white system). He began by giving his silent partner the unquestionable equality one might offer a twin—leaving an orange on the other cot, then chocolate, until it became obvious that everything brought by visitors was divided in equal shares between their beds. Gradually rebuffs decreased, then rejection ended; at last the silence was broken, the two began to talk, and friendship began. Years later when the man, now a minister and community leader, received word of Debs's death, he said, "He was the only Christ I ever knew."

Imaginative empathy, putting himself into another's place, was, as the man says, a Christ-event, what is meant by "incarnation." Compassionate empathy can start with a shared orange and grow to a shared world. Debs's decision to transpose himself into the feeling, thinking, and acting structures of a deeply wounded man enabled him to become a guest in the other's angry inner world. By restructuring his responses to the common language of kindness and consideration of the other's pain, Debs offered his empathic understanding and asked for nothing in return. Slowly he entered the forbidden structures of a fortified personality, not by intrusion but by hard-won invitation.

Empathy, a word coined in English to translate the German concept of *Einfühling*, or to "feel one's way into the experience of another," has become our way of naming the difficult process of putting oneself into another's place. The most recognized theorist of empathy in recent discussion, Heinz Kohut, referred to empathy as the capacity to think and feel oneself into the inner life of another person. He offers three definitions: (1) the recognition of the self in the other, (2) the expansion of the self to include the other, and (3) accepting and understanding the other as a human echo given to confirm another or received as nutriment from another, which sustains our lives (Kohut 1978, 705).

In empathy, Kohut theorized, one listens not only to the other's words but to the music behind the words, to catch the spirit beyond the letters, the true meaning beyond the verbal content. Words of hate may cloak a deep longing for reconnection, restoration, and justice. The background may be filled with yearning for reunion while the foreground speaks of rejection. Enemy empathy is the work of enemy love that seeks the possible reconnection where only disconnection is visible.

The empathic person becomes a bridge—a bridge from soul to soul. A bridge is only a useful bridge when firmly fastened to sturdy abutments at both ends. It cannot be built from one side of the chasm without equal construction on the other. The abutment on this end is built of deep self-understanding, of learning to know the self, its attachments, and loyalties. The abutment at the other end is built by presence, attention, and listening. Respect for the wide stream between helps us distinguish our own projections and expectations (the first planks we extend from our abutment) from the hard reality of the other. When both banks have solid bases, the span can be extended and made firm for initial empathic ventures between worlds. A bridge usually carries two-way traffic, and we come to know ourselves authentically through exchange and encounter. Empathy offers not static truth, but growing truthfulness. Empathic engagement changes us, changes not just perceptions, but rationality, affect, commitments, and actions. We cannot see, think, feel in the old way.

The empathic person becomes a bridge, and a bridge is meant to be walked on. As she passes over and returns in mutual understanding, she invites first the other, and then more to explore the other side.

Chapter Nine

Justice, Mercy, and Hate:
Contempt Becomes Compassion

We are, each of us angels with only one wing and we can only fly by embracing each other.
—Bartholomew I, Bishop of Constantinople

If my devils are to leave me, then I am afraid my angels will take flight as well.
—Rainer Maria Rilke
(On withdrawing from psychoanalysis after learning of its goals)

Way to a Christian Virtue: Learning from one's enemies is the best way toward loving them for it makes us grateful to them. If you have an enemy, do not requite evil with good and put him to shame, rather prove that he did you some good.
—Nietzche

Proposition for Chapter 9

The goal of maturation is the transformation of destructive hate to constructive compassion, to move beyond retributive and rationalized hatred to discover "just hate." "Just hate" appears to be essential to true spirituality with its concern for authentic justice and compassion for the neighbor, which transforms the anger and resentment into contempt for evil and concern for justice. In this chapter we will integrate concepts of justice, mercy, and concern for others using the Psalter as a test case for religious experience and practice. A theology of justice, reconciliation, and peacemaking does not deny hate; instead, it metamorphoses hate into empathy, compassion, and commitment to seek what is truly good for friend and enemy alike.

The Jacob-Joseph story, comprising almost one-half of Genesis, is one of the earliest psychological epics of family rivalry, domination, hatred, trickery, and alienation; it also contains surprising turns toward forgiveness, healing, and reconciliation. Greed, guile, deceit, and malice run in the family of Jacob. Hate smolders between the six unblessed sons of the unloved wife, Leah, and the two blessed youngest sons born to Jacob's first and only love, Rachel. The family is frozen in malice (vividly flagged by each child's name, pitting pride and self-justification against insult and accusation with Hebrew witticisms that point fingers between Leah and Rachel, the competing siblings' mothers*).

Joseph, his father's favorite, acts with unbounded arrogance and astounding naïveté, flaunting his favored status without prudence or shame, and the competition turns rivalry to hostility. "When his brothers saw that their father loved him more than all his brothers, they hated him, and could not speak peaceably to him" (Gen. 37:4 RSV). Without considering the consequences, Joseph tells of his recurring dreams of superiority—picture ten older half brothers bowing down to him in servitude—the scandalous cultural reversal of elder serving younger. "So they hated him yet more for his dreams and for his words" (37:8 RSV).

Sent as Jacob's emissary, Joseph encounters his older brothers at a distant sheep camp, far from patriarchal protection. They seize him and plot his death, but irony wins over violence. The one who boasted of being their lord is instead sold as a slave to a caravan of traders, who carry him to be sold on the market in Egypt. "We'll see what comes of his dreams," his brothers sneer (37:20). (In later Jewish law, selling a brother into slavery is a capital offense; see Exod. 21:16.)

As a slave, Joseph quickly wins his master Potiphar's trust, becomes the household administrator, and catches the mistress's wandering eye. When her sexual overture is rebuffed, she falsely accuses Joseph of approaching her,

---

*Leah, the unblessed wife, names her first four sons: Reuben (see, "do you see? a son!"); Simeon (God heard that I am hated); Levi (my husband is now joined with me—I have won); Judah (I praise Yahweh). Rachel now offers the surrogate womb of her servant Bilhah, and the fifth and sixth sons receive the retaliatory names: Dan (God has judged in my defense); Naphtali (I've played a trick on my sister). Leah, not to be upstaged, offers her maid Zilpah, and two sons appear: Gad (good fortune); Asher (happy am I). Leah, again fertile, triumphantly bears: Issachar (God has paid me my due); Zebulun (God has made me rich). At last, Jacob's beloved Rachel gives birth to Joseph. The name is a Hebrew pun (God has taken away/God has added, i.e., "God took away my shame; may He add another son"), followed by Benoni (son of my bad luck), a name changed after her child-birthing death to Benjamin (son of my good luck).

and he is imprisoned in the king's Round Tower where he repeats his rise to responsibility. As prison master he befriends two of the king's servants, temporarily out of favor, one of whom survives to return to the palace. When the king is later troubled by dreams, Joseph the dreamer and interpreter of dreams is remembered by the former prison comrade and brought to consult with the king. His brilliance wins him a role as administrator. Now Joseph possesses authority, wealth, power, family, and multinational influence beyond even his youthful dreams. But he has not forgotten his brothers, and the injustice he suffered haunts him. His first son is named Manasseh, "causing-to-forget," for, he said, "God has caused me to forget all my troubles and my father's family" (Gen. 41:51). Twenty-two years have passed. Joseph, at thirty-nine, is now administrator of Pharaoh's Nile River food reserves, while the whole Middle East is in famine.

One day, overseeing the distribution of grain, Joseph sees ten foreigners appear in line. He recognizes his brothers instantly; they see nothing but an Egyptian official. His treatment of them becomes exacting, interrogation follows, then strategic testing with harsh imprisonment of one of them as an example. Now the brothers experience their powerlessness. Is Joseph toying with them in a despotic game of incipient revenge? Or subjecting them to the threat of slavery, like the slavery they once dealt to him? Or testing character to see if they who ask for merciful aid are now capable of mercy themselves? Speaking in their native Aramaic/Hebrew, which they assume he cannot understand, they say to each other, "No doubt we deserve to be punished because of our brother, whose suffering we saw; for when he pleaded with us we refused to listen. That is why these sufferings have come upon us" (42:21).

Joseph, hearing his mother tongue, understanding their fears, turns away in tears, but then intensifies his trickery to induce in them the terror he once knew. He keeps one of them as a hostage in the Round Tower, sends the others homeward, and the emotional captives return to their father. Only if they bring his father's blessed youngest, the boy who is Joseph's full brother, can they return, reclaim their hostage, and receive more food. The hard rule of *lex talionis*, an eye for an eye—retributive justice (to each what one has coming in payback)—is being worked out in a family where the practice of blood revenge is obligatory (42:37).

But Joseph now introduces new kinds of justice he has learned as an assistant to the Pharaoh of Egypt—attributive justice (to each according to merit, to what is earned, deserved, appropriate to status, to ability to pay for survival) and the earliest beginnings of distributive justice (to each according to needs). In turns he taunts, twists the options, tests, and retests his former tormentors. Fritsch notes "the feeling of unbridled, ruthless power in the actions of Joseph as he lords it over his cowering, fearful brethren, and plays with them as a cat plays with a mouse. They are at his mercy, and he can do anything he wants to them" (Fritsch 1955, 28). He invites them to an exclusive feast; observes seating rituals according to age that reveal he knows the family secrets; then, in a master stroke, entraps the youngest—the only innocent one, his beloved little brother, Benjamin, into slavery. In the final showdown, when all are before the bar of justice, Judah, the clan leader and the mastermind of Joseph's slavery in Egypt, offers himself as slave if only the boy can go back to the father who dotes on him above all else.

At last, when all ten join Judah in offering their freedom in exchange for that of their little half brother, Joseph reveals himself in a flood of emotions.

> Joseph could no longer control his feelings in front of his attendants, and he called out, "Let everyone leave my presence." So there was nobody present when Joseph made himself known to his brothers, but so loudly did he weep that the Egyptians and Pharaoh's household heard him. Joseph said to his brothers, "I am Joseph; can my father be still alive?" His brothers were so dumbfounded at finding themselves face to face with Joseph that they could not answer. (45:1–3)

Then Joseph redefines the moral impasse that separates them:

> I am your brother Joseph whom you sold into Egypt. Now do not be distressed or take it amiss that you sold me into slavery here; it was God who sent me ahead of you to save men's lives. (45:4–5)

He then assumes his role as clan leader in the position of feudal sovereign over the extended family, relocates the clan, allocates land, and guarantees food and support. The dream has come true.

No mention of forgiveness occurs at this point—the word has not yet occurred in the Pentateuch.* Instead, Joseph offers a settlement from the

---

*There are several Hebrew words for forgiveness: "to bear, endure, tolerate, lift up, or carry away" is *nasa'*, used for both human and divine forgiving and appearing later in the story; "to cover" the sin is *kapar*; "to let go" is *salach*, used only for God's forgiveness; "to not remember" is *zakar*; "to find favor" is *masa'*. The four different pictures of forgiveness are: carrying a burden for another, covering up, blotting out, and canceling a debt.

bench, distributive justice of equal opportunity and resources to each. The great disparity in their social positions drives the fear, suspicion, and guilt of the dark family drama into the murky underground of this deeply wounded clan. Thirty years of hate deposits have settled in the collective family soul.

The discussion of the attempted fratricide—limited as it is—is apparently kept between Joseph and his brothers. The closed family system is not opened. There is no evidence in the story, or in Jacob's deathbed poem of blessing and anticipation in which he predicts each son's destiny and fortune, that the patriarch knows that the ten elders sold their brother into slavery. Instead, everything indicates that the old man is not informed; the mystery of Joseph's abduction to Egypt is left unexplained. The buried secret is a metaphor for the unfinished issues among the brothers.

It is no surprise that following Jacob's burial the brothers reapproach Joseph, suspecting that the time has come for settling the old grudge. At last the one with absolute power will exact retributive justice. Repayment for enslavement*—they will be enslaved—awaits them after seventeen years of a silent truce in respect for the late patriarch, Israel (Jacob). "It may be that Joseph will hate us and pay us back for all the evil which we did to him" (50:15 RSV).

They offer a persuasive story, likely fictional, concocted as a negotiating point. Israel, their father, knew all, and he left a final plea in their behalf that they now bring to Joseph:

> I ask you to forgive your brothers' crime and wickedness; I know they did you harm.

And the brothers plead:

> So now forgive our crime, we beg; for we are servants of your father's God. . . . You see, we are your slaves. (50:17–18)

---

* It is interesting how the Hebrew word *'abadim* (slaves/servants) is used here. The brothers seem to begin with an appeal for complete exoneration, based on an alleged word of their father. They claim to be "slaves" of the God of Joseph's father, and when Joseph's response is delayed by emotion, they also weep and go further, saying, "We are your slaves." Is this contrition? desperation? negotiation? Joseph refuses to accept their submission to "slavery." However, a new pharaoh will later use these very words. (Exod 1: 13–14) (Personal note from Professor James Butler)

There is no evidence that Jacob knew of their crime. Joseph apparently had refused to create a relational triangle with his brothers and his father while Jacob was still alive; now the brothers draw Jacob into a triangle after his death, and then create a second one involving not only Jacob, but Jacob's God as well. The law of revenge is their expectation—retributive justice—but they plead for the generous gift of forgiveness, for him to "bear or endure the offense." This is not our full concept of forgiveness, but a hope for something bordering on redemptive justice.

Joseph's response, tearful and empathic, is clear. He says: (1) "Do not be afraid," offering comfort and reassurance. Then asks: (2) "Am I in the place of God?" as he at last surrenders his youthful dreams of his brothers' bowing down to him, and marks the beginning of the Hebrew tradition that God alone can forgive evil. He is clear in naming their crime: (3) "You meant evil . . . but God meant . . . good" (v. 20 RSV). The Genesis epic opened with the tree of temptation offering "the knowledge of good and evil," now it ends with someone who demonstrates it. He concludes with the promise: (4) "Do not be afraid. I will provide for you," pledging his continuing good will (50:21).

Joseph, "perhaps the only true saint in the Tanakh," reveals in this faithful kindness his trust in a God who is kind; as Miles notes, "God is kind, as Joseph is kind" (Miles 1995, 80–81).

> But if God is implicitly like Joseph in the closing chapters of Genesis, we can only note that he was not like Joseph in the opening chapters. The Lord who did not forgive Adam and Eve for their single act of disobedience was not like the forgiving Joseph. Neither was the Lord/God like Joseph when he sent a flood that "destroyed all flesh" in retribution for scarcely named offenses in Noah's generation. The Lord God in those scenes is maximally powerful and minimally kind, whereas the God mirrored in Joseph is maximally kind and minimally powerful. (Miles 1995, 81)

The Joseph story reveals, for the first time in the Pentateuch, the kindness of God—what will later be called *ḥesed*, the stubborn love of steadfast loyalty that characterizes the God of the Hebrews. Here, in a story of love lived out in a manner that mirrors God's good intentions toward those who act hatefully, we catch a first glimpse of a God who does not deal out punishment for shortcomings, demand repayment for old injustices, or exact retributive justice against those who deserve retribution.

Justice, an Answer to Hate

Just hate, the form of hate that expresses passion about evil along with compassion for the evildoer, has made its first appearance in the Joseph story. We will see it all too rarely in the broad sweep of the Hebrew and Christian Scriptures. Visible in the Joseph story are a whole range of conceptions of justice. The brothers fear the retributive; Pharaoh offers a welcome that is attributive justice; Joseph administers national welfare that is distributive justice; and toward the brothers' evil past, he rises to redemptive justice. We shall explore these particular types of justice further after first looking at several inclusive definitions.

Justice is a human construction; it has as much to do with being and doing as with having. It is doubtful that justice can be constructed in only one way. Justice is a plural thing, and its principles cannot be reduced to such maxims as "From each according to ability, to each according to needs," as Marx attempted. However, there is wide agreement that "justice as equal rights" and "justice as fairness" are two very useful ways to address the issues that arise in each culture (Rawls 1971). Justice, no matter how ardently sought, is attainable only in part. Justice among humankind is a journey, not a destination, and our best attempts are seldom more than partially successful or satisfactory. Yet we seek a return to some semblance of rightness in relationships because human community cannot rise above cyclical hatred without it.

Michael Walzer argues that the goal of justice is not equality (an essentially negative goal to eliminate differences), which would create a level, conformist, hopelessly boring society, but the creation of a society free from any and all domination and tyranny. We become equals when no one possesses the means of domination. The goal is to distribute goods by three distributive principles: free exchange among individuals, open-ended deserts (rewards and punishments), and the consideration of need. All these are dependent on membership, the issue of who is a member in the society— the difference between member and stranger is central to our sense of humanness, to our belonging to any accountable group, and our criteria for sharing, redistributing, and seeking justice (Walzer 1983, xii–xiv).

When Aristotle praised justice as the first virtue of political life, he was asserting that a community that lacks agreement on what is just is not capable of being a community. Following his premise, philosopher John Rawls argues, "Justice is the first virtue of social institutions, as truth is of systems of thought" (Rawls 1971, 3). Rawls argues that the principles of justice are those which would be chosen by a rational agent "situated behind a veil of ignorance" (who would not know what place, privilege, or entitlement she herself would possess and thus be neutral in applying the principles of just distribution) (136). These principles are: (1) "Each person is to have an equal right, and (2) Inequalities are to be arranged to the greatest benefit of the least advantaged and offer equal opportunity" (302). This is an expression of faith in rationality as the guarantor of justice. However, in order to reach such equal justice, we would need to share a common tradition of rationality. We cannot argue convincingly that reason and rationality can produce a truly universal idea of justice; we must admit that even the best is conditioned by particular traditions (MacIntyre 1981, 229).

Since the Enlightenment, justice has usually been tied to the notion of rights distributed according to uniform impartial and impersonal standards. For some, these rights are God-given, for others they belong naturally to human beings, and for still others they are the products of reason. It is clear that the notion of "rights" has given us a powerful language with which nations of the world can demand a more equitable worldwide practice of justice. What is not clear is the goal of this elusive thing called justice. What does it seek?

> To give to each according to merit or works?
> To give to each according to needs?
> To give to each the same thing in spite of needs?
> To give to each similar treatment for similar cases?
> To give to each what is missing or lacking, to live productively?
> To give to each what is necessary for transforming future relations
>   into parity and security?

What constitutes justice? What form does it take? What does it give to each? Each vision of justice is shaped by a particular social location, by social context and process.

Attributive justice: Give to each according to what we are or can claim to be, according to social status, position, or role. This is a justice of entitlement. It functions within and assumes or creates hierarchy. It serves to render appropriate deserts according to status, position, and power. It rarely challenges such entitlements of status; it is the *quo* of status quo. It can be the servant of hate as well as tolerance, of contempt as well as respect.

Retributive justice: Give to each the equal proportion of what we deserve—"an eye for an eye" punishment; penny for penny deprivation; exact repayment for action or inaction; a justice of *lex talionis*. Retributive justice—similar treatment—seeks to stipulate that what is right for one person cannot be wrong for another who is similarly circumstanced. The immediate impulse for revenge is to apply a different—more severe—standard to a wrongdoer, even though similarly circumstanced, thus repaying a wrong with further wrongdoing. In retribution, one is sorely tempted to judge one's own behavior by the motive, the other's by its consequences. "What is right for me, because my intentions are good, obviously, is not right for you because the consequences of your action are evil, undeniably." So the repayment must always exceed the original act. It is the standard process of political, penal legal systems (similar treatment in similar cases). It offers a quid pro quo of various elements—satisfaction, repayment, restitution, retaliation, revenge—according to situation, context, responsibility, motivation, and consequences. At its best it "pays an appropriate debt" to society and restores civility. At its worst it feeds the emotions of revenge, with little ability to alleviate the hate, horror, or grief of a heinous act of wrongdoing.

Distributive justice: Give to each an equal proportion, regardless of their resources or need. This justice of share and share alike is more complex in that it seeks to bring together the principle of equality with a measure of attributive justice, offering equity within context, recognizing that needs will vary according to context—climate, location, productivity, population mass.

Redemptive justice: Give to each according to what is needed to restore what is lacking and to bring the person to equal well-being and fulfillment of potential. A justice of reparative equal rights seeks to respond to and repair what has been broken or injured. Its focus is on the rescue of the alienated, release for the oppressed, and it tends to address the pain of the victim, rarely addressing that of the perpetrator. Its twin, *restorative justice*, takes the redemptive concern even more widely, to include all parties in the injustice or evil situation.

Restorative justice: Give to each the opportunity and resources to recover a life of fairness and equality in a just community. This is a justice of transformative change for both oppressor and oppressed, for victim and victimizer. Both redemptive and restorative justice seek to "make things as right as possible," but the latter is more concerned for both the victim and the perpetrator. Both view crime as primarily an offense against the neighbor, an assault on human relationships, and secondarily as a violation of law. (Laws exist to protect the integrity, safety, and equity of human relationships.) When crime is perpetrated, the probability is that both the perpetrator and the victim will emerge more alienated, injured, devalued, and dehumanized by the total response of society. Restorative justice seeks to fully recognize the injustice done at all levels—the victim, the perpetrator, the community, the justice system—to fully pursue the restoration of equity and to clarify the future, the consequences of the wrongdoing, and the safety and security of all participants.

Whereas retributive justice sees crime as a violation of the state defined by lawbreaking and guilt, restorative justice views it as a violation of people and relationships. The former assigns blame and administers punishment in a contest between the offender and the state by the rules of "the game of law"; the latter is a search for solutions that promote repair, reconciliation, and reassurance (Zehr 1995, 181).

Restorative justice, motivated by a commitment to be unconditionally constructive, is rooted in the union of love for neighbor and a passion for justice in community; its taproot is in spirituality: spirituality is at the center. A spirituality of justice has a communal goal, a vision of harmony and health in relationships, a concern for equal opportunity and mutual privilege. Until these have been restored, we have achieved only a justice of satisfaction for the more powerful, articulate, connected, and privileged. Justice without this spiritual component is subject to the undertow of "eye for an eye" retribution, or "making the punishment fit the crime." The search for what is just, transcending human differences, and the quest for what is spiritual, the transcendent, are inseparable. The work of Simone Weil can help clarify this idea of spirituality in pursuit of justice.

Justice and Compassion as a Spiritual Way of Life

Simone Weil, the radical French philosopher and Christian activist, spoke of justice in a fascinating way:

> What we need is for the spirit of justice to dwell within us. The spirit of justice is nothing other than the supreme and perfect flower of the madness of love. . . . The madness of love draws one to discern and cherish equally, in all human milieu without exception, in all parts of the globe, the fragile earthly possibilities of beauty, of happiness and of fulfillment; to want to preserve them all with an equally religious care; and where they are absent to want to rekindle tenderly the smallest traces of those which have existed, the smallest seeds of those which can be born. (Weil 1987, 9)

The madness of love is the purest possible expression of this new virtue of justice that draws us to see another's pain or hurt and to seek to help.

"To the extent to which at any given time there is some madness of love amongst men, to that extent there is some possibility of change in the direction of justice: and no further" (1987, 9). Any understanding of justice, she argued, must be linked to a spiritual way of life. The search for authentic spirituality is a kind of madness with a radical commitment.

Madness, for Weil, is a passion for love and justice and the belief that without love and justice we banish God from the world. Madness is the awareness that God, and here she uses Wittgenstein's words, is moving around in the grammatical background. God is embodied in the grammar of one's very life. God is the Divine Compassion who is the "in between," the middle term in whose company one discovers one's neighbor. God is present in the person within whom God's love is alive because "compassion is the visible presence of God here below" (Weil 1970, 103). The love of God and the love of neighbor cannot be divided; love and justice become one in compassionate neighbor love. Justice for her is compassion and nothing less. "Any talk of rights is empty unless it is filled with compassion for human need. Compassionate love is the only just love" (1970, 95).

"Justice may be *in* this world by virtue of the supernatural, but justice is not *of* this world," Weil argues (1970, 176). By this she means, justice is not a human construction; it transcends human inventions. It is the concern for human need that seeks equity and fairness, not dispassionately, but with compassion. For Weil, compassion is spiritualized suffering; justice is spiritualized love. When compassion becomes a way of spiritual life, it is "able without hindrance, to cross frontiers, extend itself over all countries in misfortune, over all countries without exception; for all peoples are subjected to the wretchedness of our human condition" (Weil 1970, 174). Compassion has no boundaries; it is a universal concern for human need and suffering wherever it occurs. The mark of true justice is this concern, commitment, and profound care for human need. Weil, with her "madness" that these two central concerns be thought of and acted upon with profound spirituality, stands in the prophetic tradition—the tradition of seeing Justice and Mercy as indivisible if they are authentic.

Justice and Mercy, Complementary Antonyms of Hate

Justice that limits revenge, and mercy that transforms hostility, are two complementary antonyms of hate. The two come together in the pursuit of redemptive justice and restorative justice, since their shared goal is reformation and transformation, not restoration of the original precipitating situation.

Mercy, by definition, is a heartfelt compassion in the face of need, aroused in those who need not yet wish to help, and do so. Although mercy may be equated with kindness, grace, pity, compassion, help, forbearance, and "forgiveness," it must link emotion and action or the sentiment one feels is merely sympathy. "Mercy is an *action*, or more precisely, a *reaction* to someone else's suffering, now interiorized within oneself—a reaction to suffering that has come to penetrate one's own entrails and heart" (Sobrino 1994, 16).

If we are seeking to do justice and love mercy, as the Hebrew prophet Micah phrases the task, how do the two relate? Mercy is not the opposite of justice; the opposite of mercy is cold revenge or unemotional retribution. The opposite of justice is injustice. Mercy and justice are two sides of the same virtue, like sides of a coin, and the coin is neighbor love. So merciful justice and just mercy become one in love of the neighbor or enemy. Neither is valid or complete without the other. In Paul Tillich's classic paradigm "Justice is composed of love and power in unity and in balance. Loveless power cannot work justice, nor can powerless love. It is powerful love and loving power that unite to produce justice" (Tillich 1954, 13). In Micah's paradigm, both justice and mercy are forms of power. Justice confronts mercy to discern with fairness, mercy challenges justice to act with compassion; each fulfills the other in the practice of neighbor love.

Mercy is a dominant theme in the Hebrew and Christian Scriptures. God is merciful (Exod. 34:6: Deut. 4:31; Pss. 51:1; 116:5; 145:9; Lam. 3:22; Dan. 9:8–9). Key references to mercy in the Christian Scriptures are found in Luke 6:36; 10:37; 2 Corinthians 1:3–4; 1 Peter 2:10; Romans 9:15–18; Ephesians 2:4; Titus 3:5; and Hebrews 8:12. Jesus says, "Blessed are the merciful" in his Beatitudes, speaks of hungering and thirsting for justice-righteousness, and includes three or more forms of humility in the list (Matt. 5:1–12). But mercy is not held up as the exclusive virtue; the tensions between mercy, justice, and righteousness are not minimized. What if help given in mercy takes away the dignity and self-determination of the helped? What if a judgment must be made between two equally needy persons? Are there limits to mercy? Jesus showed mercy to the lepers, the tax men, the prostitutes, the sick, the mentally ill; mercy is so characteristic of him that we must be reminded to recall how merciless he could be toward the Pharisees in his diatribes, toward an arrogant and dismissive Pilate, toward the symbolic fig tree.

"Mercy," according to Jean Hampton, "is the suspension or mitigation of a punishment that would otherwise be deserved as retribution, and which is granted out of pity and compassion for the wrongdoer" (Murphy and Hampton 1988, 158). What is "deserved" here refers to what is perceived as necessary to humble the wrongdoer and vindicate the victim's value.

In colonial New England, it was the practice to urge a criminal sentenced to hang for his crimes to repent of his acts before execution. If he did so, the community would hold a reconciliation feast in his honor, welcoming him back into its midst as a forgiven member of the group, but nonetheless it would follow up this feast by hanging him the next day (Murphy and Hampton 1988, 158). Reconciliation was not considered inconsistent with consequences; the value of the victim was exacted from the victimizer, but the victimizer was valued as a person. Was this loving mercy, or doing justice, or an attempt to do both? If mercy is an action, not an emotion, then the community praised the sacrificing of mercy for the sake of retributive justice and failed to grasp the theology that was grounded in redemptive, not retributive, justice. Mercy applies a different standard to one accused. The difference is that retribution, in anger, tends to increase the offender's punishment; mercy, in contrast, leads to the betterment of the other. Mercy involves compassion on undeserved pain, help to the distressed, relief of debts, kindness to enemies. Mercy offers value where value has been diminished; eases pain where pain is deserved; restores relationship where relationship is broken; distributes proportionately according to needs, not merits. At the foundational level, mercy is motivated by empathy with and compassion for the suffering of individuals in this world (Sobrino 1994, 16).

I have been exploring, in this chapter, the nature of that justice and mercy which are involved in *just hate*, and argued that redemptive and restorative justice unite mercy and justice more effectively and are able to separate more completely the offender hated from the offense condemned. Some scriptural texts that address hate can help us in this difficult task of discerning the fine boundary between person and action that characterizes just hate. We shall look at the early narrative descriptions of hate, then turn to the Psalter, where its expression in the worshiping life of the Jewish community has been echoed by its constant presence in the liturgy of the various Christian churches. The focal psalm, Psalm 139, one most often cited in hymns, devotional literature, and public worship, contains the most vivid and vitriolic words of hate, words that are most commonly omitted or avoided in Christian piety. It will serve as a test case in exploration of the varieties of hate.

Throughout the Hebrew Scriptures, instigations to hate are interlaced with injunctions against its expression. In a wide range of narrative accounts, the Scriptures provide models for hate and its varied resolutions: mandates for hate and their pursuit in violence and warfare; laments that ventilate hate against oppression and injustice; and prohibitions to pursuing the path of hatred. The first occurrence of premeditated *murderous rage*—that of Cain for his brother, Abel—is not called hate, but anger (Gen. 4:6). The earliest use of the word *hate* refers to the *competitive enmity* of the Philistine chieftain Abimelech for the patriarch Isaac, which ends in an eventual treaty of coexistence (Gen. 26). The intense sibling rivalry of Jacob and Esau leads to *vengeful hate* (Gen. 27:41) that drives Jacob into exile and sets the stage for a long story of fear, avoidance, confrontation, and ultimately reconciliation. The familiar hostility of legitimate sons for the illegitimate Jephthah reveals an *excluding hatred*. The family's united front of exclusion breaks open when Jephthah's military abilities are needed to protect the clan (Judg. 11:1, 7). *Reactive guilty hate* is exhibited by Amnon, Israel's crown prince, toward his sister Tamar immediately after his assault and incestuous rape (2 Sam. 13:15). *Murderous hate* is harbored by her brother Absalom for Amnon's despicable double betrayal. Absalom plots and carries out the execution of the rapist and avenges his sister (2 Sam. 13:22, 28).

The God of the Hebrew Scriptures is effectively involved with the destiny of his people. God pledges eternal friendship and loyalty and to share their enemies and their enmity. The covenant that establishes the identity of the Hebrews has a codicil in which God guarantees: "If you will only listen . . . and do all I tell you, then I will be an enemy to your enemies, and I will harass those who harass you" (Exod. 23:22). We cannot avoid noting in the Hebrew Scriptures the six hundred passages speaking explicitly of individuals or nations attacking, destroying, or killing others. And there are another thousand passages referring to God's punishments by destruction and death, to threats of annihilation and promises of vengeance. In yet another one hundred passages God expressly gives commands to kill persons. Indeed, no other human activity—be it worship, work, sex, sport, commerce, politics, religion, or family—is mentioned as often as violence. Intriguingly, the book of Psalms addresses this God of violence and compassion with a wideness of emotional expression and a great range of frank requests for God's violent support as a means of both safety and salvation. The meeting point of human experience and the religious vision is nowhere more clear in the Scriptures than in the Psalms, and especially those which contain both longings for connection, laments about disruption, and cries for vindication between humans.

The Psalter: The First Confessional Psychology

The first book of confessional psychology—the Psalter—will serve as a series of focal texts for our examination of the interface between hate and compassion. The book of Psalms, standing outside the prophetic tradition with its patterns of critique of both self and other, does not edit human experience. It deals frankly with the dark side of the human psyche as it seeks to bring all of life into the presence of God. To be true to the psalmist, we must resist any attempts to "tidy up" the psalms, to interpret away the hate and rage and improve their piety. As Brueggemann observes in discussing what he calls "Psalms of Disorientation" (Brueggemann 1984, 55): "The stunning fact is that Israel does not purge this unguardedness but regards it as genuinely faithful communication. . . . There is no attempt to protect Yahweh from how it really is. . . . We should not think to pray that way very often, but it is thoroughly biblical" (71–72). "Hatred is one mode of access to the God who cares for his majesty" (87). The Psalter records a wide spectrum of human emotions, including a broad range of varieties of hate, among which are (1) hate with no moral cause (Pss. 35:14; 69:4), which is a "wrongful hate" (38:19); (2) social-political hate of those who hate the Psalmist as a representative of a people (18:17; 21:8; 25:19; 34:21; 41:5, 7; 44:7); (3) a true moral hatred of evil (97:10), of falsehood (119:163), of a false way (119:104, 128), of perverse behavior (101:3), of double-mindedness (26:5); (4) the hatred of God and of God's people (82:2); (5) the hatred of Zion, the city of God's special choice and blessing (129:5). The moral person who fears God, according to the Psalmist, hates those who threaten the safety and security of loved ones and of the community that provides their safety and security. But even more fundamental, evildoers are hated because they threaten the divinely established order of justice and seek its destruction (22:13–17; 57:5; 73:6–9). What sort of prayers are these poetic demands for violent retribution by a God of presumed infinite mercy? How can a God of eternal compassion be invoked to requite human violence with even more vicious divine violence in the name of justice? How can God be challenged to prove God's identity, integrity, and veracity by retaliating fully in kind—doing the same evil to evildoers that evildoers are doing against him? How can these outpourings of hatred, which go beyond lament to bloodthirstiness, be models for or the medium of our prayers? We who have come to understand that the God of the Hebrew Scriptures is characterized by unfailing love, compassionate grace, and steadfast faithfulness are left with puzzling questions to answer. To read the Psalms as literature, to experience their emotions as the psychology of triumph and defeat, of victory or loss, of reward and revenge is a rich exploration into the deep dynamics of the human experience, even as the Psalms are an undeniable affront to our civility and human fellow feeling.

To recite them in public, communal prayer seems incongruent to the liturgical event; but their appropriateness becomes more understandable when seen in the context of abuse or atrocity. The situation of these psalms can be described tersely: People in catastrophic suffering, overwhelmed by pain; knowing themselves to be powerless, facing massive injustice and certain oppression; outraged by impending evil, staring in the faces of ruthless enemies; crying out in passionate distress to God, pouring out their souls in desperation; gripped by terror at the heinous evil being perpetrated on them; venting their rage; demanding the destruction of their foes; crying for justice. But, we ask, how can this explosion of rage be an appropriate prayer to a God of goodness? "Unpleasant and repulsive psalms," they have been called; they seem out of place in cathedral or monastic oasis or the inner chambers of the soul, because they are to be prayed in the midst of a hostile world of enemies. Norbert Lohfink has put it most succinctly: "The one praying *and* his or her enemies—that, in short, is the dominant theme of the psalms" (Lohfink 1988, 36). Their most colorful and complex vocabulary is employed to describe enemies—ninety-four words are used—and no less rich are the metaphors of God's angry judgment on the foe. Hatred, enmity, hostility, violence, retaliation, revenge are central themes of the Psalter from Psalm 1 to Psalm 149.

The psalms of outrage are not only cries against specific evil acts, they are also a passionate struggle against oppression, structural violence, and systemic evil. Unpleasant in emotion and intention, repulsive in their graphic visualizations of the annihilation of the enemy, they stir up the longings for retributive justice and the passion for further violent injustice that answers rage with outrage. "Those who permit the images, scenes, and life context of the individual psalms to affect them will be shocked that there is so much outcry *against* violence, but also so much shrieking *for* violence—and especially at the hope that there is a God of retaliation, vengeance, and destruction" (Zenger 1996, 4). Key examples of the most explicit retributive prayers, sometimes described as repulsive psalms, are: Psalms 5:5–10; 12:12; 41:11–12; 44; 58:7–12; 79:11–12; 83:13–17; 94:1–2, 23; 109:2, 5, 7–20; 137:7–9; 139:19–22.

These troubling psalms serve multiple functions for those who pray them, Zenger argues. (1) They protect victims from becoming voiceless, speechless, and apathetic. (2) They repudiate the idea that the suffering are sacrificial victims of an incomprehensible divine wrath. (3) They keep us open, keep us wrestling with our faith, keep us questioning God and questing for God in the midst of violent reality. As they exemplify the struggle with God against God for the sake of justice, they awaken passionate dialogue. (4) They expose the reality of violence in human community and cry out for change. They personally confront God with the outrage of this world. (5) They stand alongside the other texts in both First and Second Testaments that struggle with violence by insisting that nonviolence is the true way to overcome violence (Zenger 1996, 85).

A major obstacle to our understanding of these difficult texts rises from our modern social location as rugged individualists. We immediately focus the psalms on a particular foe. We can hardly direct our thinking away from individual enemies as we pray these lines that were originally written as corporate expressions of persons with sociocentric "corporate personality" formation. Today we must use the language of systems or of structural good and evil to capture the collective experience of the millennium B.C.E.

The enemy in the retributive psalms, Bernd Janowski argues persuasively, is not simply a personal opponent, an individual enemy, but instead, "all who oppose God," all the evil of chaotic power, and the psalms are less after personal vengeance than the pursuit of justice (Janowski 1995, 162). The main message of these psalms, he argues, is that rage belongs before God, not in a reflectively managed and impeccably worded form of confession, but in a prereflective outburst that wells from the depths of the soul. "They are a cry for justice in a world full of injustice" (1995, 171). We must note, however, in the most poignant and powerful of all the imprecatory psalms, Psalm 139, the perfect confession and the ultimate expression of hate come together.

Psalm 139 as Paradigmatic

The most eloquent, the most theologically nuanced, and the most troubling psalm is the 139th, which we shall examine as a case in point for our discussion of *moral hate*, and perhaps find in it a foreshadowing of *just hate*.

The psalm opens with an affirmation of God's complete knowledge of the psalmist—thoughts, words, behavior, internal self, physical development from conception—and concludes with the recognition of God's infinite capacity for intimate knowledge of each creature. The psalm, in twenty-four verses, unites all the genres of hymns in Hebrew liturgical literature, combining elements of a creation hymn, a psalm of trust, a lament, and a wisdom saying, and connecting to themes in Genesis, Job,

Isaiah, and Jeremiah (Harder 2001, 130). It offers a rich understanding of human nature, its place in the created order and in the presence of God. In midsong, however, comes the outpouring of the darkest hate:

> O God, if only thou wouldst slay the wicked!
> If those men of blood would but leave me in peace—
> those who provoke thee with deliberate evil
>   and rise in vicious rebellion against thee!
> How I hate them, O LORD, that hate thee;
> I am cut to the quick when they oppose thee;
> I hate them with undying [a perfect] hatred;
>   I hold them all my enemies.
>   (Ps. 139:19–22)

Having exposed the shadow side of the self in this explosion of inner reserves of raw hostility, the psalmist, in a virtual bipolar mood shift, immediately requests ruthless examination, radical accountability, and firm correction or redirection toward right thought, feeling, and action:

> Examine me, O God, and know my thoughts;
>   test me, and understand my misgivings.
> Watch lest I follow any path that grieves thee;
>   guide me in the ancient [or everlasting] ways.
>   (Ps. 139:23–24)

This is a fascinating text to deconstruct. It begins in (1) a context of encounter with the infinite and transcendent that is (2) expressed with awe, wonder, and complete humility before the utter otherness of God, and in which (3) there is a radical self-disclosure to the God who already knows the most intimate secrets, even the unconscious depths of the soul. This confession seeks to own the whole truth of what is totally known by the Other. (4) Hatred erupts with uncontrolled malevolence—yet the psalmist asks for God to destroy those hated, and does not claim the right to annihilate them himself. (5) At this point the moral focus of the hate becomes explicit. The psalmist hates those who stand in adamant hate against God and do deliberate evil against goodness, order, and right relationships; he feels radically wounded, cut to the pain center of the soul by their actions against God; he pledges undying, steadfast hate (the mirror opposite of "steadfast love"); he identifies with God over against these foes. Those at enmity with God have become his enemies.

But, and here is the crucial sign of *moral hate* becoming *just hate*, the psalmist recognizes the precariousness, the arrogance, the fatal ambiguity of hate. Realizing how other forms of hate mask themselves behind righteous pretensions, he reopens his deepest emotions, antipathies, hostilities to God's examination, recognizing that in the moment of absolute judgments and total commitments one is most subject to distortion and deranged evil. He invites God to sift, test, and pass judgment on his inner thoughts and desires. This is not an "Oops, I have gone too far" ellipsis, this is an integral part of experiencing just hate. It is truly *just* when the one passionate about justice is as concerned for his or her own integrity of just behavior as for that of the enemy. The reciprocity of justice has entered the soul of the hater, and demanding justice for the other as you wish it for yourself or expecting justice from the self in the same measure as you expect it of the other is the action of reciprocal agape—agape is equal regard that values both ends of the interpersonal equation equally.

The psalmist ends by asking for correction from any action that grieves God's intentions for us, for direction toward that which is everlasting, toward the virtues that endure, toward the paths that lead us to transcend short-term goals. Here the psalmist has come to the end of *moral* hate, has risen above it to discover a motivation that transcends its limits—a *just* hate. Such just hate seeks correction of—not ratification of—his perspectives. This self-criticism is revealed sharply by interlining the two parallel texts, vv. 21–22 and 23–24. The steadfast assertions of radical loyalty are each critiqued by the self-reflective examination of motives, and suggest a suspicion of unconscious and unknown depths to one's own intentions, although no idea of the unconscious processes appears for another two millennia. Self-assertion in loyal hate can be done justly only when there is also humble self-doubt.

> How I hate them, O LORD, that hate thee;
> *Examine me, O God, and know my thoughts;*
> I am cut to the quick when they oppose thee;
> *test me, and understand my misgivings.*
> I hate them with undying hatred;
> *Watch lest I follow any path that grieves thee;*
> I hold them all my enemies.
> *guide me in the everlasting ways.*

Just hate walks a "narrow ridge" between condemning another and examining the self; a depth critique of the enemy is best done in a spirit of necessary self-doubt that resists the impulse to absolute judgments or actions. It views both the arrogance of principled hate and the high ground of moral hate with suspicion. The psalmist of Psalm 139 confesses his own fallibility and frailty while crying out in outrage. This is not an isolated occurrence of self-critique in the Psalter, but here it occurs on the fault line of rage. A hateful eruption in the midst of liturgical prayers is permissible, but prayer before God requires the one praying to look into the abyss of his own destructiveness. Lydia Harder comments here: "Praying Psalm 139 in its entirety will encourage us to go beyond a superficial identification with the feelings of the psalm to probing into the unresolved hatred and anger within us. The plea for justice will then not be based on a projection of evil onto others, but will become a real wrestling with evil both within ourselves and others" (Harder 2001, 135). In the process within Psalm 139, outrage is confessed to God, confronted before God, and ultimately yielded up to God. The case for hate and rage is presented bluntly, then referred to the highest court. The solution to overwhelming rage in the book of Psalms, Brueggemann concludes, is not to repress hate, anger, and rage but to state them clearly and forcefully to God, to "speak [rage] honestly to the throne," to submit and relinquish rage to God, to reject an easy or cheap forgiveness that comes to terms too easily by remembering and speaking the rage, and yet leaving the vengeance itself to God (Brueggemann 1984, 76–77). Volf carries this argument further by seeing within it the seed of hope.

> This is no mere cathartic discharge of pent up aggression before the Almighty who ought to care. Much more significantly, by placing unattended rage before God we place both our unjust enemy and our own vengeful self face to face with a God who loves and does justice. Hidden in the dark chambers of our hearts and nourished by the system of darkness, hate grows and seeks to infest everything with its hellish will to exclusion. In the light of the justice and love of God, however, hate recedes and the seed is planted for the miracle of forgiveness. (Volf 1996a, 124)

The vision of justice is the central hope of the Psalter. "The LORD loves righteousness and justice" (Ps. 33:5), and the hope of seeing justice done on earth as it is in heaven motivates the laments as well as the hymns of praise. This hope drives the cries for retribution and the prayers for reconciliation. *Just hate*, when it appears amid the struggles for survival and security, is grounded in the abhorrence of all that is duplicitous and destructive, and steadfast adherence to the conviction that injustice in any form is outside the character and will of God. It is in the continuing pursuit of justice, the recognition that justice is a journey, not a destination, that life is ennobled by any effort to do justice without compromising mercy and that the search for such merciful justice is long, hard, and always a step beyond the best we are able to conceive or create.

So what are our next steps in this journey?

What Shall We Say, Think, Do to Address Hate?

What above all shall we do in rethinking our responses to hate? As we conclude this exploration of the darker regions of the soul, we might still be tempted to think that there is little that can be done to redirect a human dynamic so deep, endemic, indeed epidemic across cultures. Or we can seize a renewed hope by incorporating the signal directions we have noted along the way of this study.

There are crucial and pivotal things that we can do.

1. We can think more clearly about hate, not as a single, unified common behavior, but as a spectrum of emotions and actions stretching from raw and unconsidered negation to careful and thoughtful pursuit of justice, and commit ourselves to seeking cognitive and emotional change in ourselves as well as fostering them in others in pursuit of justice. *From hate of others, to hate of those who hate us, we can grow until we hate* hate *itself.*

2. We can seek to learn the difficult art of facilitating transforming moments where subjective hatred breaks through to a new world of objective hatred, if we recognize that we only prepare the way, we do not work the miracle. *Conciliation is our work, reconciliation is God's work; owning and dealing with hatred is our gift, the transforming moment when hate breaks through to empathy is God's gift.*

3. We can seek to foster, teach, model, and reinforce nonretaliatory ways of dealing with threat or conflict. We can create and employ conciliative patterns of learning and teach how to respond constructively to provocation and violation. *If we learn how to hate, we can unlearn how we hate: if we know constructive ways of responding to threat, provocation, or violence, we are less likely to regress to old destructive ways.*

4. We can learn and practice methods of neutralizing memories, reframing resentments and finding a useful place in the soul for our

recollections of violation or violence that transforms painful stories into commitments to justice. *We can forget the anger-demands if we seek to remember the justice-demands; we can cancel our demands for retribution when we commit ourselves to conflict transformation.*

5. We can stop living unexamined lives, acting out of the unconscious, and end the blind obedience to reflexive and reactive defenses by doing our own hate-work, the work of courageously owning and exploring the inner underworld of our own souls. (See Appendix I.) *When we come to understand more of our private souls, we will live less out of the shadow side of the personality; when we come to know more of our depths, we are less reactive and more responsive in difficult situations.*

6. We can give up pretensions to possessing the absolute, learn to question our natural tendencies toward dogmatism, finality, or fanaticism, and stop giving ourselves rationalized permissions to take absolute actions. *When we follow the "demon of the absolute," we become not absolute, but demonic.*

7. We can face how deep is the history of human evil, make our social, economic, and political decisions in awareness of its power, rethink our religious convictions in light of its pervasiveness and horror. We will not forget the holocaust and the many holocaust echoes that continue to happen all around the world, and cease the blind rush to repeat them. *We must remember, recall, review the heinous events in our past and repeat again and again, "Never again, never again."*

8. We can place enemy love at the center of all religion and faith and learn its practice in personal, social, economic, political, and religious life. This is the minimal benchmark for judging religious doctrine and practice: *No false religion teaches enemy love; no religion that blesses hatred of the enemy is worth a second thought. (We must be able to make this declaration without either absolutism in judgment of a religion's shortcomings or hatred for its proponents.)*

9. We can commit ourselves to do justice while loving mercy and, without exception, be strenuous in self-critique of all our claims to just hate. *"Search, try, know my heart, lead me in eternally just paths. May I come to see myself, O God, more nearly as you see me, to know myself as I am known by you."*

These are minimal steps in applying the paradigm of multiple hatreds which we have been pursuing together in this study. They are not a final examination for maturity, but entrance requirements for joining truly human community.

Three Crucial Issues in Reducing a Culture of Hate

Further, we can take countercultural steps of swimming against cultural tides—in actuality tidal waves—that nurture primitive hate patterns. These include our (1) resisting the constant return to trusting in retaliation and retributive justice as the bottom line in addressing wrongdoing; (2) opting out of the reliance on redemptive violence as the last word in our search for solutions to human conflicts and tragedies; (3) refusing to settle for superficial understandings of reconciliation. Let's look again at these three patterns.

1. The Return to Relying on Revenge

We must challenge the movement of Western culture from its already exaggerated trust in retributive justice to its renewed reliance on revenge and retaliation as the inevitable answer to wrongs suffered or evil done. The demand for quid pro quo settlements of injury has become routine news. Following the terrorism of 9/11, the expectation of the nation was for the president to fulfill his immediate promise of swift and forceful retaliation for the thousands of lives lost. The so-called war on terror took vengeance on an Arab nation that could not retaliate, ignoring the nationality of a majority of the terrorists, who came from a powerful nation friendly toward the U.S. and on whose oil we are heavily dependent. Then the focus quickly turned toward Iraq, although no link to the attack on America could be demonstrated. World press has, with few exceptions, inferred that the desire to avenge his father lies behind the president's policy. "Saddam is said to speak frequently of 'Bush the son' being driven to avenge 'Bush the father's' failure to take him out once and for all in 1991." Former President George H. W. Bush said in a September 2002 meeting in Houston that "I have nothing but hatred in my heart" for Saddam Hussein (Johnson 2002, E-1). No matter where, why, or by whom revenge is advocated, we can refuse to honor it as a valid motive, and reject it as a legitimate institutional process in our society or world.

For several centuries it has been the common wisdom that revenge is no longer a part of civilized society. Phrases like "objective rule by law" and the "universal brotherhood of man" had replaced family-versus-family vendettas. "Revenge developed to preserve the integrity of the family, because out in the isolation of the desert or in the jungle or in the grasslands, no one could defend himself alone," Blumenfeld argues. "And so revenge ensured survival. It's the ultimate instrument of collective identity in terms of giving everybody in the group an identity. But it also helps preserve the group." In aboriginal Siberia revenge is so embedded in the concept of kinship that the word for kindred families means "a collection of those who take part in blood revenge" (Blumenfeld 2002, 15).

The goal of revenge is to teach the perpetrator what pain feels like, but the punished perpetrator feels his own pain, not the victim's. Nothing was taught, nothing learned. There are ways to teach empathy, or reach remorse and reconciliation, but revenge is not one of them. When revenge gets even, evil has won a double victory. Since violence always wounds the victimizer as well as the victim, retaliation injures both giver and receiver. Revenge negates the humanity of the avenger, violates the humanity of the avenged, reduces both to common inhumanity. Revenge creates a new act of aggression, which it maintains is justified, but in defending an act of aggression as justifiable it prepares the way for the next act of aggression to be justified. Revenge does not acknowledge the history of victimization that instigates the original acts of the aggressor, or recognize the exploitive system that created the unjust context. In blaming the victimizer it refuses to see that the perpetrator was previously a victim, and after revenge will continue to be a victim, who will in time again be a victimizer. By focusing on the most recent violent action it ignores the related injustices, diverts attention from the totality of the injustice that needs to be addressed and the systemic or institutional change that is needed. So revenge provokes revenge which demands revenge which elicits revenge which requires revenge which evokes revenge which deserves revenge.

2. The Reverence for Redemptive Violence

We can challenge the elevation of redemptive violence in contemporary culture that sacralizes revenge, retributive justice, and retributive hatred as the primary paths to healing.

Hate, rather than love, has become the popular religion of contemporary culture. As I write, I have just seen the movie *In the Bedroom*, adapted from a short story by Andre Dubus III. The story, centered in the murder of a young man by his lover's ex-husband, revolves around the inconsolable grief of the dead boy's parents. The murderer is indicted, but out on bail and likely to go free. In spite of all their grief-work, the parents are consumed by the demand for "justice." Their differing ways of coping with rage erects an impenetrable barrier between them. When the father hits on a private plan for the perfect crime—kill the murderer but set up clues to indicate that he has skipped bail and disappeared—he tells his wife nothing. Only his old military buddy is in complicity. All proceeds by plan. He stealthily returns to the bedroom in the middle of the night to find his wife awake. "Did you do it?" she asks. He nods. In the quietness, they lie in silent satisfaction. "The story is ultimately redemptive," the ads for the movie assert. An intriguing choice of words—they use theological language to sell a story of revenge.

The myth of redemptive violence has become the sacred story of the resolution of hatred in our Western culture. Walter Wink is the most incisive and prophetic critic of this phenomenon. In summary, Wink argues: "Violence is the ethos of our times. It is the spirituality of the modern world. It has been accorded the status of a religion, demanding from its devotees an absolute obedience to death. Its followers are not aware, however, that the devotion they pay to violence is a form of religious piety. It, not Christianity, is the real religion of America" (Wink 1992, 13).

The dominant myth of redemptive violence in contemporary America is a continuation of the central beliefs of ancient Babylon religion. It was a celebration of violence that affirmed that evil is prior to good, that it is an ineradicable constituent of ultimate reality, that violence inheres in the Godhead, that creation is an act of violence, that the world is formed by the god Marduk from the cadaver of the god Tiamat, that humanity is created from the blood of this murdered god, that killing is in our blood since our origin is violence. It offers a theology of war, the virtue of suffering by the hero, redemption through the extermination of the enemy, an ethic of might makes right. Contemporary Western culture has enshrined this cult of violence. It is at the heart of public life, and even those who seek to oppose its dominance often do so using the very same means (Wink 1992, 13–17).

The myth of redemptive violence pervades popular culture. The simplest form, Wink observes, is in children's comics and television cartoon shows. "An indestructible good guy is unalterably opposed to an irreformable and equally indestructible bad guy. Nothing can kill the good guy, though for the first three quarters of the strip or show he (rarely she) suffers grievously, appearing hopelessly trapped, until somehow the hero breaks free, vanquishes the villain and restores order until the next installment. The psychodynamics of the television cartoon or comic book are marvelously simple: children identify with the good guy so that they can think of themselves as good. This enables them to project onto the bad guy their own repressed anger, violence, rebelliousness, or lust, and then vicariously to enjoy their own evil by watching the bad guy initially prevail (allowing ample time for indulging the dark side of the self). When the good guy finally wins, viewers are then able to reassert control over their own inner tendencies, repress them, and reestablish a sense of good-ness. Salvation is guaranteed through identification with the hero" (Wink 1992, 17–18).

The myth is replayed in movies, television, and novels and reenacted in real-life dramas of the pursuit, capture, or hostage dramas of urban crime. The myth of redemptive violence is the spirituality not only of entertainment, but of increasing litigiousness, and above all of militarism. All war is metaphysical; one can only go to war religiously. "The real faith of National Securocrats is redemptive violence" (Wink 1992, 27). "The myth of regenerative violence is the structuring metaphor of the Ameri-can experience. . . . It is nationalism become absolute" (30).

Hate has found a home in the culture through this permeating myth. It provides the cultural base for creating scenarios of violent solution, vio-lent resolution, that serve as rationales for retributive justice. The princi-pled justifications are woven into the plots that convince us emotionally as well as rationally that there is no other logical alternative, no other pos-sible outcome.

If one believes Jesus, and believes what Jesus believed, rather than "believing in Jesus" (the Christianity that has made him a captive of each nation and its agenda), then one refuses the myth of redemptive violence in any form. In returning to what Jesus actually taught, lived, died, one gives up the dream that violence can answer violence, hate will stamp out hate.

3. The Reduction of Forgiveness to Civility and Tolerance

We can challenge the devaluing of authentic forgiveness: refuse to join the popular psychological and theological trends that reduce genuine for-giveness to a therapeutic technique, tolerant civility, or individual release from resentment; return to the biblical and theological understandings and practices that recognize the true goal of forgiving is, first of all, work-ing at interpersonal change which, when achieved, results in intrapersonal release.

For millennia, the central function of forgiving has been transforming relationships. Its primary function was in between, not within, persons. When forgiving resulted in a change within persons, this new willingness to accept the other again was seen as a consequence of returning trust, regaining respect, and achieving camaraderie and love. In collective cul-tures, the historic bonding function that renegotiates the web of relation-ships and the justice that spins and sustains their attachments are still definitive of "forgiving." In Western cultures, however, the word has been devalued to an intrapsychic idea of therapeutic, not relational, change. Forgiveness has become "the gift you give yourself," individual, private, personal—not interpersonal. This indicates not just the evolution of language; it is a glacial shift to radical individualism in human relationships. "Forgiving" has mistakenly become the popular language for a process of dealing positively with hatred. Rarely does it mean the reconciling of alienated relationships; rather, it is a reordering of personal attitudes toward the other so that one no longer ruminates over the alienation. Hatred must be resolved by recognition of the other's humanity and a return to the mutuality we call neighbor regard. It is a restoring of essential acceptance of the other as a fellow human traveler. This is what neighbor love, not forgiveness, is about.

Our denial of hate, indeed our inability to deal with hatred, has seduced us to redirect the process of forgiving from its actual task and claim it as the means to taking the primary step, the pre-forgiving move of restoring basic recognition of the other as a human. We begin to deal with hate when we admit that the other is a man or woman, not a monster; a colleague, not an animal or object. Further, our fear of addressing our outrage at injury has led us to abbreviate the process of forgiving to an unconditional tolerance for actor and act, rather than the painful process of working toward, or when possible working through to, reconciliation. When forgiveness is seen as an unconditional release of demands against the offender, as the common cultural misunderstanding currently tends to perceive it (indeed this is the process being researched by such projects as the Campaign for Forgiveness Research), then its focus moves to internal changes in perceptions and cognitive behaviors that facilitate a therapeutic release of hatred. This is an important issue for research, but in reducing "forgiveness" to its introductory step and blending it with enlightenment tolerance for diversity, we have lost a central and powerful healing process, an essential necessity for community life.

This individualistic concept of forgiveness as a therapeutic process that offers uncritical absolution is not how the Jewish or the Christian Scriptures defined forgiving or how it has been expressed in theology or philosophy in the last two thousand years. Forgiveness cannot be split apart from repentance, justice, and some resolution of differences without emptying the concept or practice of any depth of meaning or function in community. When forgiveness is understood as the mutual recognition of appropriate repentance and an affirmation that right relationships are being committed or are achieved, then its authentic interpersonal character is visible to both the offender and the offended as well as the surrounding community. Those who use the word for the individual process of release refer to the interpersonal dimensions as "reconciliation" and view them as desirable consequences, but not essential to forgiving, and argue that there can be forgiveness without reconciliation, but there cannot be reconciliation without forgiveness. This splitting of the two—which are interdependent aspects of the same process—allows for a private reframing without any act of returning toward the other.

The restoring of neighbor regard and fellow feeling is the prerequisite step prior to the beginning of the process of forgiveness. Theologically, this prerequisite is the restoration of compassion for the offender. Wrongdoing is not a valid reason for withholding compassion or love from the other. The moral status of the offender may be in question, but this does not diminish or reduce the other's inherent worth as a human being. The return to valuing the other as a human and recognizing worth in a person as a person opens the door for conversation about the injustice perpetrated, the injury done. Such valuing is not forgiving, because the issues of loss, pain, or violation still remain to be addressed. When we do not recognize the presence of hate, when we deny its existence within self and society, then we seek to address its outcry by leaping across the wall of rage and claiming the latter process to resolve the primary feelings of outrage. This mislabeling creates misunderstanding, which leads to misapprehension of what is actually needed, and mistaken attempts to find an immediate "closure." The popularity of the word "closure" is revelatory of this devaluing of forgiving in the healing process. Closure is a psychological term from Gestalt psychology for achieving a clear perception as the figure of attention emerges from the ground being observed. "Closure" is a business term for completing the purchase of a property and taking ownership of the house. Neither of these metaphors is appropriate to the complex and multilevel process of healing and restoration. We can address the issues of our hate—in empathy, in compassion, in a return to enemy love, in honest recognition of the fellow humanity of the offender. Then we may be prepared to do the work of seeking forgiveness together.

Perhaps the most prophetic expression of the rejection of hate was embodied by Nelson Mandela. After emerging from twenty-seven years in prison, he announced that he had forgiven those who jailed him. "That example has been enormously influential in South Africa," says Alexander Boraine, deputy commissioner of the Truth and Reconciliation Commission and New York University professor. The strong cultural conception in South Africa of *ubuntu,* the idea that we are all one, makes it hard to separate oneself from someone who has done wrong to you. The Truth and Reconciliation Commission, with its mandate to resolve the atrocities of the apartheid era committed by both sides of the racial divide, has accepted public acknowledgment and remorse as the requisite and final completion of reviewed cases of atrocity. This concept would never work in the United States, Archbishop Desmond Tutu has said, until the nation abolishes the death penalty, renouncing retributive justice (punishment as resolution) and embracing restorative justice (reconciliation as the goal). "Human beings," says Tutu, "despite the fact that we have the capacity for untold evil, are ultimately made for goodness, for love, for gentleness, for forgiveness, for peace, for reconciliation" (Clark 2001, F-4).

Nobody Left to Hate

In the novel *Birdy*, William Wharton's protagonist, Sergeant Alfonso, develops an instant dislike for an obnoxious, overweight enlisted man, a clerk typist named Ronsky. At the top of his list of gripes about this annoying grunt is Ronsky's revolting habit of continually spitting. He spits all over his desk, his typewriter, his papers, and those who venture too near. Alfonso is only waiting an excuse to punch him out. Then the sergeant learns Ronsky's story. He was an infantryman on D-day, and saw his buddies shot down in the surf before they even reached the beach of Normandy. And his constant spitting, it seems, is a physical manifestation of his attempt to get the nauseous foulness of war and death out of his mouth when anything reminds him, as virtually everything does, of its acrid smell and putrid taste. Sergeant Alfonso suddenly sees Ronsky with new eyes. What yesterday had irritated him unbearably, today wins his total respect. He sighs with regret, and thinks: Before you know it, if you're not careful, you can get to feeling for everybody and there's nobody left to hate (Wharton 1979).

Empathy does that. Compassion leaves so few to hate. Once you let them into your inner world of understanding, you change, and they are no longer the people you previously despised. Your world grows larger, the spiritual solipsism breaks open. Solidarity becomes more than a word. Compassion opens us to *things as they are*. Albert Einstein, describing this transformation in what he called "widening the circle of compassion," said:

> When a human being experiences himself, his thoughts and feelings as separated from the rest of humankind, it is a kind of optical delusion of consciousness. This delusion is a prison, restricting us to our

personal desires and to affection for the few persons nearest us. Our task must be to free ourselves from this prison by *widening our circle of compassion*, to embrace all living creatures and the whole of nature in its beauty. Nobody is able to achieve this completely, but the striving for such an achievement is, in itself, a part of the liberation and foundation of our inner security. (Einstein, in Aronson 2000, 89)

Basic Introduction to Hate-Work

Hate-work is hard work. It is easy to simply add restraints or prohibitions against hate, but this inevitably boomerangs. Any increase
in prohibitions evokes an equal and opposite increase in drives, and when
the restraints are not enforced, the drives win. And the last state is more
powerful than the first.

Hate-work is liberating work. The way to end hating or oppressing
others is not by further oppressing oneself. Adding restraints only
increases the drives of hostility. The secret to release is found not in
adding restraints, but in taking away old drives to hate. We move toward
freedom by discovering what it is that *drives* our hate—the drives are the
needs, the fears, the past injuries, the beliefs, the familial and communal
instructions, the prejudices and stereotypes that press us from within.

Hate-work is daily work. It involves uncovering, discovering, recovering, and removing our drives to hate, one by one. Release is the result of
taking away, not adding to, decreasing not increasing internal pressures.
Change comes from reducing these drives, eliminating the old inner
instructions and commands, allowing the possibilities of understanding,
of empathy, of fellow feeling and of cohumanity to slowly emerge. The
work is hard because it is not easy to let go, give up, let grow, pull up.

Hate-work is also hope-work. As I come to see rightly how I have seen
others wrongly, and begin to perceive them in a new light, I may look at
my world and at myself seeing through a ray of hope.

What Hate-Work Is *Not*

Hate-work is *not* overlooking, ignoring, or tolerating evil.

Hate-work is the process of looking the evil suffered fully in the face, feeling the pain again and again, but refusing to be controlled, dominated, imprisoned, determined, consumed, or re-created in its hateful image.

Hate-work is *not* emotional amnesia.

Hate-work is an unfolding memory metamorphosis, an emotional breakthrough to empathy that sees the other as a broken human not totally dissimilar to aspects of many people one has known and accepted, including oneself.

Hate-work is *not* memory fatigue.

Hate-work is gradually moving beyond the burnout of anger to rework, reenvision, reframe the hated person and the hated act until the monster shrinks to puny, stunted, or average human size again.

Hate-work is *not* excusing evil.

Hate-work is progressively refusing to use evil as an excuse to return evil for evil. Hate-work reverses the downward spiral of violence and revenge in order to turn upward in a widening spiral of mutual humanity.

Hate-work is *not* giving up the right to justice.

Hate-work is stubbornly seeking to move beyond retributive justice that returns legal evil for illegal evil. Hate-work seeks restorative justice that, where possible, lets both sides make a new beginning.

Hate-work is *not* inviting the evildoer to do evil again.

Hate-work is continually challenging evil by reaching out to the evil-doer as a fellow human while despising, rejecting, and, when possible, confronting and intervening in evildoing.

Hate-Work: Exploration and Recognition

Process 1. Exploration—Uncovering, Discovering, Recovering

For individual self-exploration, since the webs of hate are secluded in the shadows within, the following issues are starting-point questions, useful in beginning a longer process of unmasking:

1. Are there persons that I avoid, persons who are invisible to me in my family, work, church, or community?
2. Are there members of my family, work, or church systems whom I have emotionally cut off, who were previously connected with me but are no longer so?
3. Do I have a pattern of placing blame on another or on others for painful injuries to my self-esteem, success, or safety?
4. Do I have hurtful relationships that I cannot stop reviewing? Are there painful events that I repeatedly revisit to renew my resentment of the person(s) who caused me pain?
5. Do I realize what payoff I get from brooding? Can I identify what I get out of rehearsing an offense over and over? Why do I insist on replaying the history of injury?
6. How often have I told and retold the story of the offense to others to gain their support and validation of my role or position as victim?
7. What fantasies have I created about the offender—visualizing her suffering or relishing the idea of his feeling similar pain?
8. How have my feelings of rage at the offender permeated other areas of my life, bleeding into other relationships, coloring my spirituality?

9. Does this situation affect my attitude toward other people, other situations, or other circumstances that are similar in some way?
10. Do I let the hateful act take over and define how I see the perpetrator? Am I aware that, in doing this, I allow the act to also define me as victim?
11. Is it possible that the hateful emotions within me have begun to usurp my identity and are now taking on a life of their own?
12. Do I want to risk harboring hatred, when I see how hatred can consume a person until it is the only truly personal possession one has within, and eventually becomes a substitute core identity?

Process 2. Recognition—Facing, Owning, Risking

For recognition of hidden hate, the following questions provide opportunities for facing, invitations to owning, possibilities for risking decision and change:

1. Can I admit that my negative feelings are hurtful to me, but in reality have no power to hurt the other?
2. Am I willing to explore how subjective my judgments are, how influenced by my pride, how they defend me against shame, how they minimize my part and maximize the offense of the other?
3. Can I own the hostility within me and recognize that holding on to it is not useful or functional for me?
4. Can I risk talking to a counselor or a significant other about how I am feeling stuck, or how I feel as if I were being held hostage by hostility?
5. Can I make a mental and emotional commitment to think empathically about the other person's perspective, to see the situation from the other's point of view?
6. Can I begin to see the other in a wider, broader, more human frame of reference, to think of our cohumanity as fellow strugglers?
7. Can I enter the other's experience by asking what losses, what pressures, what past injuries may have influenced him or her at the time of the altercation?
8. Can I recall similar experiences in which I acted hurtfully toward another, where I was party to a similar breach of trust or caused a parallel injury, when I was guilty of even the same failure?
9. Do I really want justice to be done? If so, what kind of justice? Am I willing to move beyond retributive justice to ask what would be

redemptive or transforming for me, for the other, for the relationship, for our future in community or in the world?

10. Do I see myself, not as alone, but as a part of a wider world of persons who have survived and even transformed suffering into strength to care?

11. Can I let go of my subjective feelings of hate that are fixated on the offender and on my being offended and think objectively about how I hate all acts of injustice and injury of any kind, anywhere, against anyone?

12. Can I give up my attachment to my own anger about this instance of being unjustly treated or violated, and choose a new stance that is determined to speak, act, work for justice whenever and wherever possible?

13. Can I identify any benefits that have come to me through this loss, injury, or conflict that have strengthened or deepened my understanding of life?

14. Can I absorb a significant piece of unjust suffering, realizing that life is not always fair and someone must take the initiative and bear the injury if there is to be healing or hope for the future?

15. Can I visualize the other as moving toward the light of God's grace and healing, even as I know myself to be—although this person travels by a different path, perhaps a twisted and troubled path, and then wish her well on her journey?

For group process, you may use the preceding items as experiences for increasing awareness, as questions for group conversations, as joint exercises in letting go of self-justification and reactive defenses. For reflection on masked hatred in any group to which you belong, the issues for beginning conversation and reflection include:

1. Do we exclude persons who differ on the basis of stereotypes about character, minority status, race, sexual orientation, gender, religion, or some other factor?

2. Do we tribalize as a group by telling stories, making jokes that use language that excludes, trivializes, or demeans members of another group?

3. Do we gain in cohesiveness, feel more solidarity, by contrasting ourselves with another group whom we oppose?

4. Do we retell stories of injustices borne or indignities suffered at the hands of the other group?

5. Do we profit from another group's lesser status? Do we assume entitlement to our situation, our status, or personal advantage?
6. If we come to see the cohumanity of the enemy, can we begin to visualize the possibility of shared life in a world without the hostility and hatred that has divided us from each other in the past?
7. Since all lasting change takes place within relationship, does change in prejudice, fear, and hate require the shared practice of empathy? (Enright 1998, 53; Patton 1990, 173–75, 184–86; Augsburger 1996, 165–68)

Hate-Work: Working through Our Hate

The relationship between doing hate-work and forgiving is often blurred by the many ways in which the word *forgiveness* is used to designate the change from negative to positive attitudes. The long list of definitions stretches from "forgiveness as the practice of simple civility" to "forgiving as authentic repentance and genuine reconnection." It is helpful to group common definitions and compare or contrast their goals with those of hate-work.

1. Is the goal to somehow get free from it, get past it, get over it all?
The popular idea of "forgiveness as memory fatigue" equates forgiving with the "eventual exhaustion of memories." The common wisdom is that distance and the passage of time "heals all," so that one chooses to "put the anger or pain behind oneself in 'closure.'"

One evicts the event, refuses to be held hostage by memory or resentment, and "gets on with life." So forgiveness is enlightened social tolerance, necessary civility, mature politeness that excuses an offender or an offense by offering an immediate, automatic pardon without consideration of responsibility or guilt.

2 . Is the goal somehow to give up simple, malicious, or retributive hate?
Forgiveness is "the willingness to abandon one's right to resentment, negative judgment, and indifferent behavior toward one who unjustly injures us, while fostering the undeserved qualities of compassion, generosity and even love" (Enright 1998, 47).

Forgiveness is a matter of a willed change of heart, the successful result of an active endeavor to replace bad thoughts with good, bitterness and anger with compassion and affection (North 1987, 506).

3. Is the goal to give up principled rationalizations for hate?

Forgiveness is breaking free from bondage. An act of transgression locks the perpetrator to the victim; every offense creates human bondage: evil acts create chains—largely unconscious—of debt, guilt, obligation. Forgiveness is a complex process of "unlocking" painful bondage, of individual or mutual liberation (Mueller-Fahrenholz 1996, 24).

Forgiveness is an act of laying aside one's rational arguments for retaliation, one's legal arguments for repayment, my principled arguments for my being truly in the right and you being wholly in the wrong, and at last offering a full and complete pardon to the other, whether or not there are any believable signs of authentic remorse or repentance in the perpetrator. In granting the other person release, one receives one's own.

4. Is the goal to give up the moral high ground and reach out in cohumanity?

Forgiveness is not something you do, it is something you discover: you discover you are in no position to forgive; you are more like than unlike the one who hurt you (Patton 1990, 15).

I doubt that when forgiveness is offered the gaze is cast on the specifics of the deed. Forgiveness, while not disregarding the act, begins not with it but with the person. Forgiveness recognizes the deed, its impact having been and continuing to be lived by the victim, but transcends it (Gobodo-Madikizela 2003, 95).

Forgiveness is the restitution of the human, the recognition of cohumanity. One human being chooses to accept another—in spite of a terrible past—as another human being (Yevtushenko 1967, 26; Mueller-Fahrenholz 1996, 32).

Forgiveness is morally possible because of the inherent value of all persons. The moral status of the offender may be in question, but this does not diminish the person's inherent worth as a human being. Forgiveness is a relational stance of accepting the inherent worth of another person even after judging the wrong action (Kellenberger 1995, 407).

Forgiveness is an increase in our internal motivation to repair and maintain a relationship after it has been damaged by the hurtful actions of the other (McCullough, Sandage, and Worthington 1997, 22).

5. Is the goal an active search for justice, concern for the enemy, and change of evil?

Forgiveness is the mutual recognition that repentance is genuine and right relationships have been restored or achieved (Kimper 1972).

Forgiveness usually begins with the perpetrator's giving some "sign" that invites forgiveness. Forgiveness is a kind of revenge, but revenge enacted at a rarified level. Forgiveness may appear to condone the offense, thus further disempowering the victim. But forgiveness does not overlook the deed—it rises above it. "This is what it means to be human," it says. "I cannot and will not return the evil you have done to me." And that is the victim's triumph (Gobodo-Madikizela 2003, 117).

Forgiveness is a process that includes both perpetrator and victim, occurring when the offender asks and the offended grants it, not unilaterally, but in an appropriate measure of mutuality, with both sides recognizing, owning, moving, changing, releasing, healing, redeeming the past, renewing the present, opening the future to a more just relationship.

In repenting, one returns to stand in the painful point of time—the remembered evil act—feels the shame of abuse or victimization, owns the hatred or wish for revenge, relinquishes actual and illusory power in reciprocal repentance, and finally feels the internal release of all demands on the event, the self, and the other person.

Forgiveness is a habit, a practice, a craft. It is not simply an action, an emotional judgment, or a declarative utterance—though Christian forgiveness includes all of these dimensions. Rather, forgiveness is a habit that must be practiced over time within the disciplines of Christian community. . . . Forgiveness is a habit, a practice alongside other practices, including baptism, Eucharist, confession, repentance, excommunication, prayer, and healing (Jones 1995, 163, 165–66).

So, hate-work becomes the practice of forgiving love.

Views of Forgiving: Alternative Perspectives

The many perspectives on forgiving provide a progressive range of views, from minimal social civility to restored relationship. Find your preferred understandings and goals on the following chart, recognizing that different relationships call for differing goals and diverse responses.

Table 5	*Perspectives on Forgiving*					
Civility	**Tolerance**	**Acceptance**	**Pardon**	**Cohumanity**	**Process**	**Connection**
politeness, courtesy, "niceness"	denial, overlooking, "closure"	unconditional positive regard, benevolence	unilateral pardon & release	equal regard, shared humanity	reach out, risk, & work thru	reconnect, re-create, reconcile
Offer immediate polite association without question of guilt or respon- sibility	Overlook insult or injury by refusing all judgment, foreclose on "closure," and "put it behind us"	Accept the other as fallible yet of worth ("in the wrong, but I will overlook it for peace")	Release of demands vs. offender, setting self free of review or resentment by an act of will	Restitution of the human; acknowledge the other as another human being in spite of failure in our past	Validating repentance by one or both in mutual intention, action, & behavior	Mutual recognition; repentance is genuine and right relationships are restored or achieved

Table 5   Perspectives on Forgiving, continued

Goals of One or Both Parties:

Democratic Way	Superior Way	My Way	The Right Way	Our Way	Open Way	A New Way
enlightened tolerance; respect for human fallibility, frailty, oddity	superiority, competence, anger management, pride of my being "big about it all"	condescension, being "one up," putting the other in debt, boosting one's own ego & self-image	refusal to "get back" or "get even" in review, retaliation, revenge, or hate-speech	empathy, reciprocity, mutuality, cohumanity, compassion —basic though weak	work at relating, deal with hurt/guilt/ shame/pain in self or other	risking trust, open future, discern reality, settle for the truly good rather than what's "right"
Practice personal civility	Practice individual tolerance	Model acceptance & generosity	Practice generosity of pardon	Express mutuality in mercy	Live out shared agape	Live within integrity of justice/grace

Moving across the spectrum may sometimes mean:
Hate hidden—hate present but denied—breakthrough—release and recovery

From Hate-Work to Hope-Work:
For Group Discussion

The following affirmations are a set of declarations for doing Hope-Work. How many of them can you, as a group, come to a consensus of commitment to pursue?

We are all in need of the grace of God (knowing that we are accepted by God, and humbly accepting God's acceptance at the very point where we know ourselves to be most unacceptable).

We can recognize that all true religion is grounded in grace and is characterized not by hatred of any other, but by enemy love.

We can come to see that neighbor love and enemy love are the two undeniable evidences of the experience of grace. It may well be that the only way to God is through our enemy.

We can discover that as we reaffirm the humanity of the enemy, we realize that our own true humanity lies in seeing the cohumanity of all persons.

We learn that giving and receiving grace are two aspects of the same reality—we exist in all relationships because of the grace of others, we enter human community as responsible adults when we extend grace to others.

We can assimilate the truth that the path of reconciliation is the one and only pathway to a future with few walls, with less fear, and with little hate.

The Oslo Declaration on Hate (1990)

This ancient scourge, whose origins remain hidden in darkness, knows neither barriers nor frontiers. It strikes all races and religions, all political systems and social classes, and because hatred is willed by man, God Himself is unable to stop it. No nation may consider itself protected against its poison; no society is safe against its arrows. Both blind and blinding, this hatred is a black sun, which from under an ashen sky hits and kills all those who forget the greatness of which they are capable and the promises once bestowed upon them.

Hatred has no mercy for those who refuse to fight it. It kills whoever will not try to disarm it.

Parents, teach your children that to hate is to mutilate their own future.

Teachers, tell your pupils that hatred is the negation of every triumph that culture and civilization may achieve.

Politicians, tell your constituencies that hatred is, at all levels, your principal enemy, and theirs. Tell all those who listen to you that hatred breeds hatred and can breed nothing else.

To hate is to refuse to accept another person as a human being, to diminish him, to limit your own horizon by narrowing his, to look at him—and also at yourself—not as a subject of pride but as an object of disdain and of fear.

To hate is to opt for the easiest and most mind-reducing way out by digging a ditch into which the hater and his victim will both fall like broken puppets.

To hate is to kindle wars that will turn children into orphans and make old people lose their minds from sorrow and contrition.

Religious hatred makes the face of God invisible. Political hatred wipes out people's liberties. In the field of science, hatred inevitably puts itself at death's service. In literature, it distorts truth, perverts the meaning of the story, and hides beauty itself under a thick layer of blood and grime.

Today, at the threshold of the twenty-first century, this is what we must tell all men and women for whom we wish a future as bright and smiling as the faces of our children. If we do nothing, hate will come sneaking perniciously and slyly into their mouths and into their eyes, adulterating the mutual relations between people, nations, societies, and races. If we do nothing, we will be passing on to the coming century that message of hatred known to us as racism, fanaticism, xenophobia, and anti-Semitism.

Democracy means dialogue. Without the other, neither is conceivable. Together, they contribute towards that "brotherhood of nations" mentioned by Alfred Nobel in his last will and testament as man's only hope of peace and survival. This then is our appeal:

"We appeal to governments, organizations, the media, educational institutions to find measures to follow up the essence of this Oslo Declaration in ways which can help lead mankind away from hate and vanquish the indifference to hate."

These words do not only mean that we have decided to oppose the flood of ugly, violent hatred that is still inundating our society. By signing them, we first of all confirm our certitude that humanity is strong enough to stem it and worthy of such a victory.

Oslo, Norway. August, 1990
(Wiesel 1999, 376–77)

Reference List

Abrahamson, Irving. 1985. *Against Silence! The Voice and Vision of Elie Wiesel.* New York: Holocaust Library.

Abrams, Jeremiah, and Connie Zweig, eds. 1991. *Meeting the Shadow: The Hidden Power of the Dark Side of Human Nature.* Los Angeles: J. P. Tarcher.

Aho, James A. 1994. *This Thing of Darkness: A Sociology of the Enemy.* Seattle: University of Washington Press.

Alinsky, Saul D. 1971. *Rules for Radicals.* New York: Vintage.

Allport, Gordon. 1954. *The Nature of Prejudice.* Reading, Mass.: Addison-Wesley.

Altman, L. L. 1977. "Some Vicissitudes of Love." *Journal of the American Psychoanalytic Association* 25:35–52.

Americas Watch. 1985. *Human Rights in Nicaragua: Reagan, Rhetoric and Reality.* New York: Americas Watch.

Arden, Nicky. 1996. *African Spirits Speak: A White Woman's Journey into the Healing Traditions of Sangoma.* Capetown: Inner-tradition International.

Armour, Ellen T. 1999. *Deconstruction, Feminist Theology, and the Problem of Difference: Subverting the Race/Gender Divide.* Chicago: University of Chicago Press.

Aronson, Elliot. 1991. *The Social Animal.* New York: W. H. Freeman.

———. 2000. *Nobody Left to Hate: Teaching Compassion after Columbine.* New York: W. H. Freeman (Worth Publications).

Ashkenasy, Hans. 1978. *Are We All Nazis?* Seacaucus, N.J.: Lyle Stuart.

Auden, W. H. 1940. "September 1, 1939." In *Another Time.* New York: Random House.

Augsburger, David. 1992. *Conflict Mediation across Cultures.* Louisville: Westminster/John Knox Press.

———. 1996. *Helping People Forgive.* Louisville: Westminster John Knox Press.

Baird, Robert M. and Stuart E. Rosenbaum, eds. 1999. *Hatred, Bigotry and Prejudice: Definitions, Causes and Solutions.* Amherst, N.Y.: Prometheus Books.

Baldwin, James. 1955. *Notes of a Native Son.* Boston: Beacon Press.

Balint, Michael. 1952. "On Love and Hate." In *Primary Love and Psychoanalytic Technique.* London: Maresfield.

———. 1979. *The Basic Fault: Therapeutic Aspects of Regression.* New York: Brunner/Mazel.

Barton, R. 1919. *Ifugao Law.* Berkeley: University of California Press.

Ben-Ze'ev, Aaron. 2000. *The Subtlety of Emotions.* Cambridge, Mass.: MIT Press.

Berdyaev, Nicolas. 1944. *Slavery and Freedom.* New York: Charles Scribner's Sons.

Berger, Peter. 1994. "Hatred under Ice." *First Things* 42 (April): 11–12.

Bergmann, Werner, and Rainer Erb. 1997. *Anti-Semitism in Germany: The Post Nazi Epoch Since 1945.* London: Transaction Publishers.

Bierce, Ambrose. 1999. *The Devil's Dictionary.* New York: Oxford University Press.

Blackman, N., K. Smith, R. Brokman, and J. Stern. 1958. "The Development of Empathy in Male Schizophrenics." *Psychiatric Quarterly* 32:546–53.

Blue, Rose, and Corrine J. Naden. 1994. *Working Together against Hate Groups.* New York: Rosen Publishing Group.

Blumenfeld, Laura. 2002. *Revenge: A Story of Hope.* New York: Simon & Schuster.

Bly, Robert. 1988. *The Little Book on the Human Shadow.* New York: Harper & Row.

Bonhoeffer, Dietrich. 1963. *The Cost of Discipleship.* New York: Macmillan.

———. 1970. *No Rusty Swords.* London: Collins, The Fontana Library.

Bowen, Murray. 1978. *Family Therapy in Clinical Practice.* New York: J. H. Aronson.

Bowlby, John. 1982. *Attachment and Loss.* New York: Basic Books.

Braham, Randolph L., ed. 1986. *The Origins of the Holocaust: Christian Anti-Semitism.* Boulder, Colo.: Social Science Monographs and Institute for Holocaust Studies of the City University of New York.

Brockway, Allan R. 1982. "Religious Values after the Holocaust, A Protestant View." In *Jews and Christians after the Holocaust*, ed. Abraham J. Peck. Philadelphia: Fortress Press.

Brown, Norman O. 1970. *Life against Death: The Psychoanalytical Meaning of History*. Middletown, Conn.: Wesleyan University Press.

Brown, Robert McAfee. 1983. *Elie Wiesel: Messenger to All Humanity*. Notre Dame, Ind.: Notre Dame University Press.

Brueggemann, Walter. 1984. *The Message of the Psalms*. Minneapolis: Augsburg.

———. 1993. *Texts under Negotiation: The Bible and Post-Modern Imagination*. Minneapolis: Fortress Press.

Buber, Martin. 1957. *Pointing the Way*. London: Routledge & Kegan Paul.

———. 1970. *I and Thou*. New York: Charles Scribner's Sons.

———. 1971. *Between Man and Man*. New York: Macmillan.

Buechner, Frederick. 1993. *Whistling in the Dark: A Doubter's Dictionary*. San Francisco: HarperCollins.

Burneo, Jose. 1996. "The Legalization of Impunity: An Obstacle to National Reconciliation." In *Impunity*, ed. Charles Harper. Geneva: WCC Publications.

Butler, Joseph. 1726. *Fifteen Sermons*. Reprint, 1749. London: J & P Knapton.

Butler, Judith. 1993. *Bodies That Matter: On the Discursive Limits of Sex*. New York: Routledge.

———. 1995. "Burning Acts: Injurious Speech." In *Deconstruction is/in America: A New Sense of the Political*, ed. Anselm Haverkamp. New York: New York University Press.

Byatt, A. S. 1967. *The Game*. New York: Charles Scribner's Sons.

Bychowski, Gustav. 1968. *Evil in Man: The Anatomy of Hate and Violence*. New York: Grune & Stratton.

Carter, Jimmy. 1999. "Rid the Justice System of Racism." *Los Angeles Times*. November 2, sec. B, p. 9.

Cather, Willa. 1943. *The Song of the Lark*. Boston: Houghton Mifflin.

Chambers, Whittaker. 1952. *Witness*. Chicago: Henry Regnery.

Charlesworth, James H., Frank X. Blisard, and Jerry L. Gorham. 1993. *Overcoming Fear between Jews and Christians*. New York: Crossroad.

Charny, Israel. 1969. "Marital Love and Hate." *Family Process* (March): 1–24.

———. 1972. *Marital Love and Hate*. New York: Macmillan.

Chesterton, G. K. 1928. *Generally Speaking: A Book of Essays*. London: Methuen.

Chicago Commission on Race Relations. 1922. *The Negro in Chicago: A*

Study of Race Relations and Race Riot. Chicago: University of Chicago Press.

Chrysostom, Saint John. 1857–66. "Homilies against the Jews." In *Patrologia Graeca* 48:843–942. Paris: Garnier.

Clark, John. 2001. "The Long Road to Reconciliation," a review of the documentary "Long Night's Journey into Day," *Los Angeles Times,* June 11, sec. F, p. 4.

Clutton-Brock, A. 1985. "Christmas, 1914." Cited in *In a Dark Time: Images for Survival,* ed. Robert J. Lifton and Nicholas Humphrey. Cambridge, Mass.: Harvard University Press.

Cobb, Sanford H. 1902. *The Rise of Religious Liberty in America.* New York: Macmillan.

Cohn, Norman. 1975. *Europe's Inner Demons.* Brighton, England: Sussex University Press.

Cooley, Charles Horton. 1902. *Human Nature and the Social Order.* New York: Charles Scribner's Sons.

Copjec, Joan. 1996. *Radical Evil.* London: Verso Press.

Cushman, Phillip. 1995. *Constructing the Self, Constructing America: A Cultural History of Psychotherapy.* Reading, Mass.: Addison-Wesley.

D'Arcy, Martin. 1947. *The Mind and Heart of Love, Lion and Unicorn: A Study in Eros and Agape.* New York: Henry Holt.

Daly, M., and M. Wilson. 1988. *Homicide.* Hawthorne, N.Y.: Aldine de Gruyter.

Dicks, Henry V. 1972. *Licensed Mass Murder: A Social-Psychological Study of Some S.S. Killers.* New York: Basic Books.

Dijk, Tuen A. van. 1995. "Elite Discourse and the Reproduction of Racism." In *Hate Speech,* ed. Rita Whillock and David Slayden. Thousand Oaks, Calif.: Sage Publications.

Djilas, Milovan. 1958. *Land without Justice.* New York: Harcourt, Brace.

Doi, L. Takeo. 1976. "Psychotherapy as 'Hide and Seek.'" In *Culture-Bound Syndromes, Ethnopsychiatry and Alternate Therapies,* ed. William Lebra. Honolulu: University of Hawaii Press.

Dorrien, Gary. 1997. *The Word As True Myth.* Louisville, Ky.: Westminster John Knox Press.

Doub, Christopher Bates. 1999. *Racism: An American Cauldron.* New York: Longman.

Dovidio, John F., and Samuel L. Gaertner. 1986. *Prejudice, Discrimination, and Racism.* Orlando, Fla.: Academic Press.

Eckhardt, William. 1913. *Compassion: Towards a Science of Value.* Toronto: Canadian Peace Research Institute.

Elizondo, Virgil. 1986. " I Forgive but I Do Not Forget." In *Forgiveness*, ed. Casiano Florestan and Christian Duquoc. Edinburgh: T. and T. Clark.

Ellis, Marc H. 1990. *Beyond Innocence and Redemption: Confronting the Holocaust and Israeli Power*. San Francisco: HarperCollins.

———. 1994. *Ending Auschwitz: The Future of Jewish and Christian Life*. Louisville, Ky.: Westminster John Knox Press.

———. 1997. *Unholy Alliance: Religion and Atrocity in Our Time*. Minneapolis: Fortress Press.

Ellul, Jacques. 1965. *Propaganda: The Formation of Men's Attitudes*. New York: Vintage Books.

Elster, J. 1999a. *Alchemies of the Mind: Rationality and the Emotions*. New York: Cambridge University Press.

———. 1999b. *Strong Feelings: Emotion, Addiction and Human Behavior*. Cambridge, Mass.: MIT Press.

Engel, David. 1999. *The Holocaust: The Third Reich and the Jews*. New York: Longman.

Enright, Robert, and Joanna North. 1998. *Exploring Forgiveness*. Madison: University of Wisconsin Press

Everett, Robert. 1986. Cited in *The Origins of the Holocaust*, ed. Randolph L. Braham. Boulder, Colo.: Social Science Monographs and Institute for Holocaust Studies of the City University of New York.

Feingold, Henry L. 1981. "Determining the Uniqueness of the Holocaust." *SHOAH* 2, no. 2.

Fine, Reuben. 1990. *The History of Psychoanalysis*. New York: Continuum.

Fornari, Franco. 1975. *The Psychoanalysis of War*. Bloomington: Indiana University Press.

Frank, Michael. 2001. "The Human Stain," a review of *Neighbors*, by Jan T. Gross. *Los Angeles Times Book Review*, Sunday, June 17:4–5.

Freud, Sigmund. 1937. "Analysis Terminable and Interminable." *The Standard Edition of the Complete Psychological Works of Sigmund Freud*, vol. 23. London: Hogarth Press.

———. 1960. *Letters of Sigmund Freud*, ed. Ernst Freud. New York: Basic Books.

Friedman, Maurice. 1964. "Hasidism and the Love of Enemies: A New Approach to Reconciliation." *Fellowship*, November.

Fritsch, Charles T. 1955. "God Was with Him: A Theological Study of the Joseph Narrative." *Interpretation* 9, no. 1 (January): 25–30.

Fromm, Erich. 1956. *The Art of Loving*. New York: Harper & Brothers.

Frye, Northrop. 1990. *Words with Power: Being a Second Study of "The Bible and Literature."* San Diego, Calif.: Harcourt Brace Jovanovich.

Fugard, Athol. 1997. "A Playwright in Love with the Theatre." *Performing Arts*, April.

Gadamer, Hans G. 1982. *Reason in the Age of Science*. Cambridge, Mass.: MIT Press.

Galdston, R. 1987. "The Longest Pleasure: A Psychoanalytic Study of Hatred." *International Journal of Psycho-analysis*, 68:371–78.

Gandhi, Mohandas. 1961. *Non-Violent Resistance*. New York: Schocken Books.

Gibbs, N., and T. Roche. 1999a. "The Columbine Tapes." *Time*, December 20:25.

———. 1999b. "A Week in the Life of a High School." *Time*, October 24: 17.

Gibran, Kahlil. 1925. *The Madman*. New York: Alfred A. Knopf.

Gilbert, G. M. 1950. *The Psychology of Dictatorship*. New York: Ronald Press.

Ginger, Ray. 1949. *The Bending Cross*. New Brunswick, N.J.: Rutgers University Press.

Ginzburg, Ralph. 1969. *One Hundred Years of Lynchings*. New York: Lancer Books.

Girard, Rene. 1986. *The Scapegoat*. Baltimore: Johns Hopkins University Press.

Glover, Jonathan. 2000. *Humanity: A Moral History of the Twentieth Century*. New Haven, Conn.: Yale University Press.

Gobodo-Madikizela, Pumla. 2003. *A Human Being Died That Night*. Boston: Houghton Mifflin.

Goleman, Daniel. 1995. *Emotional Intelligence*. New York: Bantam Books.

Gordon, S. L. 1990. "Social Structural Effects on Emotions." In *Research Agendas in the Sociology of Emotions*, ed. T. D. Kemper, 145–79. Albany, N.Y.: SUNY Press.

Greenberg, Irving. 1982. "Religious Values after the Holocaust: A Jewish View." In *Jews and Christians after the Holocaust*, ed. Abraham J. Peck. Philadelphia: Fortress Press.

Greenwald, Anthony G. 1980. "The Totalitarian Ego: Fabrication and Revision of Personal History." *American Psychologist* 35:603–18.

Gross, Jan T. 2001. *Neighbors: The Destruction of the Jewish Community in Jedwabne, Poland*. Princeton, N.J.: Princeton University Press.

Gruber, Howard. 1991. "Foreword." In Robert W. Rieber, *The Psychology of War and Peace*. New York: Plenum.

Hagedorn, Herman. 1921. *Roosevelt in the Badlands*. Boston: Houghton Mifflin.

Hallett, Garth. 1989. *Christian Neighbor-love: An Assessment of Six Rival Versions.* Washington, D.C.: Georgetown University Press.

Harder, Lydia. 2001. "Reading Psalm 139: Opting for a Realistic Reading." In *Reclaiming the Old Testament,* ed. Gordon Zerbe. Winnipeg: CMBC Publications.

Harper, Charles. 1995. "Exigences œcuméniques pour la réconciliation." *Université de Paix* 52 (September), Belgium.

———. 1996. *Impunity: An Ethical Perspective.* Geneva: WCC Publications.

Harrell, Camara Jules. 1999. *Manichean Psychology: Racism and the Minds of People of African Descent.* Washington, D.C.: Howard University Press.

Heer, Friedrich. 1971. "The Catholic Church and the Jews Today." *Midstream* 17 (May).

Henderson, Charles. 1972. *The Nixon Theology.* New York: Harper & Row.

Heschel, Abraham J. 1962. *The Prophets: An Introduction.* Vol. 1. New York: Harper & Row.

Hiebert, Paul. 1999. *Missiological Implications of Epistemological Shifts: Affirming Truth in a Modern/Postmodern World.* Harrisburg, Pa.: Trinity Press.

Hillerman, Tony. 1993. *Sacred Clowns.* New York: Harper Torch.

Hillesum, Etty. 1981. *An Interrupted Life.* New York: Pocket Books.

Hitler, Adolf. 1942. *Mein Kampf.* New York: Stackpole Sons.

Hofstadter, Richard. 1966. *The Paranoid Style in American Politics.* New York: Alfred A. Knopf.

Holbrook, David. 1972. *The Masks of Hate.* Oxford: Pergamon.

Howard, Michael. 2001. *The Intervention of Peace: Reflections on War and International Order.* New Haven, Conn.: Yale University Press.

Hukanovic, Resak. 1996. *The Tenth Circle of Hell.* New York: Basic Books.

Isaac, Jules. 1964. *The Teaching of Contempt: Christian Roots of Anti-Semitism.* New York: Holt, Rinehart & Winston.

———. 1971. *Jesus and Israel.* New York: Holt, Rinehart & Winston.

Jacoby, Susan. 1983. *Wild Justice: The Evolution of Revenge.* New York: Harper & Row.

Janowski, Bernd. 1995. "Dem Loewen gleich, gierig nach Raub; Zum Feindbild in den Psalmen." *Evangelische Theologie* 55:155–73. Bern, Switzerland: Christian Kaiser/Guetersloher Verlagshaus.

Jervis, Robert. 1976. *Perception and Misperception in International Politics.* Princeton, N.J.: Princeton University Press.

Johnson, Reed. 2002. "Revenge: a Family Affair." *Los Angeles Times.* December 11, sec. E, pp. 1, 10.

Jones, L. Gregory. 1995. *Embodying Forgiveness.* Grand Rapids: Wm. B. Eerdmans.

Jones, James M. 1972. *Prejudice and Racism.* Reading, Mass.: Addison-Wesley.

Jung, Carl G. 1917. "On the Psychology of the Unconscious." *Collected Works.* New York: Pantheon Books.

_____. 1946. "After the Catastrophe." *Spring,* 4–23. Also in *Collected Works,* vol. 10, 11.

_____. 1953. *Psychological Reflections,* ed. Jolande Jacobe. New York: Pantheon Books.

_____. 1954. *The Development of Personality.* New York: Pantheon Books.

———. 1969a. *Psychology and Religion: West and East.* Translated by R. F. C. Hull. Princeton, N.J.: Princeton University Press.

_____. 1969b. *Collected Works.* Vol. 11. Princeton, N.J.: Princeton University Press.

Kahn, R. L. 1972. "The Justification of Violence." *Journal of Social Issues* 28:155–76.

Kaplan, Justin. 1966. *Mr. Clemens and Mark Twain.* New York: Simon & Schuster.

Keen, Sam. 1986. *Faces of the Enemy.* San Francisco: Harper and Row.

Kellenberger, James. 1995. *Relationship Morality.* University Park: Pennsylvania State University Press.

Kernberg, Otto. 1980. *Internal World and External Reality: Object Relations Theory Applied.* New York: J. Aronson.

———. 1984. *Severe Personality Disorders.* New Haven, Conn.: Yale University Press.

———. 1995. *Love Relations: Normality and Pathology.* New Haven, Conn.: Yale University Press.

Kim, Seyoon. 2002. *Paul and the New Perspective.* Grand Rapids: Eerdmans.

Kimper, Frank. 1972. Lecture and class notes, Claremont School of Theology, Claremont, Calif. Unpublished.

Kinzer, S. 1999. "A Sudden Friendship Blossoms between Greece and Turkey." *New York Times.* September 13:1.

Kleg, Milton. 2001. *Hate, Prejudice and Racism.* New York: State University of New York Press.

Klein, Melanie. 1940. *Love, Guilt and Reparation.* London: Hogarth Press.

———. 1986. *The Selected Melanie Klein,* ed. Joliet Mitchell. New York: Free Press.

Klein, Melanie, and Joan Riviere. 1962. *Love, Hate and Reparation,* Two Lectures. London: Hogarth Press.

Kohut, Heinz. 1978. "The Psychoanalyst in the Community of Scholars." In *The Search for the Self,* ed. Paul Ornstein, 704–705. New York: International Universities Press.

Lacan, Jacques. 1977. *Ecrits: A Selection.* New York: W. W. Norton.

———. 1978. *The Four Fundamental Concepts of Psycho-Analysis.* New York: W. W. Norton.

Laing, Ronald D. 1965. *The Divided Self.* Baltimore: Penguin Books.

———. 1967. *The Politics of Experience.* New York: Ballantine Books.

———. 1970. *Knots.* New York: Pantheon Books.

———. 1972. *The Politics of the Family.* New York: Vintage Books.

LaMothe, Ryan. 1996. "Hatred, Hostility and Faith: A Theological Perspective." *Pastoral Psychology* 44 (January): 185–98.

———. 1998. "A Psychodynamic Perspective and Theological Implications of Hate and Hostility in Pastoral Counseling." *American Journal of Pastoral Counseling* 1, no. 3: 27–40.

Leach, Edmund. 1977. *Custom, Law, and Terrorist Violence.* Edinburgh: Edinburgh University Press.

LeDoux, Joseph. 1966. *The Emotional Brain.* New York: Simon & Schuster.

Lens, Sidney. 1987. *Permanent War: The Militarization of America.* New York: Schocken Books.

Letelier, Francisco. 1998. "Now the World Will Know the Truth." *Los Angeles Times,* October 2, sec. B, p. 7.

Levin, Jack, and Jack McDevitt. 1993. *Hate Crimes: The Rising Tide of Bigotry and Bloodshed.* New York: Plenum Press.

Lifton, Robert Jay. 1967. *Death in Life: Survivors of Hiroshima.* New York: Random House.

———. 1979. *The Broken Connection.* New York: Simon & Schuster.

———. 1986. *The Nazi Doctors.* New York: Basic Books.

Lifton, Robert Jay, and Nicholas Humphrey, eds. 1984. *In a Dark Time.* Cambridge, Mass.: Harvard University Press.

Lifton, Robert Jay, and Richard Falk. 1982. *Indefensible Weapons: The Political and Psychological Case against Nuclearism.* New York: Basic Books.

Lippmann, Walter. 1922. Reprint 1961. *Public Opinion.* New York: Macmillan.

Loder, James. 1989. *The Transforming Moment.* Colorado Springs: Helmers & Howard.

Lohfink, Norbert. 1988. "Review of Decoding the Psalms." *Journal for the Study of the Old Testament* 37:41.

Lyotard, Jean-François. 1984. *The Post-Modern Condition: A Report on Knowledge.* Minneapolis: University of Minnesota Press.

Lyotard, Jean-François and Jean-Loup Thebard. 1985. *Just Gaming.* Minneapolis: University of Minnesota Press.

Maccoby, Hyam. 1986. "The Origins of Anti-Semitism." In *The Origins of the Holocaust,* ed. Randolph L. Braham. Boulder, Colo.: Social Science Monographs and Institute for Holocaust Studies of the City University of New York.

MacIntyre, Alasdair. 1981. *After Virtue.* Notre Dame, Ind.: University of Notre Dame Press.

Macmurray, John. 1961. *The Form of the Personal.* New York: Harper & Row.

Martin-Baro, Ignacio. 1994. *Writings for a Liberation Psychology.* Cambridge, Mass.: Harvard University Press.

Marvilo, Sam. 1993. *Ending the Cold War at Home.* New York: Lexington Books.

May, Rollo. 1969. *Love and Will.* New York: W. W. Norton.

———. 1972. *Power and Innocence.* New York: W. W. Norton.

McClendon, James W. Jr. 1986. *Ethics.* Systematic Theology, vol. 1. Nashville: Abingdon Press.

McCullough, Michael, Steven Sandage, and Everett Worthingon. 1997. *To Forgive is Human.* Downer's Grove, Ill.: Intervarsity Press.

McFeely, William S. 1999. *Proximity to Death.* New York: W. W. Norton.

Menninger, Karl. 1942. *Love against Hate.* New York: Harcourt, Brace.

Merton, Thomas. 1961. "The Root of War." *Catholic Worker* 28 (October): 1.

———. 1991. "The Root of War." Cited in Tom Hempson, *Tales of the Heart: Affective Approaches to Global Education.* New York: Friendship Press.

Miles, Jack. 1995. *God, A Biography.* New York: Random House.

Miller, Alice. 1981. *The Drama of the Gifted Child.* New York: Basic Books.

———. 1986. *Thou Shalt Not Be Aware.* New York: Meridian.

Miller, Marjorie. 1999. "Family Feuds Are No Game in Albania." *Los Angeles Times,* July 12, sec. A, p. 1.

Miller, Michael V. 1995. *Intimate Terrorism.* New York: W. W. Norton.

Miller, W. I. 1997. *The Anatomy of Disgust.* Cambridge, Mass.: Harvard University Press.

Miranda, Jose. 1974. *Marx and the Bible.* Maryknoll, N.Y.: Orbis Books.

More, Paul Elmer. 1928. *The Demon of the Absolute.* Princeton, N.J.: Princeton University Press.

Mueller-Fahrenholz, Geiko. 1996. *Vergebung macht frei: Vorschlaege fuer eine Theologie der Versoehnung.* Frankfurt: Otto Lembeck.

Murphy, Dean. 1997. "A Victim of Sweden's Pursuit of Perfection." *Los Angeles Times,* September 2:1, 8.

Murphy, Jeffrie. 1982. *Evolution, Morality and the Theory of Life.* Totowa, N.J.: Rowman & Littlefield.

Murphy, Jeffrie G., and Jean Hampton. 1988. *Forgiveness and Mercy.* New York: Cambridge University Press.

Murphy, Kim. 1999. "Last Stand for Aging Hate Groups." *Los Angeles Times,* January 10, sec. A, p. 1.

Neihardt, John G. 1907. *The Lonesome Trail.* New York: John Lane.

Niebuhr, H. Richard. 1941. *The Meaning of Revelation.* New York: Macmillan.

———. 1960. *Radical Monotheism and Western Culture.* New York: Harper.

———. 1963. *The Responsible Self.* New York: Harper & Row.

———. 1989. *Faith on Earth.* New Haven, Conn.: Yale University Press.

Nietzsche, Friedrich. 1924. *The Complete Works of Friedrich Nietzsche.* New York: Macmillan.

Nixon, Richard M. 1980. "America Has Slipped to Number Two." *Parade* October 5.

North, Joanna. 1987. "Wrongdoing and Forgiveness." *Philosophy* 62:499–508.

Nouwen, Henri. 1972. *The Wounded Healer.* New York: Doubleday.

Nygren, Anders. 1953. *Agape and Eros.* Philadelphia: Westminster Press.

O'Connor, Flannery. 1956. *Everything That Rises Must Converge.* New York: Farrar, Straus and Giroux.

Orwell, George. 1938. "Homage to Catalonia." In *The Collected Essays.* New York: Harcourt, Brace.

———. 1966. *Collected Essays.* London: Heinemann.

Paton, Alan. 1958. *Cry, The Beloved Country.* New York: Charles Scribner's Sons.

Patton, John. 1990. *Is Human Forgiveness Possible?* Nashville: Abingdon Press.

Paz, Octavio. 1991. "The Absolute." Cited in Tom Hempson, *Tales of the Heart: Affective Approaches to Global Education.* New York: Friendship Press.

Peavy, Fran. 1985. "Us and Them." *Whole Earth Review,* no. 49 (winter).

Perlmutter, Phillip. 1999. *Legacy of Hate: A Short History of Ethnic, Religious, and Racial Prejudice in America.* Armonk, N.Y.: M. E. Sharpe.

Perls, Frederick. 1969. *Gestalt Therapy Verbatim.* Lafayette, Calif.: Real People Press.

Phillips, Robert. 1941. *American Government and Its Problems.* Boston: Houghton Miflin.

Pirandello, Luigi. 1988. *Collected Plays.* London: John Calder.

Planalp, Sally. 1999. *Communicating Emotion.* Cambridge: Cambridge University Press.

Rawls, John. 1971. *A Theory of Justice.* Cambridge, Mass.: Belknap Press.

Redekop, Vernon. 1990. *A Life for a Life.* Scottdale, Pa.: Herald Press.

Ricoeur, Paul. 1992. *Oneself as Another.* Chicago: University of Chicago Press.

Rieber, Robert W., ed. 1991. *The Psychology of War and Peace: The Image of the Enemy.* New York: Plenum Press.

Rieff, David. 2001. "In Dreams Begin Responsibilities." *Los Angeles Times Book Review,* June 3: 4–6.

Rittner, Carol, and John Roth. 1997. *From the Unthinkable to the Unavoidable.* Westport, Conn.: Greenwood.

Rogers, Carl. 1975. "Empathic: An Unappreciated Way of Being." *The Counseling Psychologist* 2:2–10.

Rosenfeld, Alvin, and Irving Greenberg. 1978. *Confronting the Holocaust.* Bloomington: Indiana University Press.

Roth, John K., and Michael Berenbaum. 1984. *Holocaust: Religious and Philosophical Implications.* New York: Paragon House.

Rudin, Josef. 1969. *Fanaticism: A Psychological Analysis.* Notre Dame, Ind.: University of Notre Dame Press.

Sagan, Eli. 1988. *Freud, Women and Morality.* New York: Basic Books.

———. 1991. *The Honey and the Hemlock.* New York: Basic Books.

Salecl, Renata. 1998. *(Per)versions of Love and Hate.* London: Verso Press.

Sanders, James A. 1987. *From Sacred Story to Sacred Text.* Philadelphia: Fortress Press.

Sandmel, Samuel. 1978. *Anti-Semitism in the New Testament?* Philadelphia: Fortress Press.

Sartre, Jean-Paul. 1946. "Portrait of the Anti-Semite." *Partisan Review* 8, no. 2.

Schacter, Daniel L. 2001. *The Seven Sins of Memory.* Boston: Houghton Mifflin.

Segal, Hanna. 1973. *Introduction to the Work of Melanie Klein.* London: Hogarth Pess.

Shields, David L. 1986. *Growing beyond Prejudices.* Mystic, Conn.: Twenty-third Publications.

Shriver, Donald W. Jr. 1995. *An Ethic for Enemies.* New York: Oxford University Press.

Singer, Irving. 1987. *The Nature of Love.* Vol. 1, *Plato to Luther;* vol. 2,

Courtly and Romantic; vol. 3, *The Modern World.* 2d ed. Chicago: University of Chicago Press.

Slovo, Gillian. 1997. *Every Secret Thing: My Family, My Country.* New York: Little, Brown.

Sobrino, Jon. 1994. *The Principle of Mercy: Taking the Crucified People from the Cross.* Maryknoll, N.Y.: Orbis Books.

Solomon, R. C. 1989. "The Emotions of Justice." *Social Research* 3:345–74.

———. 1990. *A Passion for Justice.* Reading, Mass.: Addison-Wesley.

Spotnitz, H. 1976. *Psychotherapy of Pre-Oedipal Conditions: Schizophrenia and Severe Character Disorders.* New York: J. Aronson.

Stagner, Ross. 1967. *Psychological Aspects of International Conflict.* Belmont, Calif.: Brooks-Cole.

Steiner, George. 1988. "The Long Life of Metaphor." In *Writing and the Holocaust,* ed. Berl Lang. New York: Holmes & Meier.

Stevenson, Robert Louis. 1952. *The Strange Case of Dr. Jekyll and Mr. Hyde.* New York: Heritage

Storr, Anthony. 1972. *Human Destructiveness.* New York: William Morrow.

Swift, Jonathan. 1952. *Gulliver's Travels.* Chicago: Encyclopedia Britannica.

Tagore, Rabindranath. 1928. *Fireflies.* New York: Macmillan.

Taylor, Mark C. 1987. *Altarity.* Chicago: University of Chicago Press.

Taylor, Shelley E., and Jonathan Brown. 1988. "Illusion and Wellbeing: A Social Psychological Perspective on Mental Health." *Psychological Bulletin* 103:193–210.

Terkel, Studs. 1992. *Race: How Blacks and Whites Think and Feel about the American Obsession.* New York: New Press.

Tillich, Paul. 1952. *The Courage to Be.* New Haven, Conn.: Yale University Press.

———. 1954. *Love, Power and Justice.* New York: Oxford University Press.

Timmerman, Jacobo. 1982. *Prisoner without a Name, Cell without a Number.* New York: Vintage.

Tournier, Paul. 1979. *The Gift of Feeling.* Atlanta: John Knox Press.

Toynbee, Arnold. 1971. *Surviving the Future.* New York: Oxford University Press.

Trachtenberg, Joshua. 1943. *The Devil and the Jews: The Medieval Conception of the Jew and Its Relation to Modern Antisemitism.* New Haven, Conn.: Yale University Press.

Tracy, David. 1982. "Religious Values after the Holocaust: A Catholic

View." In *Jews and Christians after the Holocaust*, ed. Abraham J. Peck. Philadelphia: Fortress Press.

Twain, Mark (Samuel Clemens). 1960. *The Adventures of Huckleberry Finn*. New York: Dell.

Van Bowen, Theo. 1996. Jacket notes on *Impunity*, ed. Charles Harper. Geneva: WCC Publications.

Van den Berghe, Pierre L. 1987. *The Ethnic Phenomenon*. Westport, Conn.: Greenwood.

Volf, Miroslav. 1996a. *Exclusion and Embrace*. Nashville: Abingdon Press.

———. 1996b. "The God Who Forgets." *Books and Culture*, September/October: 11–15.

Vukovic, Zeljiko. 1993. *The Killing of Serajevo*. Belgrade: Kron.

Walzer, Michael. 1983. *Spheres of Justice*. New York: Basic Books.

Weikart, Richard. 2001. "The Roots of Hitler's Evil." In *Books and Culture*, March/April: 18–21.

Weil, Simone. 1970. *First and Last Notebooks*. London: Oxford University Press.

———. 1971. *Need for Roots*. New York: Harper & Row.

———. 1987. "Are We Struggling for Justice?" *Philosophical Investigations* 53 (January).

Wentz, Richard E. 1993. *Why People Do Bad Things in the Name of Religion*. Macon, Ga.: Mercer University Press.

Wharton, William. 1979. *Birdy*. New York: Free Press.

Wiesel, Elie. 1960. *Night*. New York: Hill & Wang.

———. 1962. *The Accident*. New York: Hill & Wang.

———. 1967. "Jewish Values in a Post-Holocaust Future." *Judaism* 16:281–85.

———. 1969. *The Town beyond the Wall*. New York: Avon Books.

———. 1970a. *A Beggar in Jerusalem*. New York: Random House.

———. 1970b. *One Generation after Another*. New York: Random House.

———. 1978a. *Four Hasidic Masters and Their Struggle against Melancholy*. Notre Dame, Ind.: University of Notre Dame Press.

———. 1978b. *A Jew Today*. New York: Vintage.

———. 1979. "A Personal Response." *Face to Face: An Interreligious Bulletin* 6:35–37.

———. 1982a. "Foreword." In *Jews and Christians after the Holocaust*, ed. Abraham J. Peck. Philadelphia: Fortress Press.

———. 1982b. *Legends of Our Time*. New York: Schocken.

———. 1990. *From the Kingdom of Memory: Reminiscences*. New York: Summit Books.

————. 1995. *All Rivers Run to the Sea: Memoirs.* New York: Alfred A. Knopf.

————. 1997. *Ethics and Memory.* Berlin: Walter de Gruyter.

————. 1999. *And the Sea Is Never Full: Memoirs.* New York: Alfred A. Knopf.

Wiesel, Elie, and Philippe-Michael de Saint-Cheron. 1990. *Evil and Exile.* Notre Dame, Ind.: University of Notre Dame Press.

Wiesenthal, Simon. 1997. *The Sunflower.* New York: Schocken Books.

Wink, Walter. 1986. "On Not Becoming What We Hate." *Sojourners,* series of articles November 1986, January 1987, February 1987.

————. 1992. *Engaging the Powers.* Minneapolis: Augsburg Fortress.

Winnicott, D. W. 1949. *Through Paediatrics to Psycho-Analysis.* New York: Basic Books.

————. 1976. *The Motivational Process and the Facilitating Environment.* London: Hogarth Press.

Yevtushenko, Yevgeny. 1967. *Yevtushenko's Reader.* New York: Avon Books.

Zalaquett, Jose. 1995. "Human Rights." *The Economist,* July 1.

Zehr, Howard. 1995. *Changing Lenses: A New Focus for Crime and Justice.* Scottdale, Pa.: Herald Press.

Zenger, Erich. 1996. *A God of Vengeance? Understanding the Psalms of Divine Wrath.* Louisville, Ky.: Westminster John Knox Press.

Name Index

Subject Index